RUNNING FROM HIPPOS

by

BD TIMMINS

First published in paperback by
Michael Terence Publishing in 2021 www.mtp.agency
ISBN 9781800942196

2nd Edition published in paperback by
Spooktacula Publishing in 2022
ISBN 9798846376205

In Loving Memory of Peter Alfred Bartlett
who passed to spirit in November 2020

This book is dedicated to everyone who has a story to tell, especially my beloved ex-husband (Big) Mick, my dear friends Peter Richards and Steve Strange, and to Paul; all of whom were taken too young and who never got the chance to tell their stories. It is also dedicated to my long-suffering mother; and to my father who I never really understood.

Grateful thanks to my partner Mick for his patience and understanding, my son Michael for his constructive criticism; and to you both for being in my life.

"Till death us do part and beyond"

Brenda Diskin

Contents

Brenda Diskin

PREFACE

Often extremely emotional, occasionally funny, sometimes thought provoking, 'Running From Hippos' is the story of my struggle with relationships, self-confidence, psychic ability and abuse. It tells of the horrors of post-traumatic stress disorder[1] and depression, and how I not only managed to bring some kind of normality back into my life but also found love and inner peace.

Victims, like their abusers come in all guises. Anyone, old or young, rich or poor, regardless of gender, sexual orientation, race or religion can become a victim. I know, because I became a victim at an early age and my only crime was being different. You are a victim if you suffered any of the following at the hands of another person, or persons:

Bullying, Psychological / Physical / Mental / Sexual / Domestic / Financial / Discriminatory abuse, modern-day slavery, or neglect.

We are frequently told that we are free to make our own choices in life, but often other people's actions make certain choices impossible. For instance, you decide to only indulge in sexual activity with the person you marry, but what if someone takes that prerogative away from you when you are unable to decide for yourself. Perhaps you may choose not to partake of illegal substances and someone spikes your drink in a pub, or at a party. Then those choices are no longer yours.

Now consider, that at an early age, something traumatic happens to you that you can't remember; but which stays lodged in the deepest part of your brain as a disassociated memory. Then you are 'blessed' with a natural gift that uses areas of your brain that wouldn't normally be accessed; causing this memory to resurface in other ways. You have dreams of an animal that you absolutely love but, after a while, your dream animal becomes a monster. You develop a phobia, become angry, anxious, depressed, possibly suicidal.

Throughout my childhood and early adult-hood I allowed myself to be a victim of other people's unhappiness, insecurities, lust and aggression. Life's course and circumstances have found me around, and near to death, more times than I care to think about. Never having been an angel, I have made a lot of mistakes in my life; some due to being young and naïve, some through illness, and some because I truly believed that I was doing the best thing for the people I loved. Although I regret many of the things I have done, I cannot change them and have paid dearly for my mistakes; but I would like to think that I learnt valuable lessons and have become a better person because of it.

Some people believe that, after death, we go on to live either in peace and love in Heaven, or in torment in Hell; it all depends on how we have lived our mortal lives. Personally, I believe that we experience Heaven and Hell here on earth; as I can truthfully say I have had several glimpses of Heaven, and a damn good look at Hell.

On several occasions I have really wanted to leave this earthly existence, but every time I have been hauled back by some unseen force. In fact, over the years, I have come to believe that I am being kept here for a purpose; although I am unsure as to what that purpose is.

I have dragged my heels while writing this book, deciding what to include and what to leave out. Which has proved difficult, as every part of it has shaped my life as it is; even the stuff that caused me so much pain and suffering. To help distance myself from certain events many passages have been written in third person, as Bren, and some can be quite graphic.

It has taken me over a decade to write this book and reliving all those memories has been one of the hardest things I have had to face.

Throughout, I have deliberated upon some of the things I have done and questioned why I did so. I have wept for the person I was, and for the person I have become.

The purpose of writing this book, other than to bury my own ghosts, is to try to help those who find themselves in some, or even all, of the situations I have been through; to show them they are not alone. The outcome of this book may just give someone that glimmer of hope that they need.

My experiences show that you can prevail and build a new life.

By fighting through the grief and pain, you can distance yourself from those memories that haunt your dreams. You may never be able to fill in some of those 'blanks. You may never forget the bad things, but you can learn to forgive yourself for the things that weren't your fault. You can try to stop 'hating' those who have wronged you. Hate is such a negative feeling, and it is only by embracing the positive things in your life, that you can learn to move on.

Chapter 1
The Early Days

"Don't you find some of the things she says a bit odd?"
My mother's work colleague asked, eyeing me up and down; her chin cupped in her hand.

All I said to her was that her mother, the lady with one leg shorter than the other, wished her happy birthday for tomorrow. Then again, most people outside of my immediate family thought me to be a strange child, as I would often say and do things that weren't considered to be 'normal'. I knew things that a four-year-old wasn't supposed to know.
Mum shook her head.
"Was she right?"
The woman contemplated her answer.
"As you know Frances, I don't talk about my personal life."
"I know, but was she right about your mother?" Mum was determined to get a straight answer.
"Yes, if you must know, she was right. My mother wore a built-up shoe."
Mum appeared to be satisfied, and we left the shop to go home.

It wasn't until the 1980s that psychic readings started to become more open and popular, so up until that time it wasn't considered to be 'normal behaviour'. If your parents suspected that you had 'imaginary friends' it was normally 'conditioned' out of you before you began school. But I came from a psychic family, both my gran and my mother were psychic. From what I was told, it appeared that the gift had been passed down through many generations.

You would think that by being so psychic I would have been aware of the dreadful things that were going to happen to me as a teenager and young adult. Perhaps I did get warnings, but I was young, naïve, and too trusting.

When writing a memoir there is the danger of it becoming a one-thousand-page saga. Rather than giving you repetitive strain injury from turning so many pages, I have tried to only include the bits that bring my story together and interlaced them with a bit of humour.

My life began at a time when Britain was still economically weakened after the war; it was a time of change for everyone. All around us were the reminders of the devastation that war causes. Loved ones had been lost, homes and businesses had been destroyed and it was a time of rebuilding; homes, lives, country and economy.

My entrance into the world was by Caesarean section on January 4th 1949 in Du Cane Road Hospital, Acton, London; weighing a whopping 9lbs 10oz. I was born to Frances Lannette Bartlett and Robert William Bartlett; the product of a second marriage for both parents.

When Mum was presented with her little 'Stanley' she was shocked to discover, that he was actually a she. She had to think of a name quickly, and 'Brenda' was the first one to pop into her head.

I may have been slow to arrive, but this Capricorn baby lived up to its birth sign. Like the little mountain goat, there was no stopping me. An inquisitive mind and a strong little body meant that I was always on the go.

For the first year of my life, I lived in Notting Hill Gate. My mother told me the reason that we moved was because the landlady charged extortionate rates. According to Mum, while collecting the rent one day, the landlady was robbed and then hung onto the iron railings by the collar of her mink coat. As a result of this and to deter further robberies, she increased everyone's rent significantly.

When I was a year old, we moved to NW10 where we lived in a

spacious second floor flat above the railway bridge. Opposite us lived a single middle-aged man who had a daughter named Gay who was a dwarf, and who would visit in the summer holidays. Below us were two more flats. On the ground floor was the entrance hall and a very large walk-in cupboard where the residents kept their bicycles and prams. It was referred to as the 'bike cupboard'.

When the trains passed under the bridge all the crockery on our dining table would rattle. You've heard the expression 'the earth moved', well, it really did in our house.

Growing up in pre-technology London, we had to make our own amusement. Imagination played a big part in all our games. With the aid of a pair of scissors and a few crayons, a large cardboard box could be transformed into something magical, spawned by pictures in the story books that we read. Of course, to anyone else's eye, it was still a cardboard box with holes cut into it.

In general, the 50s and 60s weren't bad decades to grow up in and I was lucky enough to do that growing in a city rich in architecture and proud of its heritage. It was a time when, if you were naughty, you got smacked. If you fell over your pain was kissed or rubbed better, and there was never any talk of suing your parents. You sat on Santa's lap, and accepted sweets from the kindly old gentleman who sat on the bench by the roadside.

When I was a child, a pat on the bottom or leg was considered normal from a family member or a close friend and was usually accompanied by "off you go then," or "never mind it will soon be better". Anything untoward would be dealt with by an irate parent and spread around by the town gossip.

It was a time when children knew right from wrong, honoured their elders and did what they were told. You weren't afraid to walk down the street. There were 'strange' people about but you were warned to stay away from them, and there was always a local beat copper, park keeper, or supervising teacher you could turn to if you needed help.

Sometimes when people talk about abuse, they presume that it is always the violent kind, but some abuse is so 'subtle', that you may not even realise it is happening. My personal abuse started off being almost imperceptible. Over the years it gradually escalated to violent abuse; culminating in a mental breakdown.

I believe that everything we experience during our early years shapes the adult that we become. Even the smallest trauma can have a long-term effect upon a child's mind.

This is an account of what shaped my life.

The Intruder

The entry had been so quiet that they didn't even know anyone was there. No splitting of wood, no sound of metal against metal, no key turning in the lock, no groaning hinges. Nothing.

Both mother and daughter were unaware of the person wandering through their home; entering rooms, opening cupboards and wardrobes. There was none of the usual grates and groans as doors moved against frames. Not even the creaking of floorboards; which the father had told his daughter were set on springs, to absorb the vibrations of the trains going through the tunnel under their block of flats.

As was usual for this time of afternoon, the dinner was prepared waiting to go in the oven. The heavy black enamel saucepan full of teatime spuds, was standing on the draining board. The mother and child sat at the kitchen table listening to Mrs Dale's Diary. It was just as the introductory music finished that they became aware of movement in the hall outside the door.

"Cat wants to come in." The mother said, raising her cup of tea to her lips.

The kitchen door slammed against the chair behind it. The child screeched as her mother's cup flew through the air, a fountain of tea raining down on them. The trembling, panting woman grabbed at the saucepan and lifted it above her head with God-like strength. Water and potatoes spewed across the kitchen.

He appeared in the doorway, his eyes angry slits. The saucepan clattered against the lino-clad stone floor scattering the remainder of its contents.

"Bob! What do you think you are doing? You scared the bloody hell out of us." Her mother yelled. She, an innocent almost three-year-old, stared at her father open mouthed as he barged across the kitchen and tugged open the balcony door; glancing outside before banging the door shut. He turned towards her mother his face almost in hers.

"Where is he?"

"Where's who?"

"This man you've been seeing, where is he? There are wrinkles in the bedspread."

Her father's clenched fists shook; his normally soft voice, unrecognisable. Pacing back and forth in front of them; like an enraged animal, snarling and cursing.

The child sobbed and shook; her mother held her, the tone of her voice escalating.

"Every bloomin' full moon that piece of shrapnel touches on your brain. Brenda's been playing in there. When do I get time to see other men? Why would I want to? I put up with enough from you."

His abusive onslaught continued as he checked the larder cupboard; while Mrs Dale chattered away in the background, asking her sister 'Selly' to put the kettle on.

These outbursts were a regular thing. My father's moods could change at the drop of a hat. Whenever the bedroom curtains swished loudly as he opened them, we knew the accusations were about to start.

Aggressive family arguments and erratic behaviour can be soul destroying to a child; but may seem like nothing to an adult; especially one that has never experienced it.

Introducing Bren

Brenda is my birth name, the one I connect to being a child. It is the name people call me when they are annoyed with me; and the one I associate with the bad things from my childhood. It is what people who don't know me well call me. That is, when they're not calling me Barbara, Beryl, Brendan or any other name beginning with B, bar my own. Personally, I prefer to be referred to as 'Bren'.

Like many other people with psychic abilities, I have often been ridiculed by others who say that if you hear voices, or speak in a different voice to your own, you must be schizophrenic or have a split personality.

Some psychoanalysts would probably say that what I am referring to is DID, Dissociative-Identity-Disorder; where two or more seemingly separate personalities occupy the same body at different times, each with no knowledge of the other. This is not how it is with me and Bren; I have always been aware of my 'other side'.

We are not separate identities. Bren is my spiritual self, the stronger part of me, the one that can carry on the daily routine when Brenda is snivelling in some remote corner of my brain. Bren is the business woman, the tougher, angrier side of me; the one that deals with life's problems, rolls up her sleeves and gets on with it.

She is the side of me that masks my pain, the dare-devil; the side of me that takes nobody's shit. Never have I been disassociated from Bren, because I am always aware of what is going on. She is my coping mechanism; the part of my brain that remembers all the gory details so that I don't have to. She is the one that helps me to stand up in front of a large crowd without freaking out.

I wish I could say that my childhood home was always happy, but I can't. Some of my earliest memories are of my parents having horrendous arguments, the reason for which was not revealed to me until many years later, when I was old enough to understand.

From three or four years old I survived on about four hours sleep most nights; awoken by the arguments. I remember being so afraid that I would lay in my bed trembling, unable to move. At least if I could stop the arguments, I could get some sleep. Bren was the one who was brave enough to make that scary walk along the dark hallway to my parent's room.

To this day I still cannot stand people shouting.

When I was eighteen months old it was discovered that I suffered from astigmatism; which meant that my right eye permanently stared at my nose. I was referred to Westminster Hospital for corrective treatment. Most of my infant school days found me with the left lens of my spectacles covered; a useless attempt to cure my condition, and also a cruel one for a small child. My right eye was practically sightless and being as it was the eye I was forced to use; I would fall over and bump into things which made me an easy target for bullying.

Throughout this time, I think the tougher side of me was still struggling with my childhood problems. In the meantime, I had to rely on my mum to sort things out.

Starting School

All eyes were upon her as she entered the classroom. Her curly white-blond hair hung almost to her shoulders, framing her face. She could have looked like a tiny angel if it hadn't been for the wire framed spectacles, with the pink sticky plaster over the left lens.

Head lowered; she fumbled her way to the only empty chair. The children's raucous laughter filled her head and dampened her eyes as she bumped into a table, and stumbled. The teacher, Mrs Ledbetter, put her finger to her lips and shushed the children into silence. The small figure sat down, her chin resting on her chest.

The lesson began and the teacher wrote alphabet letters on the blackboard. As the chalk moved over the shiny patches on the board it squeaked like a frightened mouse, echoing the way the child felt. Leaning forward, she tipped her head to one side straining to see what was written, but to no avail.

From where she sat, at the back of the class, she was unable to join in the chanting of the random alphabet sounds. As the morning progressed, the children paired up chatting excitedly. Only she was silent, sitting alone, drawing in her exercise book until the bell rang for lunch.

While queuing for her lunch, two girls stood behind her talking and giggling; one was named Pat. As she made her way towards an empty space on one of the tables, Pat shoved her hard in the back, she tottered spilling her orange squash into her dinner plate. Pat and her friend dashed for the remaining seats. The only seat left was at an empty table, she sat and ate her lunch alone.

After lunch she wandered into the playground behind the other children and stood on the white line that ran around the edge of the yard, watching them play. Pacing and kicking at air, she looked around her hoping to attract someone's attention. Pat, a dark-haired

girl, taller than her by a good-few inches, skipped over to her.
"Why is your eye looking at your nose?" Her tone was far too cruel
for one so young. Brenda wished she could have stayed inside.

The afternoon was no better. Some of the other children pointed
at her, giggled, and made unkind remarks. All she wanted was to go
home.

When the bell rang for home-time she made her way to the exit;
small bony fingers poked and prodded her as she walked. Tripping
over nothing, she banged into a long wooden coat rail hurting her
arm. A burst of spiteful laughter followed her. She hoped her mother
would be waiting.

As soon as she saw her mum the tears flowed. Between rasping
sobs, she managed to tell her mother about her day. Her mother took
her by the hand and marched her back into the building. Sheer
determination and garbled directions got them to the right
classroom.

"Mrs Ledbetter". I could hear the anger in Mum's voice as she
told the teacher how disgusted she was with the way her daughter
had been treated. Mum composed herself before stating.
"This ends now or I will go to the headmistress".
The teacher didn't get a chance to answer. She just nodded, as Mum
grabbed my hand and we walked away. We went home. I didn't want
to return to that place.

The next day, Mrs Ledbetter announced in class that the 'Bartlett
girl' was to be allowed to sit in the front row.
"I've had a complaint from her mother. Under no circumstances are
any of you to make fun of her, push her, or upset her in any way.
That includes you, John". Mrs Ledbetter pointed at her son, who
was also one of her students.

It stopped the bullying in the classroom. But, out of teachers'
sight, it grew worse and this time it wasn't just because of her eyes.

"Tell-tale tit, your mother can't knit. Your father can't walk, without a walking stick". Saying nothing, she learnt to live with it. She made no friends.

I hated school from day one and I don't think that ever changed; I just learnt to tolerate it.

Growing Up

Unlike a lot of children my age, I didn't have brothers or sisters to play with. My half-sister, Anna, from my mother's first marriage, was ten years older than me. I also had two half-brothers from my dad's first marriage, who were twenty odd years older and who were both married. Looking back, I believe Anna may have been a little resentful of me because I was the baby, and she had been an only child until I arrived.

For years Anna would tease and torment her, going as far as to lock her in the larder cupboard. Anna would hold the knob from outside, as Bren had discovered she could push her finger into the catch to open it.

Although quite spacious the larder was dark, and housed shadowy corners, where long limbed creatures hid while trying to grab at her. The more she thought about the creatures, the more she screamed; but Anna still held the door closed. She didn't have the strength to push the door open with Anna's weight behind it; so, she had to wait until Anna got fed up and moved away from the door. As far back as she could remember she had been terrified of confined spaces; so, being trapped by someone she loved left her trembling and confused.

It wasn't until I started junior school that the situation eased. Anna and I would do things together. We shared a love of music and drove my mother mad by singing all the latest songs; using the books of lyrics that I purchased with my pocket money. I didn't just love music; I was obsessed with it. One of my biggest dreams was to become a singer.

My Dad was a bus driver. London Transport was a good company to work for. They would organise seaside trips for the whole family, Christmas parties, and Safety-First concerts; where the bus drivers were given their awards for safe driving, and the whole family was treated to an evening of entertainment.

Dad often acquired free tickets to the London Palladium where I met many of the great music hall stars of the time. The actors and recording stars of my childhood appeared to be friendlier than those of today, and they always made time for their fans. Many of them would allow you backstage for a chat and to collect autographs. No one appeared to be worried about being accused of inappropriate behaviour. It wasn't until the 'stars' became 'idols' that the whole scene seemed to change.

The person who stood out the most, for me as a child, was Tommy Cooper. That man had the biggest hands and feet that I had ever seen. He was so tall, that for years I thought he was a giant.

Christmas was a family time; it wasn't about how much you could spend because people didn't have the money back then. My parents allowed me to have a gift I wanted up to the value of one pound.

One of our Christmas treats was a visit to the Bertram Mills circus at Olympia, but the visits stopped when I decided that I didn't like the clowns. It wasn't a phobia, or that I was freaked out by them, I just didn't like to watch people making complete fools of themselves, or being bullied.

Dad was paid weekly, so every payday he would divide his money into tins in his lockup bureau. He was very well organised putting money aside for rent, insurances, holidays, Christmas and all the other bills; but he could be quite tight. Mum used to call him Fagin because, like the character in Oliver Twist, he was always hunched over a tin counting his money. In all the years I lived with them, I never saw Dad buy my mum a card or a present for Christmas or her birthday. He would usually say.

"Here's five-bob (25p) go and get yourself a pair of stockings."

To his workmates my dad appeared to be pleasant, amiable and mild mannered, but I knew differently. Dad had a Jekyll and Hyde persona, and Hyde was frequently the most apparent.

Chapter 2
I Don't Understand

From when Bren was very young, she would climb into bed with her parents on the mornings that they didn't have to go to work. Her mother would get up to prepare the breakfast and Bren would stay in bed with her father. Snuggled into the armchair that he made with his body. She would sit in the 'armchair' and sleep or chat. One morning, her mother came into the bedroom and shouted at her father.
"You shouldn't do that, it's wrong."

Bren's mother dragged her out of the bed, and took her to the kitchen for a wash. She didn't know what else was said, but the 'armchairs' and getting into bed on her father's days off stopped after that day. Often, she would go into the bathroom with her father when he was using the toilet, but her mother said that she mustn't do that anymore either.

Sometime after, a memory of gaping pyjama bottoms crept back into her mind. Her dad always tied the drawstring in a double bow, so they shouldn't have come undone; she knew this was so, as she had watched him struggle to get the knots out.

I have no recollection of exactly what happened that day, but my mother's angry words stuck in my mind. Then there were the nightmares, whether they started as a result of something that happened that day or for some other reason, I have no idea.

Bren's mother could be very 'cold'; there were very few hugs and definitely no kisses. Bren was so desperate for affection; she would beg her mother to look through her hair for nits; just to experience the physical contact.

Their home was rarely peaceful. Bren's father was an extremely

13

jealous man who was always accusing her mother of having affairs. Their arguments could last for days and her mother was constantly threatening to leave.

When Bren was about eight years old, after one particularly bad argument that ended with her mother saying she'd had enough and was leaving. Bren asked her mother if she could go with her.
"No." Was the reply.
Crying herself to sleep, Bren wondered if her mother would still be there in the morning. Obviously, she was, because she had nowhere to go.

Bren blamed herself for her mother being so unhappy; berating herself for being a naughty child, not being pretty like her sister, having a 'lazy' eye, being her father's daughter. Her insecurity and feelings of guilt stayed with her throughout her life.

She was always using her pocket money to buy her mother gifts, thinking that if she bought her mother something nice, she would love her. On her way home one day, she saw some flowers growing on a bush by the roadside which she picked to take for her mum. Her gift was not met with the joyful response she expected. Instead, her mother began shouting, grabbed the flowers and threw them in the dustbin. How was she to know that it was considered bad luck to bring Lilac into the house?

In years to come, my desperate need to be 'loved' would lead to violent physical abuse.

Running from Hippos

We stood on the busy canal side, surrounded by other excited children, and their parents. The wind blew across the stagnant water and the stench of rotting vegetation assaulted our nostrils. Occasionally a fish appeared to nibble on a piece of furry decomposing flesh, floating on the cloudy surface, probably a bit of rat, cat or dog that found its way to a watery grave; by accident or otherwise. In my young mind everything was magical. There was no death, as we were always shielded from it in infancy; so, all things held their own form of beauty.

I watched the narrow boat as it glided slowly through the water towards the waiting crowd, fascinated by the man at the rear, as he pulled on the long metal bar which guided the boat towards the bank. The water bus scraped to a halt. A bizarre choir of children's jubilant squeals rang out over the quiet streets. Tugging at my father's hand I was eager to be the first to board.

About thirty minutes later the boat docked at London Zoo. Skipping along between my father and mother I chattered excitedly as we covered the hundred or so yards to the zoo entrance.

"Can we go and see the Hippos' first, please daddy?"

My father replied.

"There are lots of other animals to see before we get to the Hippo House."

After visiting all the other animals there was only one place left to go. The pungent, musky smell of the Hippopotamus house was always a clue to its proximity. It was strangely enticing; although I likened it to the smell of the public urinal, outside of which, I sometimes had to wait while out shopping with my father. I broke into a gallop.

"Slow down." My father shouted after me.

At fifty-six years old, and plagued with arthritis, he was having problems keeping up. My mother had no such problem as she was in her early forties. But I was desperate to see these giant creatures that looked so sleepy, harmless, and cuddly. I urged my father to hurry.

Trying to get nearer to the huge pool, that was set back from the viewing area and which housed the Hippos', I leaned forward over the barrier. My short child arms and chubby fingers stretched across the distance hoping to make some kind of contact.

My mother grabbed my hand and gently pulled me away. I glanced back hoping to get one last look, as I was led along the path towards the zoo exit and the walk to the bus stop.

The 'argument free' trips out with my parents were some of my best and happiest memories. It didn't matter where we went or what we saw, at night I went happily to bed and dreamed of Hippos.

I loved all animals but my favourite was the Hippos. From the first time I saw them at the zoo I was besotted with them, there was something about those big hulking creatures that made me feel safe. It wasn't until a few years later, when my dreams became nightmares, that I started to have mixed feelings about them.

Once again, she found herself in the same place, a vast, desolate place. The darkness, thicker and blacker than normal. Her eyes strained to penetrate the unyielding shadows, searching for signs of any other life forms. It crept up on her slowly, silently. But why was she so frightened? She loved this creature; but still the fear overwhelmed her. A quick glance over her right shoulder confirmed that it was there.

Compared to her pursuer, she was a tiny insect that could easily be crushed with one footfall of this hulking purple-grey creature. Its cavernous jaws emitted a bone-chilling roar. There was nothing to do but run, she knew that if it caught her, it would 'spoil' her.

Her heart pounded so hard she thought it would escape from her body; its pulse echoed within her ears, as she tried in vain to stifle the panting that tore through her lips. She had to get away, yet everywhere she ran the ground opened before her like a hungry mouth; blocking any means of escape. A lump rose in her throat

restricting her airway and making it impossible for her to scream,
as the creature bore down upon her.......

I woke up furiously sucking my thumb and sobbing uncontrollably. Exactly when my wonderful dreams of Hippo's turned into nightmares I cannot say, all I know is that I was still very young. It was always the same nightmare, a Hippo chasing me. Strange that I should be running from my favourite animal.

Fireworks

Living in a flat meant that we didn't have a garden, so, on Guy Fawkes Night I didn't have fireworks. I would watch everyone else's from our rear balcony and Dad would buy me a couple of packets of sparklers. He was always warning me to hold them at arms-length, as he was worried about me getting burnt.

It was Guy Fawkes night and someone had rung the bell on the street door. Bren loved to be allowed to descend the four flights of stairs to find out who was visiting; or to gather the mail from the letter cage, which hung on the inside of the door.

This particular night, she reached the bottom of the stairs and saw something sparkling in the letter cage. Curious, she edged nearer; cocking her head to one side so that she could see better. Twinkling brightly, almost at her eye level, it beckoned her to come closer.

Shuddering from the blast, the letter cage rapped hard against the door. The accompanying boom echoed through the stairwell; her agonised screams rang behind it.

Her parents rushed down the stairs to find her sobbing uncontrollably, face red and sore from the impact of the exploding banger. If she had been a little nearer and not wearing spectacles, she could have been blinded, or scarred for life. Needless to say, she was not allowed to answer the doorbell for a very long time afterwards; not that she really wanted to.

You're Weird

From a very young age, I would have dreams in which I could fly. Sometimes they would be part of the Hippo dreams, sometimes not. But there would always be something, or someone, chasing me and the flying would help me to get away quickly.

So convinced was I, that I was capable of flying, I once stood on the draining board flapping my arms wildly before leaping off. Instead of taking flight, I landed in a heap on the hard-concrete floor, much to my mother's disgust. I also believed that I could drift down long flights of stairs, without touching the banister rail. Thank goodness, I never tried it on the four flights of stone steps leading to the street door.

I was never a really naughty child. If I ever even thought about being naughty, my mother showed me the 'washing stick'; a bamboo cane that she used to push the clothes into the wash boiler. Boy did that thing sting, and it left a three-inch-long welt that was visible for days. From what I remember, I only experienced it twice and that was enough to make me reconsider the error of my ways.

The other dream also started when Bren was quite young. It didn't happen as often as the Hippo dreams, and it was more unpleasant than scary. In the dream someone, she didn't know who, put their finger in her mouth. It wasn't like when she sucked her thumb, because when she bit down on her thumb, she could feel the bone. This finger seemed to be softer and fatter and there were no joints. The worst part of the dream was when the finger kind of melted in her mouth. The texture was gritty like very soft fudge and the taste and smell were so bad it made her gag.

Although I have no idea why, I always had a 'thing' about fingers with the top joint missing, it used to make me cringe and feel extremely uncomfortable. Over the years, amputated finger joints pale in comparison to some of the things I have seen. Looking back, I seem to recall Anna's dad, or someone he worked with, had the top of his finger missing.

Whether it was my astigmatism or my psychic ability that made me most unpopular, I don't know. My being able to view events before they happened unnerved many people. What I experienced at that time, was a little like watching a blurred motion picture.

My psychic abilities first started to show themselves when I was very young. According to my mother, my first encounter with spirit was as a baby while sitting on my potty. Often whilst in the bathroom, I would hear my mother shout my name. When she denied calling me, I thought she was playing a game; it appears I even tried to rationalise things at that age. It took me a long time to fathom that my mother really wasn't calling me.

Dad and I were on our way to buy electrical parts for his radios. We had just turned onto Kilburn Lane. On the corner was a bombed out building and I always insisted that we crossed over the road; as I didn't like walking past it. Normally Dad would say nothing, but this time he decided to ask what it was I didn't like about the building. I answered.

"Because I was in there".

I was around nine years old, when I realised that not everyone could see, hear and feel the same way as I could. I had always had difficulty in making friends, so you can imagine how good it felt, when someone wanted to play with me. This girl seemed to experience similar things to me. Unfortunately, she was soon

19

stopped from playing with me as her mother said I was encouraging her to have an 'imaginary friend'.

The other kids only played with me when they had nothing better to do. A group of us were at Sara's home, playing the usual kid's games. The flat Sara's family lived in only had two bedrooms, so Sara and her brother had one each and Sara's mum and dad slept on a double bed in the kitchen come living room.

We had been exchanging ghost stories, when I saw an elderly man sat in the chair in the corner of the room and asked if the others could see him; describing what the man looked like in detail. I was met with quizzical expressions and whispering. Sara said,
"That's my grandad, and he's dead."
They told me to leave; and after that day, they didn't play with me again.

It soon became apparent that I had some kind of gift, if that's what you like to call it; sometimes it was more like a curse. I remember the look of shock and fear on those kids faces that day. It was then I understood, that I wasn't the same as the other children.

A fact that was brought home to me a few days later at school, when I realised all the kids were avoiding me. Although I was used to the whispering behind my back, now it was because they thought I was weird in a different way.

Basically, I spent the first seventeen years of my life wondering what the hell was wrong with me; and the rest of my life has been spent trying to figure out what to do with it.

Holidays

Mum and Dad acquainted me with London its majestic buildings, parks, museums and, as a matter of course, its history. I still wonder at the stories of intrigue, skulduggery and grisly murders. For me every street holds an account of its past, each building sheltering the 'ghosts' of bygone days.

One of my favourite places to visit was Hampton Court Palace, its chequered history and sheer beauty added to its magic. One day, while my dad and I were sitting in the tennis courts, he asked jokingly if I could see the people playing tennis. I told him I could see people in strange old clothing with weird shaped tennis racquets; he thought I was playing along with the game, but I really could see them.

I looked forward to our family holidays, but not for the same reasons as other kids. For me it was a week or two without arguments. Some holidays were spent at my half-brother Bob's home in Weymouth. Other holidays were spent with my dad's younger brother Tom and his wife in Essex.

Aunt Ada was of the 'old tradition'. She believed that nature had its own way of 'predicting' future events. Instead of a barometer, she had seaweed hanging in her hallway; if it became wet, then rain was on the way.

Bren remembered one visit to Uncle Tom and Aunt Ada's house in Bluebell Wood Billericay, she was probably about six or seven at the time. Aunt Ada was an extremely large lady with a broad Somerset accent; even though she was a Londoner. She always greeted them with.
"Ow be ye?" Followed by.
"Tom mate, put kattle on".

Uncle Tom kept chickens at the bottom of the garden. He was complaining that a fox had been trying to get to them. When Bren arrived, he asked her to go and look at the chickens and choose which one she wanted. She was really excited as she studied them all, trying to decide which one was going to be her new pet. Pointing

to a lovely chestnut brown hen, she happily told him.
"That one."

Uncle Tom gathered the chicken in his arms, and twisted its neck. To her young ears, the accompanying crack was like the loudest thunder clap. Tears streamed down her cheeks, her breakfast forced its way back to her mouth and she grimaced at the taste. It was the first time that she had ever witnessed death. Unsure of what she felt, she said nothing; but that night she cried for the Chicken, and the Hippo's roared.

That chicken was served up for our tea. I haven't been keen on eating chicken since.

I Make Some Friends and Have My First Panic Attack

Sometimes I would do or say stupid things that I would feel embarrassed about. When this happened, I would reprimand myself, sometimes pinching my skin really hard.

Being as I was a lonely child; I would talk to anyone who had a friendly face. That included an old tramp, who walked the streets where I lived. Often, I would see him asleep on a park bench and would share my lunch with him. One day, I decided to take him home for tea.

My mother was visibly shocked, nevertheless she sat him at the table with us and put a plate of food in front of him. She even made polite conversation. After I had seen him to the downstairs door, I went back to face my mother, who said,
"That was a kind act, but in future you can take him something to eat from the cupboard."

Mum spent the next week fumigating the flat. When I say fumigating, I mean just that. We had a cylinder vacuum cleaner which had a canister with a mesh cover that you could screw onto the blowing end, and which you could fill with para-dichlorobenzene crystals to kill moths and bugs.

I was now in primary school which was almost as bad as infant school. I had the same teacher that Anna had ten years before, Mrs Davies. She hated Anna, and now she hated me. My lesson time was often spent in the corridor, or outside the head-mistress' office; in fact, I spent more time there than I did in the classroom. Mrs Davies picked on every little thing. Although the patch over my eye was now gone, I would sometimes need to ask what was written on the board; because of my weak right eye I couldn't see the board from certain angles. If I asked the teacher I would be told off, and if I asked a classmate, I would be sent outside for talking in class. So, I went from being bullied by kids to being bullied by a teacher.

There was a good side to being in Primary School and that was the school trips. The worst ever trip was to Hampstead Heath after a week's worth of rain. Even worse, was trying to explain to my irate mother how my shoes had been lost in a muddy bog, and how I had made the journey home in bare feet.

My mother became ill around this time with a perforated duodenal ulcer.

I had become friendly with my neighbour Gay, who was thirteen and was a dwarf. During the school holidays we were inseparable. On pocket money days, we would take the bus to Kensington High Street to have coffee in the Pavilion Tea Rooms in Derry and Tom's roof garden. Where we rubbed elbows with upper class housewives and budding actors. During the time it took to drink our coffee and tuck into our shared piece of cake, we were part of that rooftop world. We were brought up with manners, so no one thought anything different. When I was about ten, Gay's dad moved to

Manchester; I was very sad, as I had lost my friend and we never did keep in touch.

Around this time Sara forgave me for scaring her with my sighting of her dead grandad, and we became friends again. A few weeks later, Sara found her mother dead in the kitchen. As a result, she became slightly interested in spirits and would often ask me questions about what I saw.

Around four or five of us kids would meet at Sara's house, where we would sit on the double bed in the kitchen and tell ghost stories. On one occasion, for some reason, we put the mattress against the wall and sat on the bed spring.

After a while the others started messing around, jumping on and off the base; while I sat staring at Sara's dead mother, who was standing by the cooker. The mattress started to topple and fell on top of me, pinning me under it. It was an old horse hair filled mattress and it was very heavy, so I couldn't move at all.

Bren started to panic because she couldn't breathe. The mattress was smothering her, restricting all movement. Nausea and the tightness in her chest threatened to drag her into darkness. The others started laughing, until she began screaming hysterically. Then, somehow, they managed to pull the mattress off of her.

I don't know whether it was due to my sister locking me in the larder, the mattress falling on top of me, or some other incident that I can't remember; but to this day, I cannot stand anything over my face, being stuck in small spaces, or stranger's bodies pressing against me.

Around this time there had been a big influx of immigrants from the West Indies, and a lot of them had moved into houses on Bathurst Gardens. One day, while walking along Bathurst, I heard music coming from one of the houses. It had a heavy beat that I hadn't heard before.

There was a group of black men stood outside the house, it was the first time I had seen a black man in person. More interested in the music than the colour of their skin, I asked what it was called.

"Blue Beat." They told me, and asked if I liked it.

"Very much." I replied, and from that moment I was hooked and have loved Reggae music ever since.

Unfortunately, not everyone was happy about the immigrants, and a series of racially motivated riots broke out in the Notting Hill area of London. My sister's policeman boyfriend was injured quite badly during the fighting. As a nine, pushing ten, year old I couldn't understand what the problem was.

Chapter 3
New School

When I was ten years old, I sat for my eleven plus exam. Confusing, I know, but the Senior schools actually enrolled pupils from the age of eleven. Being as I wanted to stay with the few classmates who I got on with, I asked my mum to put Chamberlayne Secondary, as my first and only choice.

Mrs Davies' bullying even spilled into that, and the choice was rapidly changed to a grammar school; apparently, she deemed me too intelligent for Secondary school. How she came to that conclusion I have no idea, being as most days she only saw me through the glass in the classroom door. But the exam results proved her right; I had the fourth highest score in the area that year.

I decided that when I started at my new school, I would tell nobody about my spirit friends, at least that would be one less thing that would make me a 'weirdo'.

Bren longed for when she could change schools and start afresh. She sometimes left her glasses off for vanity's sake. She was unsure of when she first started feeling so self-conscious, she presumed it must have been around the age of four; but it stayed with her throughout her life. Big nose, cross eyes, ugly; it seemed like very few people looked past her exterior.

At the beginning of April 1960, I first set foot in my 'grown up' school. I was just eleven years and three months old and was now expected to act like a young adult. Brondesbury and Kilburn High School for Girls was a school full of intelligent 'mis-fits'. Those with money got better treatment than those who were there on a scholarship.

Within days of being in my new class I made a friend, a black girl named Virginia. Her mother was a great cook and I soon learnt to enjoy spicy food. We stayed friends throughout the first year and part of the second year, until her family moved to another area and we lost touch.

My sister's 'now fiancé' Peter, practically lived at our house when he was off duty. My dad was being a complete arse, accusing Peter of touching my mum in a sexual manner, so Anna decided to get married sooner than planned. On their return from their honeymoon, they found a flat to rent in South Harrow.

With things being so difficult on the home front I threw myself into my school work and that year I was a straight 'A' student. Music was one of my subjects and my lunchtimes were spent in the music room singing to Ray Charles music, with one of the fourth-year students, Betty something or other. We gelled really well, both musically and personality wise. Unfortunately, all that changed in the third year when I became friends with a girl named Cherie.

By the second year I was suffering at school, as somehow, I had managed to alienate a couple of the teachers. My geography teacher also took me for maths, and I think the problem with her started when I mistook her for the cleaner.

I had just walked into the girl's cloakroom when an elderly woman, dressed in a green overall and sporting a thick hair net, appeared holding a bottle of Dettol. She walked from sink to sink pouring the Dettol down the plug holes; so, you can see how the mistake was easily made.

Although I had long legs, I just couldn't do high jump, which put me completely out of favour with one of the gym teachers, as she desperately needed people for her team. It didn't matter to her that I excelled at several other sports, she decided that I must be able to do high jump, and she made my life a misery.

Even though I could support my body's weight on my arms, I just couldn't lift my body high enough to clear even a three-foot-high pole. The teacher would force me to try time and again, mocking my failure and making me a laughing stock in front of the other pupils. It seemed that I couldn't get away from the bullying.

On the plus side, the English teacher loved me. She would give up part of her lunch hour to listen to my poems and stories, give her opinion and recommend books.

Outside School

My friends had been sent to other schools after the eleven plus. Although we still saw each other at weekends, we were all busy with school work during the week.

Bren picked her way carefully from pole to pole. Taking time to get her balance. Everything depends on balance when you are thirty feet up and walking across scaffolding with no boards. One slip could result in a nasty injury, or even death. Although she should have been frightened of falling, she wasn't; she enjoyed athletic things, she was good at them. Bren was only afraid of not being one of the 'gang'. Anyway, her time wasn't up yet, she knew that for certain. If you could be one of the lads you had mates for life. Girls were more fickle and bitchier. Well, that's what she thought then.

Even at nearly thirteen, Bren was fascinated by motorbikes. A lad, with a BSA, had asked her if she fancied a ride. It would be her first time on a bike; in the days before crash helmets were compulsory. She threw her leg over the bike, just as she had seen others do, how hard could it be? They rested one hand on the upper part of each leg and off they went. Well!!!!

The bike went forward and she flew backwards. Her legs went over her head, which had just made a dent in the tarmac. There was a lump the size of an egg on the back of her head, but it didn't hurt half as much as her bruised pride. Her balancing skills did get better, thanks to Mike who she met a few months later.

A skinny kid who dressed like a boy, with a sheaf knife strapped to her leg, wasn't particularly girlfriend material. The only things I had going for me, were good clear skin and long blond hair; which the lads seemed to love to touch, not that I complained. I went through boyfriends like other kids went through sherbet flying saucers. Boys cried off after the first date as their mates would make fun of them; so, I considered it a miracle if I made it to a second date. I was branded as weird, ugly or 'not up for it'. The ones who did stick around were exactly what it said on the label, 'boy friends', 'friends who were boys'. It wasn't until I turned thirteen that someone really showed interest.

I Get a Steady Boyfriend and Attend My First Funeral

It was a Saturday morning and I was walking down Harrow Road in Paddington, on my way to Woolworths. I would normally have been with Sara but she was visiting her aunt in County Durham.

When I heard the sound of a bike coming up the road, I didn't turn around to look. I just kept walking. The engine slowed, until the bike was keeping pace with me. Still, I didn't look.

"Hello Gorgeous." I ignored him; he couldn't possibly be talking to me. Again.

"Hey, gorgeous."

Once again, I ignored him. Gorgeous? Me? He had to be talking to someone else. Then.

"Oi, Cloth ears." Now that was more like it.

As I turned to look at him, he asked.

"Wanna ride?"

I didn't think I'd ever seen him before; it wasn't until he removed his helmet that I realised that I had seen him with some of the other biker lads I knew. Thinking that a boy like that wouldn't be interested in anything I had to say, I had never spoken to him. After all, it was my sister who was the silk purse. I was even outshone by the sow's ear.

"Well?" He waited for my reply.

I didn't need asking again, so I went to climb on the back.

"Hang on a minute." He said, handing me his helmet.

"Put this on, I hear you have a habit of falling off backwards."

He grinned at me, and I nearly told him where to shove his ride.

Mike and I spent nearly six months together. I was treated like a princess, he opened doors for me, gave me his jacket when it was cold, bought me little gifts. Even his family were lovely; especially his two brothers, who would often accompany us on rides out.

Bren had just finished her breakfast, when the doorbell rang. She bounded down the communal stairs ready to throw herself into Mike's arms, but she couldn't shake off the feeling that something wasn't right. The nagging in her gut had started just before teatime the night before and had disturbed her sleep. Shaking her head, she told herself she was being silly.

When she opened the door, instead of Mike, his eldest brother Tony stood there; his eyes red and swollen. His words buzzed around her head, fading in and out. Tony was telling her that Mike and his brother, Brian, had been killed in a bike accident coming back from Brands Hatch; Tony had witnessed it. He held her and they cried together.

There was no consoling her, she sobbed for days. All she had to remember Mike by was the silver cased cigarette lighter and the silver pentagram that he had bought her; and one photograph.

Those three items went everywhere with her, the lighter and photo in her bag and the pentagram on a chain around her neck.

That was the first funeral she had attended. Mike was just seventeen years and nine months old; Brian was just over nineteen.

Life goes on, whether we like it or not. I now had an interest in boys and in my appearance. I wore high heels, skirts and make up. Surprise, some boys also seemed to have an interest in me. Even some of the old gang saw me in a different light; well almost. They still thought I was weird; seeing dead people and being able to tell what was going to happen in the future.

Unfortunately, not every boy was as nice as Mike, as I was about to find out.

The Worm Turns, a Different Kind of Abuse

Almost three months after Mike's death, I met Gerry, he was nineteen. With me at only thirteen and three quarters, he was really much too old for me. But at that age the three quarters is very important, as it makes you feel a lot older. Gerry was clean and 'geeky', and nothing like Mike, but he seemed nice enough.

We would often walk to Hampstead Heath, grab a cappuccino in the Italian coffee bar and then walk back. We walked a lot. Looking back, I don't think he liked spending his money. As Mike had been a nice guy and we never went further than kissing, I was still naïve.

One day, while walking somewhere, Gerry asked me if I had any French letters. I presumed he meant letters from France and replied.

"No, but I have loads from my penfriend in Malaya."

He must have thought I cracked a joke, because he laughed. It wasn't until a couple of years later, that I found out what the French letters he referred to actually were.

We had been seeing each other for about three weeks and were walking in the direction of Harrow Road, when Gerry told me he had forgotten his cigarette lighter. I said it wasn't a problem because I had mine, but he insisted that he wanted to go home for his. Thinking it was a bit odd, I was hesitant. But when he told me his mum or dad would probably answer the door, I agreed to walk back to his flat; after all it wasn't far out of our way.

Something was troubling her as they climbed the stairs to the fifth floor of the tower block. Bren thought she was probably nervous about meeting Gerry's parents, so she kept going. When he knocked on the door of the flat and his friend Bob answered, alarm bells rang.

Unnerved, she moved towards the stairs, but Gerry grabbed her by the arms and started pulling her towards the door. He was a lot stronger than her and, although she tried to wedge her foot against the door jamb, he managed to get her inside and kick the door shut behind them.

He and Bob half dragged, half carried her, screaming and thrashing, towards the bedroom. She kicked out, and as Bob wrestled to keep his grip on her legs her shoes fell from her feet. They threw her on to the bed. Gerry was already tearing at her blouse, one of the buttons ripping a hole in the flimsy cotton material. The blouse gaped open, only one button hung by a thread, the rest had scattered about the room.

Bob gripped her ankles, holding her legs firmly on the bed, his nails digging into her flesh. Her left arm felt numb as Gerry knelt on it with his full weight, while he tugged her bra up over her breasts. She lashed out with her free arm, clawing at Gerry's face; sobs breaking through her terrified screams. Flinching from the wounds, he scowled at her before yelling at Bob.

"Get up here and hold her arms".

Bob obeyed, and Gerry shifted his weight so that her body was pinned to the bed.

With Gerry sat astride her legs and Bob holding her arms, she was powerless; her screams echoed in her ears. Gerry forced her skirt to the top of her thighs, tearing her knickers as he attempted to pull them down. Impatient, he decided to just rip them off. Bren screamed out in pain, as they cut into her soft flesh. Gerry pointed between her legs.

"What's that?"

Bob leant forward to look.

"It's a sanitary belt. My sister wears one when she's having her period." Bob shook his head.

"I thought you said she was up for this Gerry. I won't be part of rape."

Bob released his grip on her arms. Clutching at her blouse, she tried to cover her small breasts. Gerry shifted his position on the bed, trying to regain control, but instead he allowed one of her legs to become free. She was already grabbing at the remnants of her clothes.

"We can't let her go." Gerry reasoned. "She might tell someone."

Her throat tightened, almost making her choke, she was now fearing more for her life than her virtue. Gerry shifted again, she thrust her free leg forward, her foot landing heavily in his groin. Screeching, he released his hold on her. Seizing the moment, she jumped from the bed and ran towards the door. Bob just stood there, watching her retreat.

"Stop her." Gerry shouted.

But Bob didn't move.

She struggled with the door, petrified that they would grab her before she could escape. Sobbing, part-naked, shoeless, she ran down the stairs; passing a man who stared open mouthed. The boys didn't follow. Running towards Harvist Road, she only stopped when she was a safe distance away, to straighten her skirt and pull her bra down over her breasts. The blouse, ripped beyond repair, barely covered her. She couldn't go home in that state, her mother would go ballistic because she would think she had been doing things that only bad girls do; so, she ran in the direction of Queens Park.

Once through the park gates, she headed towards the field by the children's playground. It was a Sunday, so the regular gang were there, listening to Pick of the Pops on a portable radio. Ricky was the first to see her. As soon as he reached her, she collapsed in his arms, blubbering. Ricky took off his jumper and slipped it over her head, helping her to put her arms into the sleeves. He held her while she blurted out her story, eyes raw.

She didn't know whether Gerry had come looking for her, but as soon as she saw him across the field, she began shrieking again and raised her hand in his direction.
"That's him, please don't let him near me."

Ricky's older brother, Alf, stood up. Anger flashed in his eyes.
"We'll teach him, never to mess with our girls."
Three of them raced across the field towards Gerry, who turned to run back the way he came; then they all disappeared from sight.

When she was sure her parents would be watching television, she left the park and headed for home, still shoeless. Once inside, she had to make it to her bedroom without her parents seeing her.
"Only me Mum."
It was the first of many times that she forced herself to sound normal; although she felt anything but normal.

In the safety of her bedroom, her thoughts began to surface. Relieved that Bob had backed out when he did, she allowed the feeling to wash over her. She didn't know what it was like to have *sex, let alone in such a violent manner, but she guessed that it wouldn't be pleasant.*

Part of her felt guilty for the beating the boys had given Gerry, but she hoped that it would stop him from doing what he did to someone else. For a long time, she was very wary of being around people she didn't know.

I never told my mother because I was too ashamed and, besides, Gerry had been punished for what he did.

My Best Friend

My near rape left me feeling extremely vulnerable. When out in the street, I repeatedly looked over my shoulder to check who was behind me. I alternated between feelings of guilt and self-loathing. I was even wary about hanging around with the usual crowd.

My school work was suffering. When I made it into the top class in the third year, I was extremely surprised. It was in this class that I met Cherie who had been held back a year.

Cherie and I clicked straight away; we had the same warped sense of humour and I instantly liked her. She was nearly sixteen and pretty, with a very well-developed figure. Cherie had a bad reputation because she liked to have casual sex, but that was her choice and nothing to do with anyone else. We started hanging around together and had some good times.

Some weekday evenings were spent at the Mount, my local youth club, which provided all sorts of courses and entertainment. It had a very good café and the best Friday evening disco for miles. I was at the club three nights a week taking part in the photography and printing classes. In June 1963, Cherie and I joined the sword fencing classes; we were actually quite good at it. When the weekends came, we swopped our school uniforms for the latest fashions.

Our gang had a weekend routine. On Saturday morning, we would meet in the park then go to Church Street Market off Edgware Road. We would take the bus there and back, and when coming home we always got off at the same stop.

Cherie normally spent her weekends with her family but that week she had joined us for the trip to Church Street. There were only two of us girls and a group of five lads. Cherie and I were wearing low heeled shoes, full circle skirts and sporting the latest wig hats (a fake fur hat that's also a wig). We were all on the bus going home when, three stops before ours, one of the lads said he wanted to go and look at the cinema board to see what was on.

Everyone stood up, and moved towards the exit platform. All the lads jumped off the bus, just as it started to pull away; followed by Cherie. The bus was gathering speed by now and Bren was still stuck on it. Her friends were all shouting at her to jump. So, she jumped, landing on her bottom but she didn't stop, she just kept going; sliding along the pavement with her skirt over her head, ripping her knickers on the gravel. When she finally came to a halt, her skirt was up round her waist and her wig hat was now neither wig nor hat; it had slid to one side and was more like a hairy mask, covering one eye and one ear. She dared to look up. All her friends were rolling about laughing, at least Steve had the decency to pull her skirt down to save her further embarrassment.

She couldn't sit down for a week because of the gravel rash, and she never wore the wig hat again. Bren was obviously not destined to be a 'girly' girl.

Chapter 4
The Meal

It was on one of our regular nights out in London's West End, that Cherie and I met Michael (Q), a Jewish boy from a posh area of South West London. We sat on the steps of Eros, sharing a beer, chatting and laughing. Just before ten, he said there was somewhere he needed to be, and asked me if I would meet him the following Saturday; to go for a meal. As he seemed nice, I agreed.

After he left, Cherie and I went to the Wimpy bar for a burger, where we sat happily munching away while Cherie eyed up the good-looking Turkish chef; who had his eyes fixed on Cherie's boobs.

Later, we ended up in Trafalgar Square which was crowded with people dancing and singing. Having had a few drinks, we were feeling 'merry'. There was a young policeman on crowd duty, we went over to talk to him. He was very friendly, until I grabbed his helmet off his head; I only wanted to see the colour of his hair.

The policeman kept asking me to give his helmet back, saying that he didn't want to arrest me. I stupidly threatened to throw it in one of the fountains, he pleaded with me, saying that he would have to arrest me. Ignoring his pleas, I dipped it in the water. When I saw the look on his face, I realised I'd gone too far. So, I stopped, shook the water off, and gave the helmet back to him. He stared at me while considering his options.

"Get home, or I will arrest you both."

We didn't think he was joking so we headed for Leicester Square.

It was nearing midnight, as they walked towards the tube station. A gang of boys gathered around them, pushing and shoving. Bren tightened her grip on her bag, twisting the handles around her finger. One of boys tugged at the handbag. She heard her finger snap, as he tore the bag from her grip.

The boys ransacked her bag in front of her, taking all the contents. She told them they could have everything else, including the money, but please could she have the lighter and photo back; as they were special to her. They laughed, as she begged and pleaded with them. Then one of them cruelly dropped the photo down a drain, before throwing the empty bag at her and running off.

Even though Bren and Cherie got down on their knees and peered into the drain, they couldn't see anything. Heartbroken at losing Mike's photo and the lighter he had bought her; she didn't say a word on the journey home. Those items were much more than just possessions; they were memories of special days that couldn't be relived. The following day, she had to get her broken finger strapped up.

If you believe in Karma and you think I was being paid back for the policeman's helmet. Then Karma was an absolute bitch to me, and she didn't stop at my bag being taken; she went one almighty step further.

The following Saturday, I went to meet Michael (Q), he was already waiting for me at the bus station. He held doors open for me and generally treated me like a lady. We chatted and window shopped, then he asked if I was hungry; to which I nodded. He told me he was going to take me for something special and he led me through streets I was unfamiliar with.

Everything was fine, until we turned off into an alleyway with very little lighting. At first, I wasn't too worried, as some of the best cafés I had visited were hidden away in the back streets of Soho. But then I started to look around me.

Bren knew something wasn't right. The alleyway appeared to be full of factory type buildings, with boarded up windows. A voice in her head shouted a warning and her chest tightened so much that it felt like her heart was banging against her rib cage.

Before she had any chance to act Michael grabbed her wrist, and pushed her between him and a factory wall, holding her there with the weight of his body. Tugging at her arms and putting pressure on her broken finger, he forced her down into a crouching position.

She couldn't scream; the sound was in her head, and her mouth was open, but nothing came out. Shoving her sideways, he caused her to lose her balance; she fell against the cold pavement, winded. Muscling her onto her back, he sat astride her, squeezing her throat, restricting her breathing.

Flailing her arms, she tried to push him away; in a bid to make him lose his grip on her throat. His voice no longer calm, his breathing heavy.

"You are going to do what I tell you."

The pressure on her throat increased. Sweating, as a grey curtain descended, blurring her vision; she struggled to stay conscious. Shifting his body forward, until his knees pinned her arms to the ground, he had complete control over her. Bren heard the sound of a zip being undone.

As he moved forward slightly, in the half-light, she could make out the shape of his penis, in front of her face. A thought flashed through her mind, that it was the first penis she had seen other than her father's, when he was going to toilet. She remembered that Michael was going to take her for a meal; it was now she realised what was on the menu.

Gritting her teeth and holding her breath; some weird sense of logic telling her if she did this, he couldn't put that thing in her mouth. Bren searched for ideas of how she could get out of this situation. His voice was threatening.

"Open your mouth. You are going to take it all, and you are going to suck it, until I come. I have a knife and I will use it."

Although she didn't actually see a knife, something metallic glinted in the moonlight.

Inhaling deeply, her lungs desperate for air, she relaxed her jaws. It was the opportunity he was waiting for; he rammed his penis into her open mouth. She didn't want to do this, she just wanted to go home. It was wrong, good girls didn't do these things. For a split second, she could hear her mother's voice telling her so.

Releasing his grip on her throat, he forced his stiff member further into her mouth. It tasted bitter and smelt of urine. Retching, she thought about the knife and the consequences of not doing what he wanted. His legs still gripped her upper body. Traumatised, her whole being screamed silently. As he pushed his penis further towards her throat, she decided that she would rather die than suffer this.

Unable to breathe through her nose, she felt like she was choking, even so she bit down; her teeth grinding against the intruding lump of flesh. He lashed out at her face, and tried to prise her mouth open, but she bit down even harder. The taste of his blood filled her mouth and she fought against vomiting; but still she bit down. His screams and expletives rang through the night. She released her grip and he rolled away from her.

Somehow, she got to her feet and ran. The knife blade flashed through her mind; she ran faster. Having no idea where she was, she knew she had to put distance between her and him. Glad that she had worn jeans and mocs, she didn't stop until she found the bus station.

Bren couldn't believe her luck at finding her bus already there and several people waiting to board it. Breathless, she searched her pockets for money, praying that it hadn't fallen out in the alleyway.

Finding an empty seat, she curled into a foetal position. Using her arms to pull her knees close to her chest, she wished that she had someone to hold her and tell her everything was alright. Instead, she felt alone and helpless. Although legally still a child, she longed to be a child again; a child oblivious to all this, the child running towards the Hippo House.

She didn't dare breathe a sigh of relief, until twenty minutes later. Although she knew she must look terrible, she didn't care. Constantly aware of that awful taste, she longed to get home so that she could wash her mouth out, and brush her teeth. All she could think about on the bus going home, was her dream about fingers in her mouth; but she couldn't understand why.

Betrayed

Bren thought that if she talked about what had happened, she could put it in the past. Telling her mother was out of the question, as she would never have let her out of the house again. Her best girlfriend Cherie was on holiday; so, she confided in her best boy-friend, Richard.

She classed Richard S as one of her best friends, someone that she could tell anything. Richard knew about Cherie's bad reputation, but he knew Bren was a 'good girl'. Even though they really liked each other they had never dated, as they had a really good friendship and didn't want to ruin it. It turned out that Richard wasn't such a good friend after all. Instead of the comforting hug she hoped for, he looked at her in disgust and walked off.

A few days later, she found out that he had told everyone that she gave blow jobs. Then somehow people confused her with a girl named Beryl, who was having sex with everyone; and her name

41

became dirt.

That Sunday in the park, she was the only girl there. Dick Perry, the boy she had fancied for months, asked her if she would like to go for a walk. After what had just happened, she should have been less trusting, but he was one of the 'gang'; her friend. When they reached the other field, they sat on the grass and chatted. He leant forward and kissed her. She had waited so long for this moment. Then, to her horror, he pushed her down on to the grass and grabbed at her, fondling her breast.

He was practically lying on top of her, she screamed for him to stop. Shocked, he pulled away from her. She was made to feel worse when he apologised.

"I'm sorry, but I thought that was what you wanted".

He told her he had been egged on by his mates, who had said that she was 'gagging for it'; he waited for her reaction.

She explained how she thought he had finally noticed her; but he told her he wasn't interested, as he fancied someone else. He might just as well have slapped her; he would have been happy to have sex with her, but didn't fancy her enough to date.

Naturally, Dick wanted to save face, and told everyone that he had got whatever it was they wanted to hear. The other boys were quite happy to try their luck, but none of them wanted to date a 'slag'. She hadn't willingly done anything wrong.

How she wished she could go back to the time when everyone just thought she was weird. At least she didn't have to worry that rumours of that might get back to her mother. Now she was left with only one friend, and she was on holiday. The easiest thing to do was stay at home.

And still the Hippo's plagued her dreams, but this time they were competing with the 'finger in her mouth' dream.

She wondered which of them was the real villain, the boy who committed the act, or the boy who spread the rumours. They had both violated her in different ways. The sex act had terrified and disgusted her, but the rumours had almost broken her completely; so, she didn't leave the house except to go to school.

As if to add insult to injury. A few weeks later, her parents were watching Double Your Money on TV; while she sat at the table, sewing. Hughie introduced the contestant.
"Michael Q...... ......".
She finished the name and was shocked when Hughie Green echoed what she said.

Looking up, she was greeted by a familiar face staring back at her from the TV screen. To top it all, he won the £1000 Treasure Trail. How she stopped the tears from flowing was beyond her. She was glad her mother didn't question her saying the name; but then her mother was used to her saying strange things.

Up until that moment, she hadn't known if it was even his real name, or where he lived, so, he had gone unpunished. Anyway, what was the point. He was from a rich family, and it was her word against his. They hadn't really been anywhere together, so there was no proof that they had even met up that night.

Seeing him on TV made her realise, that no matter how you try to hide from things they can still catch up with you. She couldn't stay locked away for ever; so, whatever was going to happen, she would have to face it.
Not long after, Cherie's reputation led to alarming consequences.

Driven Out of the Mount

It was a Friday evening in late August, and the Mount was busier than usual. Cherie and I were dancing to disco music, and had been having a good time until Betty and Pamela walked in. Betty was the girl I used to sing with in the music room at lunchtime. Betty and Pamela were dating Alf and Dan, two of the most popular boys in the area, and the same ones who had dealt with Gerry.

Bren noticed that Betty and Pamela's attention was focused on Cherie, who was dancing in a sexy manner, her large bosom bouncing around in her low-cut top. Betty smirked and said something to Pamela, who giggled. They spoke to their boyfriends, who in turn started talking to the other lads in the club. After a while, they spoke to her and Cherie's friends, male and female.

Due to previous experiences, Bren was constantly on her guard when things didn't seem right; and there was definitely something amiss. By now, she was paying more attention to what was going on, than to her dancing. Aware that her friends were nodding and obviously agreeing to something, she reached for Cherie's arm, pulling her from the dance floor. Whispering.

"Something's not right."

Then the chanting began, first just Betty and Pamela and then everyone joined in.

"Slag, slag, slag, slag."

Bren's friends Joanne and Sara approached her and tried to reason with her.

"Brenda, come with us and you'll be ok."

"No, Cherie's a friend." Surprised that her voice was unwavering, although once again she was in a situation where she was not in control, she grabbed Cherie's arm and steered her towards the exit. Pushing through the crowd that tried to bar their way. Betty's voice shouted out, above the constant chanting.

"Brenda, last chance. If you don't come with us, you'll get the same as her."

Her heart pounded; she was scared, but she was determined to stay with her friend. Bren and Cherie passed through the swing doors and out through the school gates. They reached the corner and turned onto the main road. The mob followed, still chanting. A little further up the road, under Betty's direction, the mob split into two and moved up either side of them; grabbing their arms and forcing them apart. Once Bren and Cherie were separated, they were surrounded and forced in different directions. That was the last Bren saw of Cherie, for a few weeks.

Bren was forced along Chamberlayne Road, towards where she lived. The crowd surrounding her stopped. Noticing that there were still a few familiar faces amongst them, Bren didn't want to feel more than disappointment; but it was hard. Her so-called friends had forfeited friendship for safety in numbers, and who could blame them.

One of the lads pushed to the front. Bren had seen him in the club a few times, but didn't know him.

"So, slag, do you give a blow job as good as your friend Cherie then?"

Obviously, she now knew what a blow job was. But she was shocked by the question. The boy slapped Bren hard across the face, sending her reeling backwards. She didn't cry out and he must have thought that she was taunting him, because he slapped her again; splitting her lip and causing blood to trickle down her chin.

Then she heard a familiar voice.

"I'm not being part of this. Stopping someone from coming to our youth club is one thing but beating up our friends is wrong. I'm going and if the rest of you want part of this, then fuck you." Steve turned and walked away. The people she had called friends looked at each other and followed Steve. The boy who had hit her looked confused then he, and the others who had been milling about, also left.

She headed for home but she didn't feel relieved, just beaten. Bren phoned the police but she couldn't tell them exactly where Cherie was, because she didn't know. The police said they would send a car to sweep the area.

Cherie didn't show up at school after the summer break. One of the teachers said that she was still away on holiday. Bren called at her house a few times but there was no answer.

On her way home from Queens Park one afternoon, Bren bumped into Cherie outside the gate. Bren was overjoyed to see her friend, but the feeling wasn't mutual. Cherie hit Bren hard in the face. Before Bren could say anything, a knee found that precise spot between her legs, right on her pubis bone. As she bent forward in pain, Cherie grabbed her in a head lock and wrestled her to the ground. Once she was down, Cherie began kicking her.

Bren didn't want to fight back, because she still looked upon Cherie as her best friend, but she didn't like getting hurt either. She lay on the ground, shielding her head from the vicious kicks, then she twisted onto her back and launched a well-aimed foot at Cherie's stomach. Cherie staggered backwards, giving Bren enough time to get to her feet. Cherie shouted.

"I never want to set eyes on you again."

Bren walked away; her pain more emotional than physical. Obviously, Cherie thought she had either deserted her, or joined forces with the people who ganged up on them that night. She heard that the mob had not physically harmed Cherie, apart from pushing her around and ripping her clothes. It was also said that someone had phoned the police and they intervened. But she never got the chance to ask Cherie if any of that was true.

Regaining My Self-Respect

Having now lost my best friend, the only option for evening

entertainment was the Mount Youth Club, but I hadn't been back there since the mob had driven us out. I missed the classes and the disco, but most of all I missed the company.

Pausing at the school gate to pluck up the courage to enter, she took the plunge, it was now or never. What was the worst they could do? Gang up on her again? Ignore her? She took a deep breath, and pushed open the swing doors to the sports hall. There was no sign of Betty or Pamela. A few of the girls turned round and looked, then carried on talking. Steve came out of the café and waved to her.
"You finally decided to come back then."

He explained that after Richard S heard what had happened, he told them the full story about her sexual assault and admitted that he had spread the rumours because he was jealous; 'Too little too late, because mud sticks'. She thought.
Steve continued.
"Picked a good night for it, Sandra H and the Crescent mob are coming down for a fight. Sandra says, she's going to give our girls a right pasting".

Bren could feel her anger welling up inside at the thought of someone else wanting to inflict pain on her. She gritted her teeth.
"Have to get through me first."
By the time she realised she had actually said it aloud, Steve had already gone to tell everyone that she was going to stand up to Sandra.

Just after eight, Roger shouted that Sandra was on her way in. Bren moved nearer to the door, everyone watched her and wondered whether she really was going to take Sandra on. She had never met Sandra and didn't know what to expect.

What pushed through that door a few seconds later, she definitely didn't expect. A flame haired, twenty stone, six-footer, who would have made even the most aggressive Celtic warrior look like a pussy cat.

Sandra looked down at her, with a stare so icy that it could bore deep into your chest and freeze your heart solid. Bren could feel her blood running cold already. She feared that she would be frozen to the spot forever. Yet she couldn't run, couldn't back down, as everyone's eyes were upon her.

Raising her head, she met the greenest eyes she had ever seen. Sandra towered above her, fists clenched, an evil sneer on her lips; waiting. Bren drew a breath, that swelled her otherwise small chest. "What the fuck do you want?"

She was surprised at the ferocity in her voice and her choice of language, as she normally never swore.

Even so, she expected Sandra to flatten her with a blow from one of her sledge-hammer fists. Sandra looked straight into her eyes, bending closer to do so. Bren stood her ground, even though she felt like she was quaking in her boots. Sandra snarled.

"So, you are going to take me on, are you?"

"If need be."

Sandra roared with laughter. It was so loud it made the floor shake; or perhaps it was actually Bren's legs that were shaking. Sandra held out her hand.

"What's your name? I need to know it, so that I can tell everyone that you are the only person, male or female, to stand up to me. Put it there, girl."

Once again, Sandra offered her hand. Bren grasped it.

"Brenda. My name's Brenda."

"Come on I'll buy you a coke." Sandra put her arm around Bren's shoulders.

Bren breathed a sigh of relief and made a mental note never to do anything like that, ever again.

Now that my parents were getting older, they were struggling financially, so it made sense that I should leave school and get a job as soon as possible. My attendance had got so bad that my parents had been threatened with court action. Mum had to walk me to school every day to make sure I went.

There was still nearly eight months to go until I was fifteen and school was becoming unbearable. Some of the teachers found every opportunity to make me look bad in front of the class, so I often bunked lessons. It wasn't because I was stupid, in fact quite the opposite, I just didn't want to be there anymore.

After a couple of months, I realised the error of my ways. Being as it was a grammar school; I knew my parents would have to battle to get me released at fifteen instead of eighteen. If I wanted to leave and get a reasonable job, I needed a good report. So, for the last six months or so, I worked harder than I ever had.

Near Death Experience and Realisation

Not long after my fifteenth birthday, I got a very bad dose of flu that turned to pneumonia. I was taken into hospital and as a result of my illness my heart stopped for a short period. During this time, I had what I can only describe as a Near Death Experience.

Her NDE wasn't the same as most people relate. There were no green fields and sunshine; for her everything was dark. She was gliding down a dark tunnel, there was a light at the end of it, but not the brilliant inviting light that some people talk about. Her light was more like a penlight torch beam, miles away; if it was any smaller, she wouldn't have been able to see it at all.

Yes, she did start to walk towards it, but there were no loved ones welcoming her with open arms. There were just hands reaching out to her from the dark, some almost clawing at her, as if trying to pull her in. Although they didn't appear to be friendly, she wasn't particularly afraid. But she did know she wasn't dreaming. Then there was the voice. It was a woman's voice, but not one that she recognised.

"It is not your time yet, go back."

As soon as the voice stopped, she was sucked back at great speed; like she had been caught in the path of a very powerful vacuum cleaner.

My Dad spoke very little about his time in WW1 but he still bore the wounds both mentally and physically. The indented scars in his left leg, arm, hand, neck and head, bore witness to the horrors that he had survived. As did the pieces of shrapnel, that my mother insisted were still moving around in his brain.

Dad had worked on the buses since the 1930s and was driving them in WW2, that is where he met my mother; she was his conductorette. He shared a story with me in which he and my mother had a close encounter with death.

By deduction, it was probably mid evening around May 10th 1941. Dad was driving his bus along Great Western Road towards Westbourne Park Railway Bridge, following another bus driven by a work mate. As he approached the bridge, for some reason he felt compelled to stop his bus; even though the bus in front carried on across the bridge.

Not long after, his attention was drawn to the throb of an unsynchronised engine somewhere above him, which was followed by a high-pitched whistling. Then silence. A few seconds later, the bus shook from the impact of the explosion.

Cut by glass from the shattered windscreen, Dad swept his hand across his forehead to clear the blood dripping in his eyes. It was then, in the limited glow from the headlights, that he saw what remained of the bus in front. The bus was no more than a mass of jagged, smoking metal and bloodied rags. Sickened, he averted his gaze. He knew those people were beyond help, his concern was now for his passengers.

Climbing out of his cab he moved towards the back of the bus. On reaching the boarding platform he discovered my mother on the floor, along with all the passengers; they were all covered in broken glass. Apart from cuts, bruises and shock, everyone was alive and otherwise unhurt.

Something or someone was obviously looking after my parents that day, otherwise I wouldn't be here to tell their tale. Perhaps Dad also had some kind of latent psychic ability.

I believe that the trauma of WW1 may have contributed to my dad's erratic behaviour.

I learnt from an early age about personal hygiene and, now that I was fast becoming a young woman, I took advantage of bath nights. Our bathroom at home was huge and very cold, as the only form of heating was a square paraffin heater. Partly because the bathroom steamed up easily and partly because of the fumes from the paraffin heater, we used to leave the door open slightly when taking a bath.

Bren was drying herself with the bath towel, when she became aware of something blocking the light from the hallway; light that normally peeped through the gap made by the rising butt hinges. The shadow wasn't constant occasionally it would disappear, then reappear a few seconds later; as though someone was hovering outside the door, watching her naked body as it completed the drying process.

Thinking back, she remembered the many times she had seen her father lingering in the hallway outside the bathroom, when her sister Anna was taking a bath. Pretending to be on his way to the hall cupboard when he realised that Bren had spotted him; although, at the time, she was too young to realise what he was up to. It was only now that she became aware of his motives. Bren pushed the door closed with her foot. Fully aware that her mother would be angry when she saw the marks the ribbons of water left on the painted walls.

My psychic abilities appeared to be getting stronger every day. Being as the messages were becoming more frequent, I needed to know what was happening to me. At the time there was no advertising of spiritualist churches and the like, I had no idea such things existed so I did the next best thing; I searched for a coven.

I found one locally; an Alexandrian coven. I spent around a year there and was grateful for everything I learnt. But when it was suggested that I join the coven dancing naked in the moonlight, I decided it was no longer for me. At sixteen, I was still trying to get used to the sight of my woman's body and wasn't ready to show it to anyone else.

About the same time, I started to experience some strange sensations. Sometimes it felt like my face and body were changing shape and often my voice would sound different. Someone suggested I go and see a woman named Ivy.

When Bren got to Ivy's house, she was taken to a large summer-house at the bottom of the garden. There were around a dozen people already seated and Bren was asked to join them. Sitting in a vacant chair, she closed her eyes as instructed. One woman started giving some spiritual advice, after which Ivy thanked her.

About half an hour later, Bren heard a man's voice speaking in broken English. She was puzzled, and tried to focus on where it was coming from, then she realised it was coming from her; shocked, Bren opened her eyes. The woman who had first spoken, glared at

her. Then, to Bren's horror the woman pointed an accusing finger.
"You have been consorting with the devil."
Bren looked around to see who the finger was pointing at, and realised that the woman was talking to her.
"I haven't, really I haven't."
But the woman wasn't going to be stopped.
"You have serpents winding themselves around you, and they need to be removed."

Bren shot out of the chair and ran for the door. Obviously, she never went back and from then on her 'gift' was allowed to develop naturally.

Boys and Booze

Dick Perry had started dating Joanne, who had always said she wasn't interested in him. Perhaps Joanne thought that she was going to make Bren jealous, but she was very much mistaken; as unbeknown to Joanne and the rest of the crowd, Bren had ceased to have any affection towards Dick since the day in the park, when he tried to grope her.

While walking down Kilburn High Road one evening, I met a young man who asked me if I fancied going for a drink. I think it was The Bird in Hand pub that we went into. Although barely fifteen, I had developed a taste for brown ale and navy rum; not in the same glass though. My drinking capacity had increased and I was confident that I could drink any of the lads under the table, so one brown ale with a stranger wasn't going to be a problem.

The man turned out to be in his early thirties, and the topic of conversation was starting to make Bren feel very uncomfortable. She certainly didn't want to leave the pub with this man. Excusing herself, she went to the toilet.

After using the loo, she went to the sink to wash her hands. Glancing up, she found the answer to her predicament, an open window just above the sink. It was the type of window that opened outwards and upwards, the opening was quite small but she was very slim.

Suddenly aware of how long she had been gone, she started to worry that the man might come looking for her, it was now or never. Climbing onto the sink, she opened the window fully. Stooping, she extended both her arms out of the window, her head and shoulders just fitted through the gap. Pushing out a bit further, she stopped suddenly.

"Damn".

The belt loop of her jeans had caught on the peg that secured the window arm, and she knew it would be impossible to bring one of her hands back through the window to release it.

Sweat began to pour down her face as she realised time was running out, she fidgeted, a lump rising in her throat. 'Calm down', she thought. Inching backwards slightly, she felt the loop come loose. Moving her lower half slightly to her right so that the loop wasn't in line with the peg, she prepared to slip through the window.

There was movement outside the door to the bar; she feared that someone would come in and catch her with her lower half semi-standing in the sink. Thrusting herself forward she half slid, half fell, towards the ground below. She was so grateful it was only a few feet.

Her palms impacted against the gravel. Shuffling her hands forward, so that her back arched as her feet touched down, she moved into a crouching position, pushed herself up to standing, and was off at a sprint. Not stopping until she reached the station.

Mum must have been shocked because for once I was in early, and sober.

From the age of fifteen life became a series of parties, there was at least one every weekend. Mum always said I was like my Auntie Lil. Perhaps our similarities were due to us both being Capricorns, and because we could both drink like fish. The difference being, that I was not a nasty drunk.

Auntie Lil had a very colourful language repertoire and a foul temper which she often displayed; especially towards her husband. She didn't trust Uncle George one little bit. One evening when Uncle George was having a drink in a pub near Marble Arch, she decided he must be with a woman. Aunt Lil waited outside the pub in the hope of catching him 'at it.' What she didn't realise, was that it was an area renowned for prostitutes, and said prostitutes thought Aunt Lil was trying to steal their 'patch', so they beat her up.

Being as she was often drunk; my aunt was well known to the police and frequently took rides in a Black Maria. She and a friend once sat in the middle of the road and got run over by a taxi. They were taken to hospital by ambulance. Auntie Lil had injured her leg, and the other woman had injured her head. The doctor arrived with their X-rays, but he got them mixed up and was told so by my aunt, who informed him.

"That's not my fucking head, it's the old cow in the next bed."

Auntie Lil was the aunt I was closest to, and saw most of, until she passed with cancer of the stomach.

Chapter 5
Starting Work, a New Kind of Bullying

My fifteenth birthday fell in January, just before the new term started, so I wasn't allowed to leave school until the Easter holidays at the end of March. Around the beginning of February an appointment was made for me with the school recruitment office. Who decided for me, that I was suited to a job in accounts being as I was good at maths. I was sent for an interview for an office junior's position, at an electrical engineering company in Neasden.

A week later I received a letter to say that I was being offered the job at AEI, to start in April, at £3.19s.6d per week. To mark the occasion, Dad gave me a post office book with over £100 in it, which I was allowed to spend on clothes for starting work.

As I was due to be tested for new spectacles, I opted for the best frames that the NHS had to offer. Heavy tortoiseshell, almost round, which I thought quite suited me and took the emphasis away from my large bent nose; but apparently, I thought wrong. Is it normal, to feel physically sick at the sight of your own image? Although I often joke about being non-photogenic and how I cringe at certain photos, it goes deeper than that, much deeper.

Two of us started work on the same day. Me and a mixed-race girl named Lorraine. The office manager was a tall broad-shouldered woman, wearing a 'to the manor born' tweed suit. She showed us around the factory and offices, then led us to the mailing department, where we were to work. Our jobs consisted of sorting mail and delivering it around the factory. We had two delivery and pick-up rounds a day; dropping the ingoing mail on the way out and then picking up the outgoing mail on the way back. Personally, I didn't quite understand where accounts, or being good at maths, came into this job.

After a few days, I began to get used to the work but I hated the walk through the factory and the drawing office.

No matter how quiet she tried to be, the heavy rubber edged doors always swung to and fro behind her. Marking her entrance with an unmistakably loud 'blub-blub'; before they stilled themselves. They alerted everyone in the factory to her presence. Post bag slung over her shoulder, head down, she headed towards the metal staircase which took her up to the first office.

Bren hoped they hadn't realised it was her, but the now familiar catcalls and wolf-whistles told her they had. The crane driver was the first to start, from his seat high in the arches of the roof. His voice amplified by the cones in the eaves.

"Tawittawoo, tawittawoo, look out fellas the owl is on her way."

Humiliated, tears pooled in her eyes, but still she hurried on her rounds; unable to remove her spectacles, because she wouldn't be able to see the names on the mail. More owl sounds, followed by cruel male laughter.

She still had the Drawing Office to face, which was even worse. It was a narrow centre walkway between two rows of Drawing Boards, that seemed to stretch for a mile; it was probably more like forty or fifty feet. Several voices gave owl impressions, but she carried on walking.

"Quiet lads."

The manager gestured for his apprentices to keep the noise down, while laughing with them.

Then it was through the swing doors, into the training school/machine shop. Here they didn't dare call out, they just whispered and giggled as she passed; while carrying on with their work. As she neared the doors at the end, two boys gave her friendly smiles; but they were both geeky looking kids, who could obviously relate to teasing and bullying.

After her round, she reached the steps that took her back to the factory lower level. As she placed her foot on the first step, the toe of her shoe caught between one of the gaps in the metal tread, pitching her forward. Her arms reached out grabbing at air. The fall seemed to go on forever. All she could think about was people watching her.

The thud as she landed rang in her ears. Outstretched, feet against the bottom step, arms pinned under her chest, palms flat against the stone floor; she was unable to move. She didn't know whether she wanted to laugh or cry, but she could do neither; incapable of making a sound, as all the air had been forced from her lungs. All she could do was lie there until she could breathe again; praying that no one would use the staircase.

After what seemed like hours, she was able to lift herself from the floor. Standing up cautiously, she checked her body, nothing appeared to be broken; apart from her spirit. She was glad the staircase was in an enclosed corner. Shaking, she started to walk towards the factory floor and a repeat of the catcalls.

Outside work, in a bid to look normal, I ditched my spectacles even though I could hardly see without them. Sometimes boys gave me a second glance but I considered myself to be ugly, which seemed to have been confirmed by the males at work, so I presumed them to be critical looks.

Probably the best thing about AEI was the social club. They had some good monthly discos and I persuaded Lorraine to come with me. My second cousin Michael, Aunt Lil's grandson, also worked for AEI and would make regular appearances at the discos. One particular night, Michael and his friend stood near our table. We had all had a lot to drink, Michael and his friend were drinking shorts, which they placed on our table. While Michael was watching some girls dancing, I drank his whiskey. When he turned to grab the glass, he was so inebriated he probably thought he had already drunk it.

Michael went off to get another drink while his mate went to buy some jellied eels, from a stall outside the club. Michael put his drink on the table and carried on watching the dancing. As I went to grab the glass he turned round and caught me.

"Come outside. I want a word with you."

Like an idiot I walked outside and Michael followed. Grabbing me from behind, he held my arms tightly against my sides while his mate shoved a jellied eel in my mouth, pinched my nose and held his hand over my face so that I had no choice but to swallow. They let me go, just as the contents of my stomach decided to vacate; and to think I fancied my cousin for ages before that night.

Part of our duty at AEI, was to collect supplies from the stationary department. One day while Lorraine and I were collecting some boxes of photocopying paper, we got stuck in the lift; which had gates rather than doors. We were trapped in there for about an hour. Some of the boys from the drawing office found it extremely funny to throw peanuts at us, saying that they were feeding the monkeys in their cage. An extremely racist remark even then.

A few of the boys from AEI did ask me out on dates. Some of them actually seemed to like me, until their mates found out; then they completely lost interest. One of these boys was Terry, who worked in the drawing office. He was one of the few who didn't join in the catcalls. In fact, he would give me a wink when I passed through the office delivering the post. When I picked up the mail one morning, there was a note in his 'out' tray addressed 'to the post girl'. The note asked if I would go out with him the following Friday.

The next day there was a note asking me to wait for him by the training school lifts. I waited a few minutes, and was just about to walk away when he appeared carrying some technical drawings; his excuse to leave the office. We arranged our date and went our separate ways.

Being as he was extremely good-looking; I was surprised that he actually appeared to be really keen on me. We would take it in turns to call each other daily, via my local phone box. Everything had been going well, we had been seeing each other and visiting each other's homes for about two months, when his friend Will found out. From that moment onwards he would avoid my gaze at work, and stopped contacting me.

A few days later one of the geeky boys from the training school asked if I would like to go out for coffee, his name was George. As it turned out, he was really nice and he had a great family. We would play darts with his dad, and I became really good at the game. The problem was George was too nice, as I now had a soft spot for good looking bad-boys; so, we drifted apart.

About three or four months after he had stopped talking to me, Terry dropped me a note in the out tray asking for a second chance. But he had hurt me deeply and I couldn't be sure that it wasn't some kind of prank to make me look foolish. So, I told him.
"No thank you."
Pride wouldn't let me take that risk.

Lorraine and I began frequenting the clubs in the West End. Namely the Flamingo and the Marquee, where we would watch many of the 'soon to be famous' groups. I really loved the club atmosphere and enjoyed dancing to the current bands.

It was nearing midnight one Friday; Lorraine and I had been clubbing and I was on my way home from Queens Park station. Half way down Harvist Road a lad stopped me and gave me the handpiece from a telephone box; it still had the wire hanging from it. He told me Tom was on the line for me, then he walked away. When I looked up, he was nowhere to be seen; I presumed he must have gone into one of the houses. If I wasn't still holding the handpiece, I would have thought I imagined it all. I had never seen the boy before and I never saw him again. I found this quite odd at the time but even more so a few weeks later.

Creeping Hands and Puppy Love

Not having been on a date for months, I had resigned myself to the fact that boys just didn't find me attractive and I was probably destined to become an old maid.

Then, ironically, a few days later along came Tom. He was Irish, over six feet tall, slim, not fantastic looking but really nice. My first thought was, 'This could be someone I could get to like very much.' We had a few dates and we were getting on really well. He was everything you could want in a boyfriend, polite, charming, kind, funny and hardworking.

It was our fifth date and we were going to the Grange Cinema in Kilburn. I was wearing an extremely tight skirt and some very high heels. Trying to look my best, I decided not to wear my glasses; it was pre contact lens days, which meant I was blind as a bat.

The Grange was the 'posh' cinema of our area, beautifully decorated with all the trimmings, plush seats, fringed curtains and golden rope barriers. Tom met me outside the cinema. He was wearing a striped scarf, suit jacket and jeans. The film showing was a horror, 'The Creeping Hand'. We bought tickets and decided to sit downstairs or rather I did, as I wouldn't have been able to see the screen otherwise.

We walked down the aisle. Tom being the perfect gent let me walk in front. Next thing, I was sprawled on the floor, with my legs sticking out backwards, slightly elevated by the rope barrier that I had tripped over in the dark. It was then that Tom said something that I was to hear thousands of times over the years.

"I bet you didn't see that coming."

The evening just seemed to go downhill from there onwards.

We had been watching the film for about twenty minutes. The space ship had taken off and disintegrated. The spaceman's hand and arm up to his elbow, had fallen back down to earth and was now on a killing spree. Then Tom discovered his scarf was missing.

"I had it when we sat down, got to find it, it's my college scarf."

He seemed to think that when the people in the row behind had moved along to their seats, they must have dragged his scarf to the end of the row with them.

Off he went, crawling along our row on his hands and knees, in search of his scarf; peering under all the seats as he went. Meanwhile, the 'Creeping Hand' on the screen, was crawling along the floor looking for its next victim.

Tom spotted his scarf in the next row, right by a woman's feet. He had to lay down flat and stretch right under the seat to try and reach it, which meant he couldn't see what he was doing. His hand floundered about trying to grab the scarf. As he did so, his hand touched the woman's leg, just as the 'Creeping hand' on the screen grabbed its victim. Leaping from her seat, the woman let out a piercing scream. Tom scrambled out from under the seat, clutching his scarf and shouting.

"I've got it."

We never saw the end of the film because we were asked to leave. We didn't make a sixth date, either. Tom was too embarrassed to ask me, and I was embarrassed for him.

A few months later, I met a drop-dead amazing boy named Hal, he was almost six months younger than me, but looked a lot older than his fifteen and a half years. He lived in SW London and I was hooked from the first moment I saw him. We would meet at White City tube and go out in Shepherds Bush, or alternate going to each other's homes. His family invited me to spend Christmas with them and I didn't take a lot of persuading.

My mum and dad were going to my half-brother Bob's house for a week, they weren't keen on me staying behind, but finally relented as I had to work the day after Boxing Day.

Aware that Hal's family were gypsies, I knew that I was in for a bit of a wild time. Mid-morning on Christmas Day, I took the tube to Putney Bridge station to make the connection for SW London. The train was delayed, so by the time I got there the trains had stopped running. Being pre-mobile days, I hunted for a phone box and rang Hal. He told me to wait where I was, and he would walk up to collect me.

When we arrived at his house, his parents were already waiting to go and meet up with family members, at a pub in Southall. It was a pleasant enough few hours, which took us into early evening. Then we made our way to visit the Patriarch of the family, Hal's great grandad; it was his eightieth birthday and he was having a party.

They arrived at the three-bedroom semi, to find the party in full throttle. Most of the family members were loud and very drunk. Bren could turn a blind eye to this, as she had been to some pretty wild parties since she started drinking.

What she couldn't stomach, was Great-grandad running around the house stark naked. A very weathered, wrinkly-skinned old man, grabbing hold of all the women and rubbing his penis against them. Disgusted, she looked around, there were children of all ages present; some under three years old, all watching the shenanigans.

Bren felt sick and out of place, there was something so wrong about the whole scenario, especially being as everyone was encouraging him. She thought back to her sexual assaults and it made her feel even worse about what was going on. When the old man came near her, she could feel her whole body stiffen, she didn't want this vile creature to touch her in any way. It stirred some kind of horrible memory that she couldn't tap into; she was repulsed at the thought of this old man's body being anywhere near hers. Not being used to this kind of behaviour, she was glad when they were ferried off to another party in a pub function room.

She and Hal danced to their favourite songs and smooched a little, until a woman cut in and whisked Hal off to dance with her. A tall man in his thirties, came up to Bren and started dancing next to her, when the music became slower, he pulled Bren close and started kissing her neck. Feeling extremely uncomfortable, she pulled away. But he held on to her, as she struggled to free herself from his grip. His wife appeared, grabbed him and pulled him away while raining abuse on Bren; saying that she wasn't one of them and that she had no business being there. She really regretted not going with her mum and dad.

It turned out that the party was a two-day event and everyone was expected to stay the night. They all settled down, sleeping on the floor in sleeping bags. As soon as his wife was asleep, the man from earlier tried to snuggle up next to Bren. Terrified, she pushed him away and moved closer to Hal. As she lay awake, too uncomfortable to sleep, she realised she had another day to get through with these people; which she just couldn't face.

On Boxing Day morning, she told Hal she wanted to go home. Hal said he would walk her to the bus stop, but wouldn't go with her. They walked to Southall Broadway where Hal left her and went back to the party.

Despite being wary of his family, Bren continued to see Hal, as she was still crazy about him. One day, he made her promise that she wouldn't go into the West End anymore and she agreed. On the days she didn't see Hal she stayed at home.

Not having been to the West End since making her promise, she found herself missing it. Then one mid-January evening, while watching TV with her mum and dad, she suddenly had the urge to go to Leicester Square. She had no idea why; she just knew she needed to go. Making her excuses to her parents, she got ready and went to get the bus.

Once on Shaftesbury Avenue, Bren began walking slowly, enjoying the bustle and the bright lights. She hadn't been there long and had just reached Leicester Square, when she happened to glance across the road. There was Hal with his mates, his arm around some girl. He saw Bren and looked totally shocked. Turning to walk the other way, she expected Hal to run after her, but he didn't. Sobbing and sick to her stomach, she didn't know how she got home.

Apart from going to work, she didn't leave the house for weeks, she just got out the sewing machine and made loads of clothes. Not for any particular occasion, just to take her mind off the pain of betrayal.

Sophistication, for What It's Worth

Tired of insults and bored with being a postal clerk, I decided that a year at AEI was enough and it was now time to move on to pastures new. Now at sixteen years old, I was going to begin a new job in Jermyn Street, in the St James area of London; earning a quite healthy monthly salary.

Working in the West End had its pitfalls, the main one was that I had to use the Underground, the tube as we called it, every day. I'd probably had issues with using the tube for a very long time, but when you're a child you're usually with your parents, or a class of very excited kids. Now I had to face regular tube journeys alone, and in the rush hour.

Travelling on the first day was traumatic. The number of people waiting on the usually quiet station platform, was nothing compared to being in the tube. As soon as the train arrived there was a mad dash, and by the time Bren boarded there were no seats and very little standing room. She was pushed and shoved until she was lodged in the middle of a mass of bodies. That was when she experienced the second panic attack of her life.

The train was so crowded, she couldn't see past the sea of commuters surrounding her. All she wanted to do was to find a way out. The smell of sweat, stale perfume and bad breath from countless bodies assailed her nostrils. Chest tight, she gasped for air, her lungs felt like they were being compressed by the people pushing against her. Her vision blurred. Then the train stopped and people started leaving. Seizing the opportunity, she moved nearer to the exit.

The journey home was even worse. She soon learnt, to push herself tightly in the corner by the door, where she could at least see her escape route.

DuPont, of Lycra and Teflon fame, was an American corporation. As soon as I arrived, I was whisked away for finger printing, a mug shot, and to sign the official secrets act. The office manager gave me a tour of the workplace, and told me that in a few weeks, we would be moving to a new building in Fetter Lane, off Fleet Street. My first day was to be spent viewing our new offices, and sorting what items were making the move with us.

Carla seemed nice, she introduced herself and asked if I would like the desk next to hers. After lunch a coach arrived, which transported us all to the new building.

Our new office suite was open plan, so everyone got to mingle. The other employees were all very sophisticated and well spoken. I decided, I needed to introduce some suits and fashionable jackets, to my wardrobe. I already had a new ultra-fashionable short haircut, which my mother didn't approve of; going so far as to ask me if I had turned into a lesbian like my cousin Ann. Probably because, after Hal, I vowed I would never give my heart to another boy.

We moved to Fetter Lane and after a few weeks in my new working environment, Carla said that we had been invited to a party by one of the boys whose name was Garth.

The party wasn't quite the event I expected. Definitely not like our parties in NW London, where we consumed massive amounts of beer and laughed and danced. This party was held in the lounge of a huge apartment, where we sipped a few glasses of wine and ate pizza.

After which, the boys did their darnedest to get the girls into bed. For all their money and posh voices, they weren't at all charming, it was a case of 'drop them blossom you are up next'. Even NW London boys knew they had to do a certain amount of wooing, before they were even in with the chance of a kiss.

Contrary to some people's beliefs, I was still a virgin and aimed to stay that way; so, jumping into bed with some boring Mayfair 'IKE'[2] was not high on my list. Brassed off at their behaviour, I went home.

The day after the party Garth asked me out on a date, stating that he was engaged but his fiancée wouldn't find out because she was on holiday. I decided that he had no respect for either of us and, in true NW London fashion, I told him he could stick his date where the sun doesn't shine.

Carla had been brought up to mix with some very influential and monied people and I was soon introduced to some of them. We were given backstage passes to shows, guest passes to meet some of the stars, and free entrance to some of the best night clubs.

When I wasn't hanging around with Carla, who although nearly eighteen wasn't allowed out during the week, I was spending time in Richmond with some lovely lads; who I had met on the tube one night, when I was on my way home from a club. The Richmond lads were great fun. They were all well-educated and knowledgeable and we spent many happy hours engrossed in deep and meaningful discussions.

Chapter 6
The Seedy Side of West End Life

Perhaps it was just that I was growing up and perceiving things differently, maybe it was the 'West End' way of life that had opened my eyes, but the 60s were totally different to the 50s. People were much more open about their sexuality. I had heard my mother refer to 'nancy boys' or 'mummy's boys', but I always thought that she meant boys that were closer to their mother than their father. It wasn't until I started going to West End clubs that I became aware of the 'gay scene'. I think Carla was about as naïve as I was. She lived with her mother, and their idea of socialising was having people round to dinner.

One of the girls we worked with was secretary of the UK branch of the Gene Pitney fan club. Gene was due to appear at the Marquee club, and Carla and I were invited to go and meet him. Besides giving a great performance he turned out to be a really nice guy, who took time to talk to his fans and actually showed interest in what they had to say.

The 60s was a great time for clubbing and meeting your current pop idol, as many of them were really down to earth. Carla and I often visited the Scene in Ham Yard Soho. It was frequented by many pop stars who would always be happy to chat and dance with their fans.

The pop scene changed completely when Beatlemania was at its height. Most of the once friendly stars, were more interested in getting away from screaming fans than talking or signing autographs.

Although, only on the brink of 'flower power' I was already a bit of a hippy; but I did like to bathe every day. Some weekend evenings, we would sit around a small fire in St. James' Park, handing round a clay pipe containing cannabis, singing songs that we composed between us and trying to put the world to rights. We would talk into the early hours of the morning, when foreign backpackers would arrive to sleep in the deckchairs under the bandstand. Sometimes we would join them. Generally, the police were very good, and would not move anyone on, unless they were causing trouble. They would wake the back packers at 6am and send them on their way, before the commuters took their daily stroll to the tube via the park.

Very soon Carla and I became part of the West End Scene, frequenting the clubs, cafés and amusement arcades. I guess I was a little more hooked than her, as I spent practically every evening and weekend there.

Spending so much time in the West End, I soon got to know a lot of the locals, one girl in particular caught my eye because of her clothes. Like me she had a very unique style but her clothes weren't handmade, they were vintage. Dee and I got talking and struck up a bit of a friendship. I always remarked on her clothes and asked where she got them, but she would never let on.

A few months after we met, we were sat having coffee and strawberry gateau in the Wimpy Bar, when she told me to hurry up as we had somewhere to go. Doing as I was told, I swigged my coffee and off we went through alleyways and streets that I didn't know existed, let alone had walked down.

We stopped outside a very dingy shop with windows that looked like they hadn't been cleaned since Dickensian times. But when you went inside it was an absolute dream come true. Mostly Victorian and Edwardian clothing, hung on rails all around the shop, the prices started at £1; I was in heaven. We shopped for England.

Not long after, Dee told me she was going to dinner at her daddy's and asked me to join her. We hired a cab, and were dropped off outside a luxurious apartment block on Marylebone Road.

Daddy wasn't quite what Bren expected. He looked a lot older than her own father; she thought he was probably in his late seventies. Dee told her Daddy was the patriarch of a famous circus family. While Daddy busied himself cooking dinner, Bren and Dee chatted.

They ate their food and she and Dee washed the pots. Dee told them she was popping out to get some cigarettes. Bren wasn't happy about being left alone with a stranger, but he was her friend's dad. Daddy told Bren lots of stories about the circus and she dutifully sat and listened.

Dee had been gone quite a long time, so Bren told Daddy that she had to go, as she had arranged to meet a friend. Daddy nodded and said,

"Give me a kiss good-bye then."

Reluctantly, she gave him a peck on the cheek, not wanting to be nasty and refuse as he had cooked them dinner.

"Not like that, on the mouth, with tongues."

Bren stared at him, not sure if she had heard him correctly.

"Come on, I'll be your daddy, I'll give you lots of money and look after you."

Finally realising what kind of daddy, he was to Dee Bren was already slowly edging towards the door; although her mind was screaming at her to run. There was no way she was kissing that old man, absolutely no way. Her dinner was threatening to work its way back up her throat.

"But Dee said you would take over from her, now that she is going away."

Opening the door, Bren left.

Once again, I had fallen foul of someone's underhandedness. No wonder Dee had taken me to that brilliant shop, she was probably dangling the proverbial carrot.

Carla and I often called in at the Last Chance Saloon, in Oxford Street, which was actually a bit of a dive as clubs go. There was often trouble there and we inadvertently became involved in one particular incident.

They were on their way home, in the early hours, and as they drew near the Last Chance, they saw someone lying in the gutter. It was a boy, probably not much more than fourteen, with a horrendous wound to the stomach.

Bren stripped off her cotton shirt, and tried to hold everything in place, while Carla went to find a phone to call for an ambulance. Bren talked softly to the lad, trying to keep him as calm as possible even though she was aware that he was going into shock. People were walking by, but not one stopped to help; in fact, they turned their faces the other way. There was so much blood, that by the time the ambulance arrived she was covered in it. She didn't know whether the boy was going to make it and she never found out, but she heard the ambulance man tell a policeman that the boy had been 'gutted'.

When I got home my mother was already up. She nearly fainted when she saw the blood and wouldn't stop freaking out until she was absolutely sure that it wasn't mine, I had to tell her the whole horrible story. When I went to bed that night, I cried for that boy whoever, or whatever, he was.

My Dopplegänger and Dangerous Hobbies

They say everyone has a Doppleganger, and I actually met mine.

A Doppelgänger is a non-biologically related look-alike, or spirit double, of a living person. Some people believe them to be a portent of bad luck. There is also a myth, that if you accept food from your Doppelgänger it can take over your life and even steal your soul.

Being as I was very much into individual fashion; I made many of my own clothes and some were very 'way out'. Shocking pink satin and Tartan jackets, trousers with huge flares and different coloured legs, were my thing long before the Bay City Rollers and glam rock. The week before I met my Doppelgänger, I had designed my own hairstyle and cut it myself. It was a lopsided wedge, the left side short and behind my ear, and the right side longer and over the ear; unheard of in 1965, when everyone was wearing their hair long.

As was normal, Carla and I had spent most of the day together and I had walked her back to the tube. I decided to go for something to eat and drink, before making my way home. Just as I was about to leave the station, I bumped into a gay friend named Scot, who told me he was there to meet someone. Not long after, a girl started walking towards us. It was like looking at a mirror image. We had the same hairstyle, but she wore the right side behind her ear. Her style of dress was very similar to mine, and facially we were like identical twins; in fact, we could have been if she wasn't a few inches shorter than me. Scot stared from one to the other of us in amazement.

While we all sipped coffee, I found out that her name was Antoinette and she was a ballerina. She was nearly four years older than me, but the likeness was uncanny. The two of us were practically inseparable for the next couple of months. Antoinette lived with a Chinese man, just off Tottenham Court Road. We ate meals together, went bowling and shopping. Sharing similar interests, especially a love of the arts, we always had plenty of places to go. Then one day, I called for her and was told she had gone away.

I never saw nor heard from her again.

From a very young age, I'd had an enquiring mind, which sometimes made me want to try things I shouldn't. When I was about eight years old, I had a puff of my dad's cigarette, and being as it was before cork tips, it left nasty bits of tobacco in my mouth. I also had a sip of Dad's whiskey, which I found equally horrible.

No stranger to smoking Cannabis, which I could take or leave, I now wanted to experience every aspect of the dingier side of West End life. Well, apart from the sex act that is; which I believe I was saving for Mr Right.

Carla had gone on holiday with her mother, so it was an ideal time to experiment without her knowing. I mainly wanted to know what attraction drugs held, that made people crave them so much.

Over the two weeks that followed, I slept rough in St James' Park, took various pills and smoked an opium pipe. One night at a society party, I used heroin. It made me feel so 'out of it', that I tried to make myself sick to get rid of it, not even thinking that wouldn't work because the drug was actually injected into my bloodstream. I didn't like the way drugs made me feel during the 'high', and I certainly didn't like the 'coming down'.

But I did say I wanted to experience everything, and that included joining the homeless, sleeping in derelict houses and tunnels. This little escapade came to an end, when I discovered that I had become 'home' to several fleas. My exploits over those two weeks were never mentioned to anyone, until I started writing this book.

Because of what had happened to me when I wasn't under the influence of drink or drugs, the thought of not being in complete control of my senses and actions terrified me. That sort of life was definitely not what I wanted.

I would just like to say, I wouldn't recommend doing what I did to anyone, as I can see how easily someone could become addicted. What I did was totally reckless behaviour, and not in any way clever.

Over a period of time, I had become quite close to several of the local drug addicts and I found myself constantly grieving some loss or other. Realising that you cannot help people who don't want to, or unable to, help themselves; I decided, for my own well-being, to stop hanging around with these people and go back to frequenting the clubs and pubs.

Carla had never experimented with drugs or even touched alcohol, so it came as a major surprise when she became involved with a scruffy, smelly boy named Terry; who wasn't even particularly good-looking. They were both heavily into drugs, and Carla quit her job to bum around with her man.

Months later I saw them both on Shaftesbury Avenue, and hardly recognised Carla. She had changed from an attractive well-groomed young woman, to an aged hag with grubby skin. The last I heard of them, was that they had got married and were arrested on a drugs-related charge.

By now my hair was cropped short again, and I had started spending a lot of time in Richmond, with the boys I knew from there. They were all quite a bit older than me, but they treated me with respect. Everything was great, until I found out that one of the lads, Rob, was heavily into drugs.

He had been trying to kick the habit for some time, but because everything else he had tried had resulted in relapse he had decided to go 'cold turkey'[3] and asked the other two lads, Dave and Rick, to help. Everything was planned, time off work was booked, food stocked up, money and valuables hidden, and all drugs and alcohol cleared out of the house. I told them I would sit with Rob one night to let them get some proper sleep.

It was nearing the end of the second week, so Bren expected Rob to be through the worst of it, but the night she spent sitting with him was much worse than she could have imagined. The lads had told her she could back out if she wanted, but she insisted. Even so, they made her promise to wake them if things got too tough and she couldn't cope.

When she first entered the room Rob was asleep, but restless. After about an hour the sweat ran from his pores, she sponged his face and upper body, trying to cool him, talking to him softly. His face contorted, as he alternated between squeezing his hands into fists and relaxing them.

He opened his eyes and stared at her, as if trying to place her. Whispering her name, before turning his head to stare at the other side of the room. Sweating again, and panting, as he stared at some unseen being; moaning.

"It can't be, no, go away".

Recoiling from whatever it was that he could see, he moved his hands to his face, clawing at his skin, gouging deep enough to draw blood. Rob's body began to shake violently, undulating on the bed, his breath more like a growl. She tried to hold him, calm him, but he was too strong for her. She screamed for Dave.

Both he and Rick came to her rescue, while Rick held the convulsing Rob, Dave pushed a piece of wood between his teeth. After what seemed like hours, but was probably only a few minutes, Rob relaxed into a deep sleep. Dave went to make them all a coffee. Rick stayed with Rob, while Bren and Dave went into the living room. Dave held her as she sobbed against his chest.

At the end of the third week, when she visited, Rob was sitting in the armchair watching TV. He had found his appetite again, tucking in to a large helping of Spag Bol made by Dave. He smiled at her.

"Heard I gave you a scare hunny-bun."

Bren nodded, tears rolling down her cheeks.

"Bloody hell, don't cry, you'll start me off."

For quite a while after, Rob seemed to be doing OK; but one night when Dave and Rick went to call on him, they found him dead, with a syringe hanging from a vein in his arm. The lads said they had a suspicion that he might be using again, but couldn't prove it, as Rob had moved into a flat nearer to his mum and they only saw him occasionally.

Yet another person I cared about had gone from my life; seeing the other two only made me think of Rob, it hurt so damn bad that I backed away from them completely.

Cabs and Undertakers

In the early hours of one morning, after leaving a club on the other side of the city, I decided to take a cab to Evan's All-Night Café, to wait for the tubes to start running. I flagged down a black cab before I realised that the 'for hire' sign was turned off. The cabbie pulled over anyway, and asked where I was going. I told him, and he said that although he had finished his shift, it was on his way home so he would take me. Being as this was a black cab, any sense of foreboding was automatically shoved aside; I got in, and he began to drive. The driver was around mid-late thirties and dark haired.

Although he took a different route to the normal, I didn't think anything of it, as cab drivers often had their own shortcuts. After a while, I asked him where he was going, as he seemed to be taking a longer route.

"Been working for hours, and I'm starving, thought I'd grab a sandwich from the station café."

Unhappy about the detour, I had to grin and bear it being as he was doing me a favour; as he hadn't set the meter, I presumed he would only charge me the normal fare.

"What do you want to drink?" He asked, as we approached the station.

"Nothing thanks."

He mumbled something, that I didn't quite catch.

Bren started to become concerned, when he drove past the station. When she reached for the door handle and discovered there wasn't one, she was frantic. As the cabbie began to drive down some dark back streets, she looked around her for landmarks, but couldn't see anything remotely familiar. After what seemed like an eternity, he came to a halt in a deserted cul-de-sac full of warehouses. Petrified, she screamed for him to let her out. He sneered at her.

"Keep quiet, we're gonna have some fun. Come on, you know you want to."

She kept on screaming. But he wasn't at all worried, because the area was dark and deserted. As he made his way to the back of the cab, his laugh made Bren feel nauseous. Pounding on the window with her fists, she screamed even louder. He pulled the door open, grabbing at her. Then she heard a dog bark.

In the little light afforded by the moon, Bren could make out the shape of two people and a dog, at the top of the road. A man's voice broke through the darkness.

"Are you alright?"

The cabbie released his grip on her arms, which was her chance to leap from the cab and run towards the couple. Slamming the back door, the driver got in his cab, and without putting on his lights, reversed up the alley towards them. Swerving around them, he backed onto the side street and took off at high speed. The woman put her arm round Bren's shoulders, and led her back to their house, where they called the police.

While waiting for the police, Bren remembered making a mental note of the driver number, when the cabbie made the first detour. Maybe she had heeded the warning bells after all. Whatever the reason, the number helped the police to trace the cab driver who was found to be a suspect in previous rape allegations. This time she did the right thing, and the suspect was arrested.

That night, I asked myself, why these things kept happening to me. Did I deliberately put myself in harm's way, did I send out the wrong messages, or was I just too trusting?

A chance sharing of a taxi one night, led me to a short-lived singing career, with a band called the Undertakers. My friend Caroline and I were on our way home from a night out in the West End, when we dashed for a taxi at the same time as three lads. The lads asked where we were going, and we told them NW10. They said that was good enough for them, as they were staying in Queens Park. They asked us if we minded sharing the cab; so, we all piled in. The cab driver's radio was playing, and Caroline and I were singing along.

One of the lads remarked that we had good voices, and told us they were in a band. We spent the rest of the journey to Queens Park, singing together and arranging to meet up for coffee in Kilburn, the next day.

As it happened, I turned up, but Caroline didn't. So, I ended up hanging around with the band for a few weeks; I even sung with them on a couple of gigs. Unfortunately, it made me realise, that my voice wasn't powerful enough, to belt out rock songs from a stage. So, my dream of becoming a singer was dashed.

Even though I had been doing a few card readings for people since just before my fifteenth birthday, it was the Undertakers who made me realise I could do it professionally if I wanted to. One of the boys asked me for a reading before a gig and before I knew it, I had read for all the band, the techies and the theatre staff.

When visiting my half-sister in Rayners Lane, I saw a card in the newsagent's window which was advertising a spiritualist meeting; I decided to call the number. The lady who answered sounded very nice, and told me to come along to her house the following week. The people in the group were mainly old, but they took me under their wing. Soon my images started to become clearer, and gain more detail.

I was fed up with being a filing clerk and working with snobbish people, so I applied for another job. This one was nearer to home and working in accounts, I was in my element. Working with numbers was my passion, so balancing the books for a credit company was ideal for me.

A Certain Kind of Knowing and More Problems at Home

Although my mother was used to me saying strange things, she still found some things quite bizarre. As was the case one morning when I was leaving for work.

A news story was announced over the radio about a missing 10-month-old baby girl being found alive, but showing signs of rape. To my mother's surprise I announced.

"It was the mother."

"How can it be? She's been raped."

"It's the mother." I re-affirmed, and left for work.

Some days later, it was announced that the mother had been arrested for abusing the child, and making it look like rape. Mum was shocked.

"How did you know?"

"I just did."

This wasn't the first time I had been right about who had

committed a crime, and it certainly wasn't going to be the last.

After my sister got married, Mum and I spent more time together, shopping, laughing, and drinking coffee in Lyons Corner House; but the arguments at home carried on. Much of the time, they were so ridiculous that they would have been laughable, if you weren't involved.

As was normal on a weekday morning, Mum and I were in the kitchen, getting ready for work. Mum still had curlers in her hair, and was wearing her dressing gown. We were having breakfast, when we heard the bedroom curtains, swishing loudly. Mum and I shared a look that said Dad was in one of his moods.

The kitchen door bounced against its hinges, from the force with which it had been thrown open. Dad moved across the kitchen to the balcony door, and opened it.

"Aha I thought so."

Mum and I stared at him. Mum said what I was thinking.

"What on earth's the matter with you?"

"That's him, that's your bloke." Dad pointed through the balcony door.

Mum got up, and went out on to the balcony, I followed. There was a man leaning out of the factory window smoking a cigarette. Mum yelled.

"Do I know you?"

The poor man looked really shocked, disappeared inside and slammed the window shut; never to be seen again. Mum closed the balcony door. Dad sat at the table and ate his breakfast in silence. Then one morning, things took a really bad turn.

Bren was getting dressed, when she heard her mum screaming. She rushed into the kitchen; her mother was sat on the chair in the corner, holding her side. Bren stared at her father.

"What's happened?"

"I've stabbed her, I've stabbed your mother." Her father replied.

Bren felt the rage rising inside her. Tugging open the dresser drawer she grabbed a carving knife and leapt at her father, sending him crashing to the floor with her astride him; knife at his throat.

"Stop." Her mother gasped. "I'm alright, he only punched me."

Bren dropped the knife, shocked at how close she had come to killing her own father; but the anger didn't subside. She screamed at him.

"Why would you say that?"

For the rest of the day, she kept wondering if she would have used the knife if her mother hadn't stopped her. Did she really have it in her to kill someone?

That was the first time I had ever known my dad strike my mum, as it was normally just verbal abuse.

A Lovely Date with a Disastrous Ending

Frequenting the West End clubs had its advantages, as I occasionally had dates with boys from other areas of London. Les lived in the East End. It was Spring 1966; we had spent the afternoon in the West End and then gone for a meal in the Aberdeen Steak House. Les suggested we finish the evening with a quiet drink in his local pub, where they wouldn't bother to ask our ages.

The pub was in Jack the Ripper territory. We sat in the lounge bar because there were a few people in the public bar, and we didn't want to draw attention to ourselves.

It was gone 8pm by the time they had ordered their drinks and settled in their seats. Bren felt comfortable with Les, they laughed, discussed the latest films, and their taste in music. It was like she had known him for months.

They had been there about twenty minutes; pop music was playing in the background but Bren couldn't see a juke box. She was about to ask Les where it was, when someone entered the pub. Bren couldn't see who it was, but she heard one of the men sat at the bar make some kind of sarcastic remark. Seconds later, there were two loud pops. Shortly afterwards, there was another pop, but it sounded slightly different to the other two.

From where she was sitting, she could see a man slumped over and, what she thought to be, blood dripping on the floor. There were raised voices and the sound of doors banging, as some people left.

Aware that she had possibly just witnessed a murder, she felt her stomach heave and fought to stop herself from vomiting. She turned to Les.

"We'd better get the police."

"We saw nothing. Come on let's go."

Les grabbed her arm, and they were ushered out of the pub via a back door.

She didn't know whether anyone had seen them leave, as she knew the police would be looking for the people that were there.

Les took her to the tube station and waited with her until the train came. He touched her hand.

"Will you be alright?"

She nodded.

As she moved to step onto the train, he whispered to her. The doors closed, and she watched him walk away.

She sat on the train shaking, a terrified child trying to process what she had just witnessed. Her mind struggled to recall the exact series of events, but it was like she was staring into deep fog. She gathered that something big had gone down, but she wasn't sure what and because of Les' last words to her, she knew it was best forgotten.

"For your own safety, we were never there tonight. You saw

nothing, you heard nothing."

Les and I never saw each other again after that night, and I never mentioned what I saw and heard to anyone. It wasn't until many years later that I found out who had carried out the shooting. The person concerned was brought to justice and has now been dead for several years, but I still refuse to give names for legal reasons.

That night the Hippos had blood dripping from their jaws.

Chapter 7
If I'm Going to Marry It's the Butcher Boy for Me

It was a sunny spring morning in April 1966, three months after my seventeenth birthday and I was soon to be without a job again. While I was visiting an agency in Willesden Green, Carl came into my life.

On my way back to the bus stop, I was just approaching the butchers when I noticed a boy outside smoking a cigarette. Six foot six, slim, short dark hair and really nice looking. I pretended I hadn't seen him and hurried past.

"You've got legs right up to your arse." He shouted after me.

Being naturally shy and lacking spontaneous wit I would have normally kept going but for some reason I stopped and turned around.

"Where do you think they'd go, under my armpits?"

His mate, who had just joined him, commented.

"I think you've met your match, Carl."

With that they both disappeared back inside and I went to get my bus.

A few days later I had to go back to the agency, as they had a job lined up for me. When I was on my way back to the bus stop, Carl came out of the butchers and stepped out in front of me. Smiling down at me he introduced himself.

"I'm Carl."

"Brenda." I replied.

"Sorry about the other day but you really have got nice legs. I'm glad I've seen you again because I don't normally work here, and this is my last day. I'll get to the point; will you go out for a drink with me?"

"When?" I asked, realising that I hadn't even paused to think about it.

"Err, tonight?"

We arranged to meet at West Kilburn.

He appeared to be really nice, and looked absolutely amazing in a suit. At the end of the evening, he walked me home, gave me a gentle kiss on the lips and asked if he could see me again; cinema the following Sunday. My mum was none too happy as she said he came from a rough area, but I wasn't put off. I was falling in love.

After the cinema I was invited to his house for tea; I wasn't worried, because it felt right. When we got there his mum greeted us. She was not what I expected. Although about the same age as my mother, she was wearing a tight-fitting mini dress and high heels. With her carrot-coloured bob, her eyebrows pencilled on way too high, and her lipstick way above her natural lip line, it looked as though a clown had applied her make-up whilst under the influence of a huge amount of alcohol.

Draping herself around the edge of the door, one hand on top of it, she appeared to be flirting with her own son, fluttering her eyelids at him while addressing me.

"Do you want tea or lemonade?"

"Have you got coffee please? I don't drink tea."

Mumbling something inaudible, she disappeared. I sat closer to Carl, feeling quite uncomfortable. He pressed his lips against mine and we let our tongues explore each other's mouths for several minutes.

"Ahem."

We stopped kissing and looked at his mother, who stood in front of us in the grimy living room holding a plate of quartered cucumber sandwiches, with the crusts cut off. She put the sandwiches on the coffee table in front of us and left. Returning a few minutes later with our drinks, she put my coffee in front of me, and I thanked her.

"I'll leave you to it." She said as she closed the door behind her.

Carl kissed me and his hand wandered to my breast, although I was aroused, I grasped his hand and moved it away. It didn't feel right, not yet, especially with his mother listening outside the door as I was sure she was. Carl stared at the sandwiches.

"I'm sorry about the sandwiches. It's just that she thinks you're posh because of where you live."

When I got home Mum wanted to know all about my visit with Carl's mother. I told her about the cucumber sandwiches and in typical North West London fashion, she said,

"Who did she think she was having to tea, the bloomin' queen?"

Love Is Blind

Carl and I were an item, and we saw each other at every possible opportunity. There were certain things that happened while we were together that should have rung alarm bells, but I was young and in love. My mind made excuses for every little wrong doing, because I was besotted.

It was mid-July and Mum and Dad had gone to Uncle Tom's for a few days; I didn't go because I was working. It was a sunny evening, so when I got home from work, I took a bath.

The downstairs bell rang just as I got my undies on. Grabbing my leather trench coat, I slipped it on, belted it around me for decency, and went to answer the door. It was Carl. He smiled at me.

"I thought I'd call while I was passing, just in case you were home from work."

"Come up." I told him.

They went into the living room, and Carl sat on one of the dining chairs.

"You took a while to answer the door."

He looked so handsome and she felt so much love for him that she decided he was definitely 'the one'.

"Look."

She stood in front of him and opened her coat, thinking he would be turned on by the sight of her in her undies. A little seduction scene, like she'd seen in films. Instead, he got angry. Pushing her away from him, he demanded.

"Why the fuck were you answering the door like that?"

"I had just got out of the bath and wasn't fully dressed, so I put my coat on to cover myself while I answered the door, in case it was something important."

Tearful, trying to justify her actions, upset at his reaction to something that she had intended to be special.

He started to calm down.

"I'm sorry."

Reaching for her, he pulled her onto his lap. They kissed, and he pushed her coat off her shoulders, she let it fall to the floor. His hand wandered over her breasts, then slid down her body and between her legs; she moved his hand.

"Not here." She whispered, leading him to her bedroom.

It was the first time she had ever had intercourse. Carl was quite shocked when she told him, as he hadn't been particularly gentle. Afterwards, he told her he had to go home for tea, she was shaken; as she thought they would have laid together, savouring the precious thing they had just shared.

A few weeks later, my usually regular period late, I realised that I might be pregnant. I planned to tell Carl when he came that night, before I told anyone else. At about quarter to seven the bell rang, and when I answered the door, I wasn't overjoyed to see Joanne stood there. Even so I asked her up, knowing she had come to be nosey and to get a look at Carl. She wasn't seeing anyone now, as she had split up with Dick, so she was probably hoping Carl had some nice mates.

Carl arrived soon after, and gave me a kiss. We all chatted and played silly games. I hoped Joanne was going to go home so I could talk to Carl alone; but she stayed. It was ten to twelve when Carl said he had to go, as he had to be at work for 6am. Joanne stood up. "I'll walk with you."

Carl gave me a kiss, and said he would see me the next night. He and Joanne left together.

The following evening, she told Carl she thought she might be pregnant, he looked worried and protested.

"But it was only that one day."

She couldn't hold back the tears.

"Well, I haven't been with anyone else, if that's what you're thinking." Sobbing, as Carl pulled her to him.

"It'll be alright." He said, but he didn't sound too sure.

A few days later, Joanne paid her a visit. As soon as Joanne walked through the door she asked.

"Is Carl coming tonight?"

"No, it's his boys' night out."

"Oh." Joanne sounded disappointed.

Bren still hadn't told anyone about being pregnant, and she certainly wasn't going to tell Joanne. Joanne looked at her without smiling.

"I've got something to tell you. You remember that night when I left with Carl? Well, he walked me home and we started kissing, then we went down the side of the house and had sex."

Bren stared at her. She knew Joanne had sex with Dick when she was with him; but sex with Carl would definitely be out of order.

"Anyway." Joanne continued.

"He wants to go out with me now. I saw him last night, and I told him I would tell you."

Well, it was true that Bren hadn't seen Carl the night before, but

89

how did Joanne know? Probably guess work. Carl might have told her the nights that he and Bren saw each other; she might have told her. Bren wasn't going to let Joanne see it bothered her, because she trusted Carl. Joanne left not long after, with a smug look on her face, she turned to Bren.

"Mustn't keep Carl waiting."

Bren was livid, she had wanted to take Joanne by the neck and shake her. First Joanne had made a play for Dick because she knew how much Bren liked him, and now she was after the boy who was going to be the father of her child; the boy she loved. When Carl came the next night, she knew she needed to ask him about what Joanne had said.

After a sleepless night, there were many things that were bugging her. She and Carl never went anywhere; he would come to her home and they would sit in the bedroom. As soon as the bell rang, she went down to answer the door, she already had her jacket on. Carl looked puzzled.

"Are you going somewhere?"

"I thought we would go for a drink." She replied.

"Is it wise in your condition? If you want to go somewhere, we could go to the cinema tomorrow. Let's stay in, I've been longing for a kiss from you all day."

They went upstairs. As soon as she had closed the bedroom door, he started to kiss her and fondle her breasts. She moved his hand away.

"I need to ask you something."

"What do you want to ask me?"

"Joanne was here last night. She said that you had sex with her, and that you are seeing each other."

She could feel the tears welling in her eyes.

"Why would I want to do that? I'm not even attracted to her. It's

you I love. In fact, I was going to ask you to marry me."

Before she could answer there was a knock at the door, her mum answered it. The bedroom door opened, and in walked Joanne. She smiled at Carl but he turned his face away. Joanne looked annoyed.
"You two had a row?" She asked Bren.
"No, Carl has just asked me to marry him."
Bren watched Joanne's face; she saw traces of anger.
Joanne glared at Carl.
"I'm going now."
Neither Bren nor Carl said anything in reply.

Pushing the niggling doubts to the back of her mind, she gave Carl her answer. Happy, because Carl loved her and wanted to marry her, she was reassured that Joanne had obviously been lying.

Fixated with my baby right from the moment it was confirmed I was pregnant; I couldn't stop talking about it. That was after our parents were told and had come back down from the roof. We fixed a date for our wedding and decided to make it a small affair with just Carl's mum and dad, my mum and dad and Uncle Harry. My mum said she would do us a buffet, so that we could save money.

They say love is blind and I suppose when you're in love you ignore certain things. It was a few weeks before our wedding and I was in the kitchen ironing, when Carl arrived. We talked about our plans for the big day and what we were going to wear.
"Would your mum like me to do her hair for her?" I asked.

Bren expected Carl to be pleased. Instead, she reeled from the impact of his hand slapping her face.
"You bitch, you know it's a wig." She was too shocked, to say anything before he left. She supposed she should have realised it was a wig, but she didn't. Thinking about it afterwards, it was so obvious.

Carl called in the next day and apologised for over-reacting and we went to bed to make up.

It was Friday October 28th 1966, the day before I was supposed to be marrying Carl. I had just been to buy a Mary Quant floral print mini-dress, for my wedding. It was when I was walking back from Queens Park station that I bumped into Steve. We hadn't seen each other for months and we chatted for ages. I asked him if he wanted to come back for coffee.

"Mum would love to see you."

We went back to the flat, and I was right, Mum was pleased to see him, she greeted him like the prodigal son. Steve had never been a good-looking boy but as we sat there talking, I was suddenly very attracted to him. It even crossed my mind, that I should be marrying him instead of Carl. I think at that moment I had my first epiphany as I realised, I was not meant to get married.

The next day as we stood in front of the Registrar, I looked at Carl, handsome in his new mohair suit, and changed my mind. Even his mother in her hair rollers covered by a scarf turban couldn't change the way I felt. Despite Carl's friends saying we would only last six months, I knew we could make it work; and we did for about two years.

Mother-In-Law or She-Devil?

From the moment Carl asked me to marry him I started to buy baby things, I always knew I was having a boy; although there were no scans, or ultrasounds in those days.

After our wedding, Carl and I lived with my mum and dad, while we were saving to buy a house. Carl was still working in the butchers in Harlesden and continued to have his Friday nights out with the boys.

Carl came home one evening, and told me that a quite well-known

actress had been coming in the shop for weeks. She had been telling Carl how much she fancied him, and had made a pass at him. This particular woman, was quite a large lady in her early sixties. I knew Carl loved me, I trusted him and was sure he wouldn't be interested in a woman of that age; so, I just laughed and said,
"I hope you told her you're a married man."

A few days later, Carl told me that one of the lads had sex with a woman customer in the back of the butcher's shop. Remarking that the woman must have been desperate as I'd seen the preparation area in the back of the shop, I thought no more of it. But many years later after being reminded that Carl was a young red-blooded male at the time, probably being egged on by his mates, I began to wonder whether he had actually been referring to himself and the actress.

Carl's mother had never been a very pleasant woman, but I hadn't realised just how nasty she was. One afternoon, Carl and I had arranged to meet at his mums. I purposely arrived a couple of hours early, hoping that his mother and I could chat and become friends. Making small talk wasn't something that came easily to me back then and it didn't help when Carl's mother looked at me and snarled. "He was supposed to buy me a wedding ring, but you got it instead."

Carl's family had a German Shepherd, which spent most of its time in the yard, with the outside wash house for shelter. The dog had taken an immense dislike to Bren. She had no idea why as she loved dogs, and she had tried to make friends with her. The dog was in the yard when Bren arrived at Carl's mum's house that day. Being pregnant, she soon needed to go to the toilet which was outside in the yard. It had been snowing heavily, and there was a good six inches or more on the ground. Bren didn't bother putting her coat on, as she was only going for a wee. Carl's mum held the dog, so that Bren could go into the toilet.

After she had finished, she opened the door to leave but was greeted by a snarling dog that would not let her out of the toilet. Bren shouted for Carl's mum, but there was no answer. Several times she tried to get out, but every time she did, the dog attacked her. All the while, she kept shouting for Carl's mum, but to no avail. Having always had a fear of dark confined spaces, being stuck in a small toilet with no light, late on a winter afternoon, was one of the worse things imaginable.

Bren sat on the toilet seat and waited, surely Carl wouldn't be long. Freezing cold, chest tight, toes and fingers numb, once again she tried to get out.

It was ages before she heard Carl's voice. She thought she may have dozed off as her whole body was stiff.

"Where's Brenda, she should have been here by now."

It was such a relief, to know that he was going to let her out. Then she heard his mother.

"She was here, but I think she went home because I went in the bedroom and when I came back, she was gone."

When Bren tried to shout, her voice was as frozen as the rest of her, all that came out was a gasp. Summoning every bit of her remaining energy, she yelled as if her life depended on it, and it probably did. Then Carl was tugging at the door, which appeared to be frozen shut. When he managed to pull it open, he helped her to her feet. She croaked.

"The dog."

"Mum, get the dog locked away." Carl yelled.

He helped Bren into the kitchen and sat her on a chair, switching on the electric fire. Taking her boots off, he rubbed her feet and hands.

"Where's your coat?"

It was nowhere to be seen. Carl finally found it down the back of the settee in the living room; strange, since she hadn't been in there. Wondering how long she had been outside, she asked Carl what time it was and was shocked to realise she had been locked in the toilet for well over an hour. She thought that if she had been in there any longer, she would have had serious frostbite or worse. As soon as she was able to walk, Carl took her home.

"Aren't you staying for your teas?" His mother asked, as they were leaving.

"No Mum, I think Brenda's had enough of you for one day."

All evening she waited for her baby to move, terrified that he may have been harmed by the ordeal. At nearly bedtime she felt a kick, and a huge sense of relief.

Later, I asked Carl about the wedding ring. He told me that his mum had pawned hers and when he started work, he made her a promise that he would buy her a new one.

This was just one of many incidents of Carl's mother's hatred towards me. I sometimes wonder if she hoped I was going to freeze to death that day.

Carl had an older brother Clive who was, as it was termed in those days, backward. The story I was told, was that when he was ten years old, he was playing in a rubber Indian suit. Their mother went out taking Carl with her, leaving Clive alone in the house with an open coal fire; which he fell into. He was saved from probable death by a neighbour who was alerted by his screams, and who broke down the door to reach him. Clive was badly burned, resulting in him having mental issues.

Carl absolutely doted on his brother, and I must admit I did too. Which was more than I can say for his mother, because she appeared to hate Clive. Carl was her blue-eyed boy (green-eyed actually); looking back, it was not a normal mother-son relationship on her part.

As I've said, I was very naïve. Although I knew first-hand how you conceived a baby, I still had no idea how it came out of your body. My mum was never one to talk about anything to do with sex, so I turned to Carl's mum for help. She told me giving birth was just like being constipated. I didn't know where babies came out from and now, I thought they came out of your bottom. I was eighteen years old, eight and a half months pregnant, and terrified that the next time I took a dump I was going to flush my baby down the toilet. It was then I turned to my mum for guidance on the taboo topic and learnt an equally scary reality.

We were still saving for our own home, or rather I was. Carl spent his spare cash on drinking with his mates on Friday nights. It was about this time, that my 'little stories' started. Whenever I was home alone little scenarios would pop into my head, in which Carl was seeing another girl. I would go through the whole process of finding out about her and tackling Carl. In my stories, he denied everything and all was back to normal.

Since I was a very young, I would get certain thoughts in my head and a little while later they actually happened. I used to blame myself, because I thought that by 'making up' these 'stories', I was causing them to happen. It wasn't until I turned twenty-one, that I realised my little 'stories' were actually warning me about things that were going to happen; rather than me making them happen.

After giving birth to a beautiful son, David, I went back to work full time; while my mum looked after my precious baby boy.

While shopping in Harlesden, I saw a lovely mini dress and coat set, which I happened to mention to Carl's mum and she offered to buy me it for Christmas. The first time I wore the dress, his mum waited until everyone was out of the room, then told me I looked like a slut. This was quite normal for her, she was always sweetness and light in front of everyone and I was the best thing since sliced bread; but when we were on our own, she was abusive and nasty to me. I just took it all to heart and believed everything she said about me.

Gran passed away with throat cancer after David was born. The night before she died, according to Carl, I had been very restless and talking in my sleep. Awaking with a start in the early hours, I saw my Gran stood at the foot of our bed, she was only there for a few seconds before she disappeared. Later that morning, we found out that Gran had passed during the night.

As was normal at that time, my Gran was laid out in a coffin in her attic bedroom, and the whole family was summoned to say their goodbyes. Sherry and sandwiches were served, then the procession of family members climbed the stairs to the attic, walking in a clockwise direction around the coffin, each pausing to kiss Gran goodbye before leaving the room.

My job paid really well. So, a few months later, Carl and I found a house we liked and acquired a mortgage in Carl's name. I couldn't be put on the deeds because I was told I had to wait until I was twenty-one. Thinking back, it was a little odd being as Carl was only nineteen when he signed for the mortgage, and he was only six months older than me. How thick I must have been, I suppose it was because I was ecstatic at the time.

Out of the Frying Pan into the Fire

As I had David to look after, I had to give up my job when we moved into the house. Carl now had two jobs; he worked as a milkman in the morning and in the afternoon, he worked in his friend Charlie's greengrocery shop. Often, they would go for a drink after work and Carl would come home around 7.30pm or 8pm. To while away the hours, I concentrated on our jungle of a garden.

It was a couple months after they moved into their house, gone eight and Carl hadn't come home from work. When it got to around 10pm, Bren started to get really worried and phoned everyone she could think of, including their parents; but nobody seemed to know where he was. She couldn't go to bed because, by now, she was frantic.

At around two in the morning, she got a call from Carl's friend Peter P who told her Carl was in the police cells in Edgware Road. Carl had been caught drink driving and wanted Bren to go and bail him out. Peter said he was coming to fetch her, so she got David out of bed and wrapped him in a blanket.

Peter dropped her and David at the police station and went home. She signed all the necessary paperwork. But they still had to wait until gone 8am for the doctor to check that the alcohol content in Carl's blood was below the limit, so that he could drive them all home. They had to send his licence off, with the fine payment, to the DVLA. It came back a few weeks later with the points registered on it.

That year, I cooked Christmas dinner for my mum, Dad and Uncle Harry. After we had eaten, Mum and Dad shared our settee with Uncle Harry, while Carl and I sat in the arm chairs. Carl and Uncle Harry had a snooze, while the rest of us watched TV. Suddenly Dad started shouting at Mum.

"I can see him touching your leg."

Carl woke up with a start.

"What the fuck?"

He got the gist of what had happened, from our mumbled explanations. Carl turned to my dad.

"You're fucking mad, accusing her with her own brother. You've upset everyone, Brenda's in tears. Now you behave yourself, or I'll knock your fucking head off."

Needless to say, Dad was quiet for the rest of the day, he wasn't used to anyone standing up to him, let alone threatening him.

One evening, a few weeks into the New Year, Carl phoned Bren at 5pm to say he would be late home from work. He told her he had been stopped on the way home by police and asked to take part in a line-up. He said she wasn't to worry as he wasn't involved in anything, it was just that they wanted people who looked a bit like the suspect. When he arrived home in the early hours of the following morning, he reeked of stale beer and his aftershave didn't smell like it usually did.

That night my sleep was disturbed by the sound of the Hippos screams.

Around April 1969 Bren became pregnant again. One evening, in early May, Carl came home from work around 5.30pm. He walked into the kitchen, where Bren was cooking. She smiled at him, happy that he was home early. Carl was so tall she always felt like a midget next to him, she stood on tiptoe to kiss him and that was when she noticed it. An oval red mark, just peeping out above his shirt collar.

She had seen love bites before; in fact, she'd had one herself. A boy had done it as a joke. When Bren got home and her mother saw the love bite, she wanted to know if she had done 'naughties' with a boy. With this idea going through her head, she confronted Carl.

"What's that?" She demanded.

"What?" He answered, a lot more casually than he should have.

He moved into the hall, and looked in the mirror, studying his neck.

"Oh that, my shirt collar's been rubbing."

And she believed him. The next day, she went out and bought him some new shirts.

That was just the beginning of my problems, but I was young, stupid and head over heels in love.

Their second boy, Marty, was born in their home in January 1970. Carl was now working at the Co Op milk yard, as United Dairies couldn't keep him on with points on his licence. He was still working in his friend's shop. The after-work drinks had increased to every night, and he now came home at around 10pm.

Bren busied herself with the garden and household chores. That was when she decided that a fish pond would be nice in the front garden. One of the neighbours offered her an unused pond liner, so she set about digging the hole. Her boys watched her from their little chairs on the other side of the garden. It took her most of the day but the liner was finally in and some crazy paving had been placed around the edges. Then out came the buckets, and she filled it with water. Standing back to admire her work, she couldn't wait to get some fish to put in it.

Later that evening, Carl came home drunk as normal. Bren was cooking when he walked into the kitchen, she turned to look at him, he was dripping wet and seething.

"Who put that fucking pond there?"

She laughed inwardly.

As the weeks went on, Carl started coming home later and later; often midnight or the early hours. Bren would always wait up for him, although she knew his drinking was a problem, she didn't think anything else was wrong, because she loved him, trusted him.

But the Hippo's were invading her dreams again. They had stopped for a short while, and had only appeared occasionally since they moved into the house, now they were back every night and even more menacing than she remembered. She instinctively knew something bad was brewing.

It was then that one of the worst periods of her life began. Bren and Carl's relationship had changed, he now seemed cold and distant. His drinking had increased, and he kept her very short of money. Once the mortgage and the bills were paid, she had around £7 left for the week's food and essentials. Luckily, she received family allowance for Marty which was around fifteen shillings per week. She always made sure the kids, Carl and the animals were fed, before she even thought about feeding herself.

The goodbye kisses, when he went to work, were the first to stop. Then, when they went to bed at night, they would begin to have sex but he would stop half way through, turnover and go to sleep. Still, she refused to believe there was anything wrong.

Carl would come home late at night and demand his food be cooked fresh; he wouldn't let her warm up the meal she had cooked earlier. This caused her problems because an extra dinner each day ate into the already tight budget.

Once, when she refused to cook a fresh meal for him, his face reddened, his voice changed into something unrecognisable and he slammed his fist into the wall until his knuckles bled; all the while swearing and insulting her. She became more scared of him, with each passing day. Some nights she would have nothing herself, so that she could buy something extra for Carl. Although she had always been slim, she lost a lot of weight, dropping to about six stone. Her hip bones stuck out and she had no stomach, as it sunk in. Often, he would tell her she wasn't attractive to him because she was so skinny.

Not long after, things escalated, he stopped punching walls and started punching her. Sometimes he wouldn't talk to her, he would just click his fingers for her to fetch his food. When he was home early enough, he would click his fingers and indicate for her to sit on the settee; then he would put his legs across her lap and fall asleep. She didn't dare move, remaining there, even though she was soaking wet and stinking from him urinating on her in his sleep.

The situation rapidly became worse. He would come home so drunk he didn't know what he was doing. Often, he would urinate in the washing machine. One night she woke up to the sound of the wardrobe being dragged across the floor. When she asked Carl what he was doing, he told her he was going downstairs for a piss. She told him he was moving the wardrobe, to which he said she was fucking mad, urinated behind it and pushed it back. Other times, he would relieve himself inside the wardrobe, or all over the upstairs landing. She was constantly washing clothes and bed covers, and cleaning carpets.

In the early hours of one morning, she was awoken by something wet and warm on her face, Carl was stood astride her on the bed, penis in hand, spraying urine in all directions, including on her and the bed. Bren shouted at him, but he didn't seem to hear her, he just got back into the wet bed and went back to sleep. She slept downstairs that night.

Because she nearly always had black eyes and bruises, she stopped trying to make excuses for them. It would have been easy to blame not having anywhere to go, she could simply have admitted she had made a mistake and moved back home; but she loved Carl and thought that he would change. Every time he made a sudden move, or lifted his hand in the air, she expected a fist to make contact with some part of her body.

It was around this time that Mum became ill again. She had been admitted to hospital with another perforated duodenal ulcer. My uncle Harry's wife had died just after Carl and I were married, and Mum was doing his washing every week. So, with Mum in hospital, I took on the job of doing my parents and Uncle Harry's washing; as well as our own. This went on for several weeks, until my mum was fit enough to take their washing back on.

Bren's mind wasn't in a good place, tired, confused, scared, lonely.... It is no wonder she snapped. Carl came home drunk, and shouted at the dog, who then had an accident on the kitchen floor. Penis in hand, he pissed all over the kitchen floor and the dog, yelling.

"See how you like treading in piss."

Then he proceeded to kick the terrified animal.

Enough was enough, he could do whatever he liked to her, but when it came to her kids and her animals, that was a different story. The same anger welled up in her as it did that day when she held a knife to her father's throat. Reaching up, she grabbed the heavy frying pan from the wall hook and brought it round to connect with the side of Carl's head. He collapsed in a heap in his own urine; out cold.

When she replaced the frying pan on the hook, the panic set in. Anger turned to fear, as she realised that when Carl woke up, he was probably going to kill her. Knowing there was nothing she could do about it she went to bed.

The following morning, Carl had no recollection of what had happened, he thought that he had bumped his head, when he passed out. She said nothing, just got on with cleaning up the mess

It was only a few weeks after the points had been removed from Carl's licence, Bren was waiting for him to come home. At about two in the morning Carl rang to say he had been arrested for drink driving again. She asked if he needed her to go and bail him out, but he told her he had a friend with him, who would wait for him and bring him home. He never came home that night.

The following evening when he came home from work, she asked him for his driving licence so that she could send it off for the points to be put on. He told her she didn't need to, as it had already been done at the police station. When she queried this, Carl told her it was a new method they were trying out. And she, stupid bitch, believed him.

One afternoon, I took the kids to visit my parents, Carl was supposed to pick me up at 6pm but he was late. We'd had a big discussion that week, about our relationship, and he had been drink-free and coming home straight from work. I really thought we were getting back on track. The bell rang and I thought it was Carl. I was elated, as I now thought he was really making an effort; but it turned out to be my Auntie Lil.

"Fran, you and Brenda get your coats on, we are going out."

"But Carl will be here soon." I protested.

"We'll be back before he gets here." Her tone was abrupt.

I don't know why, but I was sure she was right, so I did as she said.

We walked towards the Queens Park Estate, but then, Auntie Lil led us down a side street. I asked her where we were going, but all she said was.

"We'll be there soon."

As we turned down another street, I spotted Carl's van outside a pub.

"Come on." Auntie Lil said, as she pushed the door to the bar open. Mum and I followed her in.

As soon as they entered, Bren heard Carl's laugh coming from a door on the left. Her mum and aunt stepped aside, so that she could enter first. There was a very fat and unattractive girl sat up close to Carl. Bren could swear that when Carl saw her, he pushed the girl away.

Same as she could swear, she heard his friend say.

"You'll have to go home tonight now."

Carl looked at Bren, his face flushed.

"That's the barmaid, she was collecting glasses." His voice

wavering slightly.

'And she needs to sit down close to you to do that?' Bren thought.

"Are you coming home?" She asked.

Carl's friend laughed.

"Under thumb, mate."

"Not at all." Carl answered.

He turned to Bren.

"Go back to your mum's. I'll be there in a bit."

   She turned to walk out, fighting back tears. It was then her Auntie Lil spoke.

"No, we came out to have a drink, and that is what we are going to do."

It was the first time she had ever seen her Aunt Lil go to the bar for drinks. Her aunt ordered three Rum and Cokes, pushed the money across the bar to pay for them and then carried them to a table.

   Mum didn't drink spirits, so she shuddered when she took a sip. Carl sat there looking worried; his mate was smirking. Bren had no idea why her aunt had brought them there, but she was sure it wasn't by chance. She didn't know how her aunt knew and she never asked, because she didn't think she really wanted to hear the answer. That was the moment she realised her little stories in her mind, could be a little bit more than stories.

   They sat there sipping their drinks slowly, although she could happily have downed hers and left. Carl sat there shifting in his seat, as the barmaid tried to get his attention. As they got up to leave Carl said,

"I'll be there in a bit."

"Don't rush." Her Aunt replied.

"We are going to another pub; the service isn't very good here."

Once outside, Bren asked.

"Where are we going?"

"Back to your mum's." Aunt Lil said. "But I wasn't going to tell them that."

Carl finally arrived, shortly after chucking out time. They went home together, but things were really bad. He was back to his usual drinking habits, and he was angry at her for following him to his 'local'. She paid for her mistake that night.

Later that week, still sore from the beating Carl had given her, Bren downed two packets of pain killers. Carl was watching TV at the time. She told him, that she didn't want to live anymore. He stared at her while she took every single pill. Carl never said a word, or tried to stop her. This was the first time she actually believed that Carl didn't love her anymore, and he really did want her to die. Emotionless, she sat there waiting for the end. Carl got up from the settee and went out, leaving her alone in the house with her boys. Then it happened; projectile vomit.

Hoping that things would get better she had hung in there. Through all the physical and mental abuse and the threats that if she ever went with anyone else, he would cut them both up in little pieces and feed them to the pigs.

She once tried leaving, tried to find a way to make a life for her and her boys, but Carl found out and stopped her. It was a crazy idea anyway, how could she expect her boys to live in one room, in a stranger's house? How could she work to support her boys, when she had no one to look after them? So, when Carl noticed things missing from the house and demanded to know where they had gone; she had little choice but to tell him. He broke down in tears promising her it would all be different, and once again she believed him.

He drove her to the house where she had rented a room; to retrieve their belongings. Once everything was back in the house Carl never spoke to her, he just went to bed. Nothing changed, if anything he was even more distant.

Whatever Carl had done to her, she had to admit that he was good with their boys. He didn't see a lot of them but when he did, he appeared to love them. The only time either of their boys were physically hurt, was when Carl came home in a bad mood one teatime. He rushed upstairs pushing David out of the way. David fell and cut his head on the skirting board. When Carl realised what he had done he drove them all to the hospital and he really did appear to be genuinely upset.

For quite some time there had been no intimate physical contact between her and Carl. Bren put up with all of it, hoping that something would change. That he would come home and be that cheeky boy with whom she fell in love, and not the nasty aggressive man that he had become. She blamed herself, for not being the type of wife that he wanted, even though she didn't know what that was. Then something happened that made her realise, she couldn't go on.

Carl came home early in a terrible mood. He walked through the door, and began banging his fist into the hallway wall. His face was red, his eyes wild and tearful. He turned to the ranch doors and punched one so hard it sent slats flying across the kitchen. Cowering in the corner, she waited for the blows to be turned to her.

He began shouting.

"The bitch, what makes her think she's so special?"

She didn't understand, and dared to ask.

"What's happened?"

His reply was malicious.

"Nothing you can put right, you're the main problem."

The tears flowed, and she sobbed out loud.

"Don't start with the fucking waterworks, you pathetic little bitch."

Carl grabbed her by the back of her neck, dragging her towards the hall mirror, which miraculously hung unscathed.

"Look at yourself, why would I want that?"

He pushed her face towards the mirror.

"Ugly fucking cow, why don't you cut your throat? In fact, I'll do it for you, put us both out of our misery."

He dragged her into the kitchen, and picked up the carving knife, holding it against her throat. Staring him in the face, her eyes willed him to do it. That was the moment she realised she had given up the fight, she really did want to die. Carl must have realised it too.

"No, you're not worth going to prison for."

He dropped the knife on the floor, and released his grip on her neck. Then he stormed into the living room.

There were no tears left to shed, it was like she had dried up inside; her heart a lump of rock. Needing to check on her boys, she had to practically drag herself up the stairs. They lay sleeping, how could they sleep through all that? She never could as a child.

Back in the kitchen, she boiled the kettle and made two cups of coffee. Carrying them to the living room, she set one of the cups down in front of Carl.

"Do you want food?"

He looked at her, and shook his head. She wasn't calm, she was numb; she felt like she was already dead.

That was when she told him that she was going to stay with her parents for a while.

"You're not taking the boys."

"Yes I am." She replied.

When the Hippos chased her that night and the chasms opened up before her, rather than avoid them, she considered jumping in.

The next day, she packed hers and the kid's belongings into the car, and asked Carl to drop them all off at her mum's. She had to leave her three beautiful cats in the house, as she had nowhere to take them. The dog had been re-homed months before, for his own safety. Carl said he would feed the cats.

He drove her to her mum's. When they arrived, she got out of the car and unloaded their belongings from the boot. Slamming the boot shut, she went to the back door to get the boy's out of the car. As she grabbed at the door handle, Carl drove off. She ran after the car, shouting and screaming, but he sped away.

Her mother found her, when she came down to buy something from the dairy next door. She was curled up on the pavement, outside the front door, sobbing hysterically. Every day for the next week, she tried to get her boys back from Carl's mother, but was met with an onslaught of violence and abuse; the last straw, was when Carl hit her mother. The day after, she found herself at a solicitor's, babbling incoherently.

We Can't Let Go, I Can't Let Go

Once under her mother's wing, she gradually got back to her normal weight, if nothing else, her outer-self was looking better. Carl would turn up at her mother's flat, in the early hours of the morning, drunk and with his neck covered in love bites. Yes, she had finally realised they weren't marks made by ill-fitting shirt collars. He would beg her to go back with him and when she questioned the love bites and asked if he had ditched his girlfriend, she would usually end up with a black eye, or at least a slap.

She was going back and forth to the house to see to the animals, while she was trying to make some arrangements for them. One day a neighbour stopped her to tell her that Carl was having a woman there, and she would often be seen naked in front of the un-curtained bedroom window. So, it was true. He really was with someone else and what was worse, he was having sex with her in their marital bed. Making her excuses to her neighbour, she dashed inside the house before allowing the flood gates to open; holding her beautiful cats close for comfort.

A few days later Carl phoned to say he wanted to meet for a drink, as he had something to discuss with her. They met up in a pub in Kilburn. For the first half an hour, they talked like a couple of strangers; she asked after the boys and he gave her a run down on their current activities, but there was no passion in his voice.

It was when they had almost finished their second drink that he told her the house was up for sale, and he wanted the cats out. Because her name wasn't on the paperwork, she had no immediate way of stopping the sale; even though she saved almost all of the money for the deposit and furnishings. Hurt and angry she asked if his girlfriend was responsible. Carl just stared at her.

Although she had been expecting it to happen at some time, she had still clung to the hope that while they owned the house, there was still a chance for them. But now he was pulling that rug from under her. She told him that she needed the loo; in the privacy of the cubicle, she broke down.

When she returned to the table, there was another drink waiting for her. As she took a sip, he dangled a bunch of keys in front of her. Her coat was on the back of the chair, reaching into the pocket she found that only her mother's keys remained; her house keys were now in Carl's hand. He told her she would no longer have access to the house and that she would find the cats outside. After delivering that emotional blow to the gut, he got up and left; leaving her sobbing, in the middle of a busy pub. She grabbed her coat and ran.

Next day she and her mother went to check on the cats, and found them as Carl said, all shut out of the house. Gathering them together, she put them in a large shopping bag and took them to the vets to have them put to sleep, she couldn't think of any alternative; her parents weren't allowed pets in their flat. She was in tatters, the *vet was horrible to her, telling her what a nasty person she was; he didn't need to tell her, she already knew. Her cats were the only thing she had left, her whole life and everything she loved was now gone.*

After a month, she forced herself to find a job, as she needed the money for her mother. Her dad wanted her to go back to working in accounts but she wasn't sure if she was able to do that. She was functioning, zombie-like. Well, that was what she wanted her parents to think, inside she was broken, lost, dying. Terrified of everything, especially living.

Around the same time Carl phoned Bren, and asked if they could try to reconcile. He told her he had changed, and that there was no one else as he realised that he loved her and would do anything to keep her. She wasn't sure that she could forgive what had happened, but she said she would give it a try. Call her stupid if you like, she was still in love with him, besides she wanted to see her kids and have things back the way they were; before Carl's drinking became a problem. They arranged to go out the next evening, so that they could talk.

One thing her mother taught her was to put your 'public' face on. Her mother never left the house without combing her hair and putting on her lipstick and rouge. That night before she went out, she applied eye makeup, styled her hair and dabbed on some perfume.

Carl had sold the house almost immediately, and with the money left over after paying off the mortgage he bought himself a flash car which he delighted in showing her.

He took her to quite a nice pub but as soon as they walked in, the barman eyed her up and asked Carl where his wife was. Carl told her that the barman had probably mistaken him for his friend, who always had his wife with him. She believed him, but not for long.

After the pub they went to an Indian restaurant; not a cheap one either. A waiter approached and greeted them in his best Calcutta accent.

"Good evening, sir. Where is your wife this evening?"

This time she wasn't swallowing any excuses. She said nothing about what the waiter had asked, but she did order the most expensive thing on the menu, and several drinks.

"Times have changed from when you would only order half of brown ale." Carl commented.

"That was before I lost everything that made life worth living." She told him.

When they had finished their meal, they went back to the pub and the same barman served them. As Carl paid, she looked at the barman, and said,

"By the way, I'm the wife, the other one is the bit on the side."

Carl's jaw dropped; he just stared at her. The barman looked shocked, but not as shocked as she was at having the nerve to say it.

As they sipped their drinks, Bren asked Carl what it was he wanted from her. He told her he wanted things back the way they were; with her waiting for him when he got home. She told him that she wanted that too, but without the drinking and his girlfriend, just him and her and the kids.

"I want you both."

Her eyes stung with tears.

"What is it about her?"

Carl told her why he fell for his girlfriend.

"Although she's no sort, she's a nice kid."

Bren thought, 'I guess he doesn't think I'm either'.

Instead of the fun-loving teen she once was, Carl had moulded her into no more than a housekeeper and a punch-bag, with no friends.

Finally, it dawned on her that when they were together sexual contact between them had become almost extinct. It was only now that she realised, it wasn't because he was tired from drink and always getting home late, it was because he was getting sex elsewhere. Then another thought came to her, he had always kept her short of money and now she knew why; he had been spending it on Indian meals and pub crawls with his mistress. He probably never even spared her a thought when he was with his girlfriend; or considered what he was doing to her, both physically and mentally.

The more Carl had wanted to be with his girlfriend, the more he hated and despised Bren. His girlfriend wanted marriage, and Bren was in the way of that. She was the dutiful wife, innocently believing his lies. Perhaps, she could have been better in bed, or insisted on going out drinking with him. Maybe then, he would have wanted her.

Carl had helped make her into a person who craved affection, in whatever way she could get it. Even being beaten and pissed on was better than being ignored. He took any self-confidence that she had, and made her hate herself. After years of being told she was ugly, useless and a failure, that is what she had become. Of course, Carl's mother knew about his girlfriend, she hated Bren so obviously she encouraged it.

May 1970, at the age of twenty-one she found herself separated from her husband and children, homeless and without any friends. Carl had sold their house and she had never received a penny from it, nor did she expect it. They had been together for four years. Although she didn't realise it then; it would take another three years before their divorce was final.

Looking for friendship, I turned to Sara and Joanne who were both married by now. Joanne and her husband Drew had twin girls. I

113

called at Joanne's one evening, but definitely didn't get greeted with open arms. She answered the door and told me to wait a moment, I heard her speaking to her husband in muffled tones. Joanne told her husband to go in the bedroom and do some sewing, she seemed terrified to let me near him. Perhaps she had a guilty conscious after having sex with Carl; as I now know she probably did. Perhaps she may have thought that I would do the same, to get my own back; the truth was, the last thing I wanted at that moment was another man.

Once Joanne had her husband tucked safely away, she let me in. I was treated to a rushed cup of coffee, then shown the door. A few days later, I got a similar response from Sara. I got the impression that it was a case of, 'lock up your husband's girls, soon to be divorcee on the prowl'.

I applied to the court for a separation order. But when the court date came around, Carl told the magistrate that he wanted to go back with me. My barrister was dumbfounded and asked me what was going on, I told him I didn't have a clue. The barrister suggested that Carl and I should go somewhere quiet, to talk things over.

They went for coffee, and talked for a couple of hours. Carl said he would give up drinking and would be faithful to her. Once again, he said he loved her more than anything and wanted them to be back together. They agreed that they would spend the night in a hotel. The following day they would find somewhere to live, away from both sets of parents, so that they could start afresh. She still loved him even after what he had done, and he promised things would be different. They arranged for him to pick her up from her parents at 8pm that evening.

Once she was back at her mum's, she packed her clothes, chatting excitedly to her mother, about the plans she and Carl had made.
"Are you sure this is what you want?" Her mother asked.
"More than anything Mum."

Her mother shook her head, her father shrugged his shoulders and disappeared into the living room. Bren knew they both missed their grand-children, so this would solve all their problems.

She waited, with her suitcase next to her for eight o'clock to arrive. Eight came, then nine, then ten, but still she waited. Eventually her mother said,

"He's not coming."

Bren practically screamed at her.

"Yes, he is, he promised." But in her heart, she knew her mother was right. He had let her down again. She lay on her bed sobbing, cuddling her pillow, praying he would still turn up. In the early hours of the morning, she must have fallen asleep.

Awake, exhausted and heartbroken, she looked at her reflection in the mirror. Swollen eyes, tear-stained face, hair standing on end. Why would he want her? She was ugly, skinny, with tiny breasts. Sobbing uncontrollably, she wished she could die.

Completely broken, she just went through the motions. Not wanting to go out, but unable to stay in. She sued for divorce on the grounds of her husband's adultery, but there were complications because, she couldn't give a name for the other party.

Looking back, it all made sense. The wanting to go back with her was a ploy thought up between Carl and his solicitor, to try to make her look like the guilty party. Who would believe she was scared of him, if she was willing to meet up with him to discuss a reconciliation? No one realised how besotted she was with him, all she wanted was her husband and kids back, she wanted the man she thought she had married. Perhaps if she had told the solicitors everything, he had done to her, maybe then they would have taken her side; but she couldn't bring herself to talk about the man she loved in that way.

Her own barrister was rubbish. He just kept talking about what his wife would do in her position, but his wife hadn't been beaten to submission, she hadn't been pissed on, and made to feel like she was the ugliest woman in the world. If Bren had been stronger, she would have told him so; but she wasn't strong, she was a frightened, heartbroken child, in a woman's body.

Her relationship with Carl had left scars. Although she acted tough, and pretended that she was alright, the fear still remained with her. So much so, that if ever anyone unexpectedly raised their hand, she would cower down, waiting for the blow to hit home.

After my break up with Carl, I couldn't be bothered to trim my hair, or style it, so I just let it grow. I know now, that I was suffering from depression, anxiety and panic attacks and had been since early childhood; I was probably, bordering on a nervous breakdown which impaired my rational thinking.

I had to accept that Carl was gone, he loved someone else. My life was worth nothing without him and my kids. Whatever friends I may have had in the past, now had lives of their own that didn't include me.

From the first moment that I became pregnant with David I hadn't consumed a single drop of alcohol, in fact the only alcohol I'd had while Carl and I were still living together was the rum and coke that Aunt Lil had bought Mum and I. Now I wasn't just wanting to drown my sorrows; I was wanting to obliterate every single memory of the past four years.

By frequenting local pubs, I got very involved with the gay scene, even though I was straight. Mainly because I felt safe with them, and nothing was expected of me. I craved male company, but not for sex, just to be with someone. Just to feel that I wasn't ugly, or a useless piece of shit that needed to be scraped off of somebody's shoe.

There were many tales that came to me through the grapevine

about arguments and blows exchanged between Carl and his girlfriend. I've got to admit that every time I heard this, I felt a little bit of pleasure.

I became friends with a twenty-nine-year-old Greek girl, who had thirteen children, a husband and a boyfriend. She would often ask me to join her and her boyfriend on nights out, as her alibi. One night, she asked me to go with them to a night club on Finchley Road. I didn't want to go but she persuaded me, telling me it would do me good. When we got there, we ordered drinks and sat down at a table. A few drinks later I needed the toilet, so I set off across the dance floor in search of the ladies' room.

On the way back she spotted Carl, standing on his own in the middle of the dance floor. It was probably the vast amount of alcohol she had consumed that gave her the bravado to stop behind him, tap him on the shoulder, and say,

"D'you wanna dance."

He turned around, looking shocked.

"Err, yeah." He replied.

They started dancing. A few minutes into the dance, she heard screaming. Turning, she came face to face with Carl's scruffy, overweight mistress, tugging at her hair and shouting.

"Get away from him or I'll kill you."

Bren replied.

"I'll dance with him if I like, after all he is still my husband."

Carl took a step towards his mistress.

"Don't start anything, Bren."

She remembered thinking, 'that's good, considering she's the one freaking out and threatening to kill me'.

The music stopped, and everyone stared at them. There was a splintering of glass, and suddenly Carl's mistress was flying at Bren with a broken beer tankard in her hand. The mistress screamed at

Bren.

"You're nothing but trash, leaving your kids."

'That's rich coming from someone who has been sleeping with their father behind his wife's back'. Bren thought.

Obviously, Carl had lied to her as well.

Carl stepped between them, grabbed the hand with the glass in, and led the screaming banshee away, saying.

"It's alright darling, it's you I want to be with."

Staring after them, she wondered what she had done so wrong that made him have affairs. She thought that she must be the ugliest, most horrible woman on the planet, because he had gone off with this awful creature, who was not at all pretty. That thought stayed with her and brought back memories of her first job, when she was constantly maligned because she wore unflattering glasses that made her look like an owl. She really was ugly and unlovable; they couldn't all be wrong, could they?

Chapter 8

Trying to Move on but not Very Successfully

One night I decided to go to the Windsor Castle pub, on Harrow Road. It was around 10pm on a late-Summer evening in 1970 and it must have been during some kind of power cut, as all the streets were dark.

The pub had candles lined up all along the bar, and there was only warm bottled beer, as the pumps and fridges weren't working. The drag artists were still performing, even though the stage was almost in darkness.

Sitting alone in the corner, downing Southern Comfort and dry ginger ale, I was trying to forget. Carl had managed to wipe me from his thoughts through drink and sex, so maybe I could wipe him out in the same way. The only problem was I didn't want sex with just anyone, for me sex was an act of love, not something that was forced upon you, or just used to satisfy an urge. Damn it, the bloody drink wasn't doing its job, I still wanted Carl.

Not long before closing time, a boy came over to my table. He was around twenty, nice looking; or at least I think he was being as my eyesight was more than a little blurred, due to a vast amount of alcohol, candlelight and the lack of spectacles.

They talked for a while and when the pub closed, he walked her home. As soon as she opened the lower door, he pushed his way in. Pulling her towards him, he kissed her while trying to put his hand up her jumper.

"No." she said firmly; she wasn't that drunk.

"Why not? I thought you were up for it."

"Why, because I'm separated from my husband, drunk and I allowed you to walk me home? That makes me up for it, does it?"

He sneered.

"Well, you ain't nothing special, I've got a girlfriend prettier than you."

"So, if you've got this lovely girlfriend, why are you messing around with other girls, or isn't she up for it either?"

He grunted and left.

Why couldn't men understand, she just wanted company, someone she could have a good conversation with, without them thinking she was desperate. She didn't expect them to spend money on her, she always paid her way, bought the round when it was her turn.

After that night she spent a lot of time at the Windsor. One night she got there before opening time and had to wait outside, before long she noticed she had started to shake and sweat; and she really needed a drink.

Bren hadn't seen the last of Carl, he still kept coming around. He even told her, that early one morning, he had woken up completely naked in the lift in his mother's tower block; not knowing how he got there. The good thing was, she felt nothing. Now, she didn't know whether she still loved him or not, as she was too numb from drink to care.

At that time, she didn't think there was any hope of getting her kids back. Although she had been granted visiting rights, every visit ended in violence and abuse, and with her and the kids in tears. It was heart-breaking to see her boys in such distress. Her solicitor was completely useless, as he seemed to be more sympathetic towards Carl and his mother, than he was towards Bren and her mother. In the end, she did the hardest thing that any mother should have to do, she walked away.

Many people would condemn her for her actions, but they were not in her shoes, they hadn't experienced what she had gone *through; was still going through. She did what she thought was best for the safety of her boys, her parents, and herself.*

Besides she was concerned about her mental state, as she had become abusive towards herself; she was drinking too much and putting herself in dangerous situations. Maybe, she was hoping that something or someone would kill her; perhaps that was what she had been wanting all of her life. Whatever the problem was, she knew that no judge would grant her custody of her boys while she was in that state, especially with Carl and his mother spreading their lies.

Her greatest hope, was that one day her boys would be home with her, but she had to try to get back on her feet and sort her life out; otherwise, that would never be. She didn't want to think of them as permanently gone, but she had to face the fact that it could be a possibility; both Carl and his mother could be very manipulative.

I had become friendly with the drag artists from the Windsor and they introduced me to a man named Edward, who lived in a student house, with a bunch of Australians. He was divorced with two kids, and seemed nice. We talked a lot and he asked me if I would like to go out for coffee. Ed was kind, attentive and full of compliments, and we seemed to get on well. I was beginning to like him quite a lot, as he made me feel fairly good about myself. He had some secrets, but he had been married with kids, so I presumed the secrets surrounded that part of his life.

Four weeks into the relationship, we were invited to a party by some gay friends, one of whom was a drag artist, and who I considered to be a good friend; being as I had been sharing his flat for the past few weeks. I was dancing and socialising when Edward disappeared into the kitchen, where the drinks were.

After a while, I decided to go and get myself a drink. A gay friend, Tony, was standing by the kitchen door.

"You don't want to go in there."

Tony put his arm out to bar her way. Bren replied that she did, as she wanted to get a drink.

"Take it from me, you don't." *He insisted.*

She pushed past him, but she really wasn't prepared for what she found in there. Edward, with his trousers round his ankles, was having sex with her 'drag artist' friend. Dazed, she forced herself to say something. Flippantly stating.

"I guess he's got something, I haven't got."

As soon as the words were out of her mouth, she made a hasty retreat.

A few days later Edward managed to catch up with her, she was still very upset and had lost faith in relationships altogether.

"Look, I'm sorry." *He said,*

Bren wasn't interested in excuses, once again a man had betrayed her; she yelled at him.

"Go away you poof."

That was when his fist made contact with her face, dislocating her jaw. Shocked and in pain, she turned and ran. After Carl, she vowed no man would ever hit her again and now this man had done just that; at least it had happened sooner, rather than later.

Betrayed and disillusioned, I stopped going to the Windsor, and went back to more familiar surroundings, namely London's West End. My jaw healed fairly quickly, but the emotional wounds refused to subside. I was just so glad that I had kept to my 'no sex without love' rule.

Peacocks

Whenever my life took a bad turn, like a Siren to a sailor, the West End called to me; drawing me in with her charms, blinding me to the perils of her rocky coastline.

Since I was a child, I have loved meeting interesting people with a story to tell and the West End is full of interesting people. No matter how sad you may feel, there is something about the bright lights, the hustle and bustle and the architecture of London, that helps raise your spirits.

George, was a Scottish lad who lived in Willesden, I liked him because he was funny. Lord knows, I certainly needed some laughter in my life; unfortunately, like me, George drank too much. We had been out drinking one evening, when he asked if he could escort me home, against my better judgement I agreed. When we reached my flats, we stood inside the outer door talking. I told him he couldn't stay and made him promise to go. But he just kept hanging about and eventually I got fed up and went upstairs to bed; leaving George to make his own way home.

The following morning, I got up as usual and had breakfast. About 8am, just after mum and dad had left for work, the sound of a woman's screams broke through the silence. I didn't even need to guess what the problem was. After dashing downstairs, I found the bike cupboard open and our next-door neighbour, Kathy, hysterical. George was curled up in her baby's pram, bum in air, with an umbrella open over the top of him. I arrived just in time to hear him say to Kathy.

"Stop screaming woman you're hurting my head."

Kathy grabbed the umbrella, closed it and started beating George with it. He leapt out of the pram and bolted for the door, with Kathy in hot pursuit.

Naturally, I denied all knowledge of him.

My Siren called, luring me with the promise of an abundance of cannabis and alcohol. For the first few months she tempted me with her music; the like of which can only be heard in sleazy back street clubs.

While basking in a false sense of security, I fell foul to having my drink spiked with LSD. That night I found myself walking across Soho's rooftops, moving from building to building as easily as stepping off a kerb. How I managed to stay alive is beyond reason, because it really seemed that I was on a path to self-destruction

In the early hours of one morning, after a party, I was really sick and happened to glance in the mirror; the face staring back at me looked older than my mother. It was then I started to re-evaluate my life. Determined to get myself back on track, I cut back on my drinking and rarely smoked cannabis. An interest in taking care of my appearance resurfaced, and within a matter of weeks the face looking back from the mirror didn't look too bad.

While in Playland, an amusement arcade, I met a lad named William 'Tommy' Thompson, he was down to earth and that appealed to me.

Late summer sunshine, warmed the busy footpath, with its afternoon glow. Sparkling sandstone lights, shimmered on the slabs, giving the impression that London's streets really were paved with gold.

Multilingual chatter filled the air, as people passed on their way to the theatres, and nightlife of Leicester Square; parading their finest 1970s West End fashion. Young men like strutting peacocks, exhibited their mating attire of coiffured hair, body hugging shirts, flared trousers and platform boots. Girls tottered on over-high heels, in hot pants and crop tops; revealing excessive amounts of flesh while staying, barely, within the bounds of decency. Hoping that some hunky male would sweep them off their pressure blistered feet.

They were on Shaftesbury Avenue. Her friend Tommy, stopped to ask two of the 'peacocks' for a light for his cigarette. Disinterested, Bren gazed at the pavement. The one with the German accent, uttered a greeting. Sun narrowed eyes, shielded by her hand, afforded her a glance at the other peacock. He flashed her a lopsided grin. Her attention had not only been captured; it had been imprisoned. Undoubtedly, he was the most beautiful man she had ever seen.

With thoughts of her mystery man still streaming through her mind, she accompanied Tommy to a small café. They sipped cappuccino in silence, while she scanned her subconscious for anything she might have missed, during those mind-blowing moments of her brief encounter with the peacock. Quick 'glimpses' of his shoulder length dark blond hair, his tall frame, his grin, only whetted her appetite for more of him. She pushed Tommy for information, but detected a jealous note in his reply.

"He's no good to you, he's gay."

Her mind wandered back to how her peacock was dressed, pink shirt, jeans and a black leather jacket. They were both 'pretty boys', so she supposed Tommy could be right. Names hadn't been exchanged, so she couldn't ask anyone else about her peacock.

For days, thoughts of him danced around her brain; but London is a big place, so she accepted that she would probably never see her peacock again. No longer being one for living in a fantasy world, she quelled the feelings that stirred within her and lost herself in life.

The idea that Tommy had any genuine feelings for me, never crossed my mind. As during the short time, I had known him, I was aware that he was seeing several other girls. In fact, he would leave me with any one of his friends, with the request.

"Take care of her for me."

On one occasion he left me with a guy named Roger, who was

quite good looking, if somewhat scruffy. His reply was.

"If you leave her with me, you won't get her back."

He gave me an appreciative look, and said,

"Come on, I'll buy you a coffee."

Roger was true to his word because a few weeks later, Tommy left me with him again. This time Roger was clean and well-dressed, and when he spoke there was a gentleness in his voice that I hadn't noticed before. I think he may have been Anglo-Indian, as his skin had a brown hue and his eyes and hair were very dark. He was nicknamed, the Mumble Man, and I found out why a while later; it seemed Roger could talk his way out of most situations.

It was a warm afternoon. Roger and I met up at Marble Arch, and made our way to one of the posh hotels; I won't say which, for legal reasons. Roger had a key to one of the rooms, so I presumed he was staying there. As he turned the key in the lock, he told me.

"Just got to pick something up."

When we entered the room, I thought that Roger was acting as though he was unfamiliar with his surroundings, even though the room was obviously occupied. My doubts diminished when he spotted what he was looking for; his wallet.

"There it is."

He opened the wallet, checked through it, then placed it in his pocket. As we left, he picked up a very expensive looking watch, and put it on his wrist. He locked the door and we went to a restaurant for something to eat.

Roger and I had arranged to meet at midnight on the following Saturday, outside the Apple club. When I arrived a few minutes before twelve, I could see Roger talking to some black guys. The conversation appeared to get heated, and one of them lifted a hand to Roger's face. Roger dropped to his knees and the men ran down the alley, bumping into me as they passed.

When I reached Roger, there was blood pouring from his left cheek, a gaping wound stretched from just under his ear to the side of his mouth. Someone went to call an ambulance. Roger shouted for one of his friends and told him.

"Get her out of here, I don't want her to see me like this."

Roger's stitches were out and the wound was starting to heal. Luckily it was quite a clean cut. We had been for lunch and were now wandering about in Piccadilly. Roger led me into one of the shops that sold souvenirs and silver jewellery. I was looking through postcards of London, and was vaguely aware of Roger looking at some rings.

Distracted from her browsing by raised voices, she became aware that Roger was being accused of stealing one of the rings. Oblivious to having done so, she had moved closer to Roger and was practically standing next to him. A store detective was telling Roger he wanted to search him. Then to Bren's horror, Roger told the store detective that he had given the ring to her. The store detective turned to Bren, saying that he wanted to search both of them. Bren spoke up.

"If you want to search me, then it will have to be done by a female police officer."

The store detective said Bren needed to go to his office, but she told him that she wasn't going anywhere, until the police arrived.

She was unsure whether it was the mention of police, or whether he was trying to avoid any embarrassment to her, but suddenly Roger took the ring from his mouth and threw it onto the counter; from where it bounced onto the floor. He grabbed her hand, and ran from the shop dragging her behind him, while shouting,

"Sorry about the ring mate, it was a joke."

They wove through the mid-afternoon crowds on Shaftesbury Avenue, the store detective didn't appear to be following. Bren thought he was probably as dazed by the whole incident as she was.

What transpired that day, did make her wonder whether there was anything illegal about the hotel room incident. Needless to say, Roger ceased to be part of her life. Joining the ever-lengthening string of other males, and females, who had hurt her or let her down.

Kidnapped-Who Can I Trust?

Since my break up with Carl I had gone through a period of wanting to lock myself away from the world. Now my overactive and enquiring brain was seeking stimulation.

The West End had become my salvation; it somehow helped to ease the pain and the loneliness. After being deceived by Ted and Roger, I was determined not to become romantically involved with anyone. Looking for company, I began frequenting the pubs and clubs again and had made a few friends amongst the regulars.

It was in one of the drinking clubs that I met a lad named Tex. He was a mine of information and I found myself enjoying the art of conversation again. There was no physical attraction which made it even better, as I thought I had finally found a friend; someone with a brain above his waist.

On a cold night in mid-December, Tex asked me if I fancied hitchhiking to Birmingham with him, as he was going to visit his parents for a couple of days. He appeared to be trustworthy and hitchhiking to another city seemed like a bit of an adventure, so I agreed.

Plans were made and it was decided they should begin their journey there and then; not even considering that she hadn't got a change of clothes and that all she had was the money in her pocket. They finished their drinks and took a tube to Hendon Central, from where they walked to the Scratchwood[4] motorway services. Tex suggested they go into one of the trucker's cafes, to see if anyone was going to Birmingham. A nice middle-aged driver offered to take them.

A few hours later, they were dropped off just outside the town centre. Even though it was the early hours of a mid-week morning, Tex insisted they walked into town. They wandered around for a while, and had a hot drink in the all-night café, before heading towards the outskirts.

Bren was surprised at the number of men wandering about, considering it was the early hours of a cold morning. It was getting light, so they headed towards Small Heath, where Tex said his parents lived. On the way he asked, if she minded them calling at his friend's house, saying that he thought she would like him, as he was an interesting man.

They stopped outside quite a nice-looking terraced house. Tex knocked, and the door was opened by a black guy. He seemed really pleasant and obviously liked his spliffs, judging by the sweet pungent smell that wafted out from the house. Standing to one side, so that Bren and Tex could enter, he asked if they would like coffee and toast as he was just making some.

Tony was as interesting as Tex said, they talked and laughed for hours, while drinking numerous cups of coffee and eating sandwiches. Before they knew, it was late afternoon. Bren was really enjoying being in the company of two men who seemed to be able to hold an intelligent conversation.

Asking them to stay for tea, Tony went to the kitchen to cook mutton stew. Tex offered to help, and Bren could hear them whispering to each other and laughing; enjoying themselves. The stew was served in a massive pot, and Tony spooned out huge helpings into soup dishes. The food was delicious.

She washed up, while the two men talked. When she returned to

129

living room, they were looking through some photos and reminiscing, Tony got up and went to the street door, locking it and putting the keys in his jacket pocket. For some reason this made Bren feel uncomfortable.

"Can't take any chances when it gets dark, too many thieves about."
Tony told them. Feeling reassured, she sat down in the vacant armchair.

Tony offered her a drink from the nearly empty bottle of Jamaican rum on the coffee table. Bren declined.

"Maybe later, thank you. Tex, shouldn't we be getting to your Mum and Dad?"
Glancing at Tony he replied.
"They stay up late."

Tony asked if she would like a smoke, once again she declined, knowing that he didn't mean a cigarette. Tex and Tony continued to chat about their school days. Then Tex turned to her.
"You know you commented about all the men walking about, that's the red-light district of Birmingham".

Puzzled, she was unsure how the conversation had turned from bad school dinners to prostitution. Not only that, the tone of his voice had changed too. Tex continued.
"Why I brought you here was so that you can work for me and Tony."
She glared at him, feeling more than a little scared, as she didn't like where this conversation appeared to be leading.
"Basically, you're going to stay here until you agree. However long it takes, whatever it takes, so you might as well have a drink and get used to it."

There was something about his tone of voice that made her realise he wasn't messing around. She thought about making a run for it but Tony was a big guy, and although Tex wasn't very tall, he was full of muscle; so, she knew she was no match for the two of them. Deciding that it was best to stay calm, she considered how she might talk her way out of it.

"I'm not like that, I can't sleep with just anyone, not even for money."

"Who said anything about sleeping?" Tex replied.

"You're going to do as you're told, as we can be very persuasive." His tone was definitely aggressive. Tony butted in.

"Lighten up Tex, let's have that drink."

Tex poured some drinks and put one in front of her. Tony fetched another bottle of rum and Tex topped up his and Tony's glasses. They lit another spliff. Sipping her drink slowly, she tried to work out what to do. They sat there making plans that involved her.

Too busy noting any means of escape, she didn't speak. No matter how much her stomach churned she had to remain rational; she couldn't allow herself to break down as it would reduce her awareness. She had to stay focused if she was going to get through this.

Another bottle of rum was opened, and they carried on drinking, smoking and talking into the early hours of the morning. Bren had re-joined the conversation, knowing that there was nothing she could do at that time. She continued to sip her drink slowly, pacing herself, telling them she wasn't used to drinking spirits. Tex was the first to pass out, followed by Tony who had consumed several more drinks by then.

The only light in the room was a small table lamp, the rest of the house was in darkness. Rising quietly from the chair, she crept across to the window; it was nailed shut. As she moved towards the other window, Tex mumbled. Her heart beat rapidly, but he settled down again. She tried the other window, that too was nailed shut and she presumed that the same could be said for all the downstairs windows. Tiptoeing to the kitchen she checked the back door; it was locked and there was no key. The only alternative was the front door.

Bren moved slowly around the room, being careful not to bump into anything. When she reached the living room door, she stepped quietly out into the hallway. She couldn't remember if there was anything in the hallway that she might bump into. So, she edged along the wall, holding her left arm in front of her in case anything was in her way.

It seemed to take forever to reach the front door. Once there, she pulled at the handle; the door was definitely locked. Sliding her hand down to the key hole, she felt for the keys. Tony grunted in his sleep, then she remembered.

'Oh god! He's got the keys in his pocket, and I've got to get them without waking him'.

Carefully moving along the hallway, she made her way back to the living room. Semi-crouching and feeling for the edge of the table, she moved around it to the chair Tony was sleeping in. Terrified that one of them would wake, warily, she slid her hand into Tony's right-hand pocket, nothing. Her eyes dampened, as she realised it was the wrong pocket. Shaking, she dreaded the thought of having to try the other one, as it was between his body and the chair arm.

Tony shifted in the chair. She thought he was going to open his eyes and catch her leaning over him, but he just changed position. Luckily, he had shifted to the right, so that the other pocket was more accessible. Feeling her way around the back of the chair, she slid her hand gently into Tony's left pocket. As she pulled out the bunch of keys they rattled slightly and Tex mumbled something. She paused ready to sit in the chair and pretend she was sleeping. As luck would have it, they both stayed asleep.

Bren slipped past the chair she had been sitting in and Tex's chair. Grabbing at the door frame for support she groped for the

opposite wall before creeping along the hallway again;
remembering that she had seen a small table with an umbrella stand
on that side of the hall, just moments before her leg brushed against
it. There were five or six keys on the ring, she hoped she would be
able to find the right one without making too much noise. The keys
jangled as she fumbled to try each of them in the lock; she was
trembling so much she didn't think she would be able to find the
keyhole. Six keys and it was the last one that fitted, she turned the
catch. It was then she realised that there was a second lock.

Her heart sank with the knowledge that she was going to have to
go through the keys again. Slimy with sweat, her hands struggled to
grip the keys; afraid she may drop them, she fought to hold back a
sob. Luckily, it was the first one she picked. When she tried the catch
this time, the door opened.

Squeezing through the smallest gap possible to avoid the
likelihood of creaking hinges, she moved into the deserted street.
Leaving the door open she ran towards, what she hoped, was the
town centre and the train station. It was still dark and freezing cold,
then she remembered she had left her jacket with her money in the
pocket. She couldn't take the chance of going back; as it was, she
kept glancing behind to make sure they weren't following her. Her
heart was pumping hard, but she just kept going.

Feeling like she had been running for ages, she was relieved when
she saw the blue sign for the police station. When she entered, the
elderly sergeant behind the desk looked straight through her.
Between sobs, she managed to tell him what had happened, but he
probably thought she was either drunk or stoned, as he told her the
best thing to do was get a train back to London.

She explained that she had left her money at the house. Now, it
was obvious that he didn't believe her. He told her to go to New
Street station, give them her name and address and they would let

her on the train. She fled from the police station, expecting to bump into Tex and Tony. By now she was near hysterical, so she just kept running as fast as she could.

In her mind, it seemed like hours before she was inside the railway station, talking to the clerk. When she had explained what had happened, she asked him if she could give her name and address so that she could get on the train home. The clerk told her that wasn't possible, as she had to get someone to pay for the ticket at St Pancras station. As soon as they were informed that this had been done, they would let her board the train.

Phoning her parents was out of the question, because they had no way of getting to St Pancras so early in the morning. So, she had to phone her half-sister. Things weren't very good between them at that time, because Anna didn't agree with her ending her marriage.

Anna and Peter were not early risers when they weren't working, and Bren knew they wouldn't be pleased at her getting them out of bed to answer the phone; especially as she was reversing the charges.

Anna did answer, and she accepted the charges. Bren didn't tell her everything, just that she had lost her money and was stuck in Birmingham. She told Anna she needed her to go and pay for a ticket at St Pancras, which was a good one-hour drive from where they lived. Peter was talking in the background.
"Leave her there." he said.
Bren was extremely tearful by then so Anna said she would do it, but Bren could tell she wasn't at all happy about it.

Informing the clerk that her sister was going to pay the money, Bren gave him the details. The clerk told her she had to wait and they would inform her over the Tannoy when she could collect her ticket.

Stuck in the middle of the station she felt totally exposed. For ages, *she wandered back and forth looking all around her, ready to run if need be. She was distraught, believing that they would catch up with her before she got a chance to get on a train.*

It took over four hours before her name was called to say the money had been paid. They issued her with a pass, but she had to wait another thirty-five minutes for the first available train. All the time she was on edge, afraid to breathe normally in case they were there and heard her. It wasn't until the train pulled out of the station, and she was sure they weren't on it that she was able to relax.

Since the Birmingham incident, I had become wary of people, realising that I shouldn't be so trusting, but some people were very good liars. Obviously, Tex had planned it all from the start and had lured me into a false sense of security, confident that he and Tony would get what they wanted in the end. I am positive that it wasn't the first time that they had done something like that.

I was beginning to think that I was a very bad judge of character.

Lost Christmas and Revelations

My pending divorce from Carl was still proving to be a problem, as I needed evidence that he had been having an affair; the identity of the co-respondent.

The information I needed came to me by a complete fluke. A male work colleague happened to be drinking in the pub where Carl's girlfriend worked. He got talking to the barman, who for some reason mistook him for a friend of Carl's and mentioned the girlfriend's name. But that wasn't all the barman told him; he said that Carl, and his girlfriend's brother, had robbed the United Dairies milk yard where Carl had worked. I was beginning to think that I didn't know the man I married at all. On the plus side, I now had the girlfriend's name and was able to complete my divorce papers.

I was now working for a company in Neasden and was living back at my parents flat. But life was far from rosy, I was still drinking too much, and struggling with losing my own little family.

It was Christmas Eve, and all fifteen staff members went for a lunch time drink. At least eight people bought a round, most of which were spirits. The drinks were downed, before they made their way back to the office to finish work. Someone had left Bren a bottle of sherry, she'd always hated the stuff but she drank it anyway and continued doing her work. Later when she went to the toilet, the room was spinning.

They left work early, and Bren went Christmas shopping. Once at home, she wrapped the presents and took them to the various houses, including dropping off presents for her boys; apparently, they were out when she arrived at Carl's mums. Back home again, she had something to eat and then went to bed.

It was the day after Boxing Day, when she finally emerged from her bedroom. Those three days were a complete blank; she couldn't recall anything about them although she presumed, she must have got up to use the toilet at some stage. Her mother said she had eaten Christmas dinner with them, but she really couldn't remember.

When she went back to work after the holidays, she discovered that everything she had entered into her ledgers was illegible. Luckily it had been entered in pencil, so she was able to rub it out and start again. Because it had affected her work and the fact that she had lost three days, she made a decision to do something about her drinking; she knew it wouldn't be easy.

Once again, I was bored and on the move. The accounts office of Swarovski London was nothing special but it promised plenty of opportunities for advancement.

While at work one day I needed to use the toilet and when I

washed my hands my rings came off; I put them on the sink and forgot to pick them up. About ten minutes later I remembered them but when I went to get them, they had disappeared and obviously no one knew anything about them. So that was the final link in my marriage to Carl gone.

During a rare heart to heart conversation with my mother she revealed the reason why she and Dad argued. Apparently, my father was obsessive about sex. His excuse to demand his 'marital rights' was that he had phlegm on his chest, and the only thing that would shift it was sex. This now gave a new meaning to when mum said. "He's got a bloody cold again".

I always thought that she was referring to Dad drinking hot toddies. My dad wasn't really a drinker, but at Christmas he would always buy a bottle of Whisky for himself. Then he would suddenly develop a cold and have a hot toddy every night. As soon as the whisky was gone the cold would miraculously disappear.

This revelation must have been very hard for my mother, as she came from a generation when talking about sex was taboo. Mum told me that although Dad wanted sex, the essential parts needed for this exercise didn't work very well so, in her words.
"He was always flicking himself off."

That was when I was struck with a lightbulb moment, about when I was a child sleeping in my dad's 'armchair'.

Marble Arch

It started with a chat over cappuccino. A while later they were walking, but not particularly by choice. What started off as a gentle stroll had been turned into a Mescaline marathon, thanks to the person who had spiked their coffee.

Alan's muscles rippled as they walked; defined by his close-fitting clothes. Studying his slightly rugged, but handsome face, she realised that she hardly knew this boy; having only met him a few times before. But here they were, sharing an experience, the like of which you would normally only share with someone you knew and trusted completely.

Tingling sensations, tiptoed slowly up her neck to the base of her skull. Pattering their way around her head like a throng of unfocused thoughts; searching for clarity and direction. Drifting along the street on a pocket of air. Kaleidoscopic images occupied her brain, pushing all rational thoughts aside. Her arms moved freely, away from her body. Rhythmically swaying, as if in time to Bach's 'Air on the G-String' played by an invisible orchestra. Walking turned to dancing, gliding and twirling to the melody. Unperturbed by the people who turned to stare. Those unlucky individuals to whom the music was inaudible.

Her dancing came to an abrupt halt as her attention focused on Alan, who was caressing a lamp post. Fingers sensuously tracing its backbone, with all the tenderness of a lover. Right leg wrapped around its waisted base, as if performing some outlandish sex act. He stopped and stared into space, as if trying to gather his thoughts. Then he turned and smiled at her.

"Come on." His East End lilt, unmistakable. He took hold of her hand, and for a while they walked normally again.

Bren had no idea how long they wandered the streets. Occasionally they stopped to stare at hideous shapes in shop windows, which were formed from their own distorted perspective of everyday objects. They sat on the steps of Eros, watching the advertising signs as they flashed on and off. Marvelling at how they reflected in the damp patches of the newly washed street. The 'Dilly' was obviously bustling with people, but it appeared grey and deserted in her altered state of perception.

They were moving again, dodging traffic now. The glare of the headlights resembled searchlights, focused on them. Like huge glowing eyes, attentively observing their progress across the busy road to Marble Arch; waiting in anticipation, for the squelch of their bodies under speeding wheels. They wandered through the arch into the square beyond. Peaceful, even though traffic flowed all around it. There was a bench to their right; they sat down, she glanced at her watch, it was 2am.

To the left of the square, the sun shone. An exquisite halo of radiant light covered the ground. Large, brightly tinted blossoms, opened, with the effortless grace of a Disney animation. Luminescent grass sparkled on an, otherwise, gloomy pavement.

She looked to her right; a thick white blanket covered that side of the square. Sparkling azure flecks pirouetted above it. Snow fell in random flakes; dancing, as she had danced. Floating and darting in every direction. The whole square glowed with an eerie brightness. In a moment of confused consciousness, she wondered how it could be both night and day, sunny and snowing, at the same time.

A tramp appeared in front of her, in tattered layers of clothing, tied around the middle with a length of old rope. A smell of stale sweat and cheap cider, hung in the air around them.
"Have you got any money? If you haven't, they can nick you for vagrancy." The tramp said, pressing a coin into her hand.

Staring at the money, it changed before her eyes. First, it was a one shilling piece, then a new 50p, a £5 note, and then a shilling again. She held out her hand to show Alan, but both the coin and the tramp had disappeared.
"Alan, did you see him? Did you see that tramp?"
Alan nodded, but she wasn't sure if he was lying. Was he actually sharing this experience with her?

A giant torch beam spot-lit where they sat; like two players acting out a scene, centre stage. The square, a huge dark theatre without an audience, abandoned and miserable. It came to her again that she didn't really know this boy. She didn't trust him. Paranoia set in.

Convinced she was about to be raped, she wrapped her skirt tightly around the tops of her legs and sat on it. Terrified, she moved along the bench, away from him, still clutching her skirt tightly and tucking it underneath her. Why did she wear a skirt? She never, normally, wore skirts. Hours passed, sitting in silence. Shaking in fear every time he moved.

Temporary lucidity, crawled purposely back into her mind, weaving its way through the maze of grey pulp, and trampling on the unruly thoughts residing there. Standing up, she seized the moment. Grabbing Alan's hand, she pulled him to his feet.
"Let's go somewhere else."

In their Mescaline induced stupor, it was difficult to focus on direction. They walked, until they found themselves back on Oxford Street. Alive with the patrons of clubs, and late-night revellers, spilling out onto the street; some unable to stand upright, without the aid of an obliging wall or fence.

Relieved to be amongst people again, she relaxed a little. Alan put his arm around her, the gentle weight of his hand and the warmth of his body were strangely comforting. Once she had felt his heat, she realised how cold she was. No longer afraid of him, she was aware of a feeling of normality coursing through her body. Her mind began to operate logically, as it returned to reality.

Bren didn't like anything that stopped her from having full control of her senses. So, when someone had spiked her drink for a second time and put her in the position where she was not in control, she was not at all happy.

Crazy Northern Boys

Her job at Swarovski had turned out to be a very boring, and she was already thinking of handing in her notice, but for now she needed the money to pay her mother; and a solicitor who was not really helping her cause.

It was a Friday in mid-January, the bustling Piccadilly streets were empty of people she knew, so she decided to pop in to the Comedy Bar for a drink. It wasn't a pub that she normally used, but she saw a sign for the Cellar Bar and having always had a fascination for cellars, decided to take a look.

The 'Cellar Bar' was heaving with crowds of commuters, grabbing after work drinks, before travelling home on claustrophobic tube trains.

The hum of numerous conversations, resounded above the clinking of the glasses being collected from random tables; a barman, balancing them precariously, dodged through the mass of bodies.

While her eyes were following the barman's progress, imagine her surprise when they rested on her gorgeous peacock, who was stood at the bar. Pushing her way through the crowds to stand right next to him, she pretended she hadn't seen him.

As she ordered her half pint of light ale, he turned and looked at her. He recognised her and gave her a cheeky smile. He handed the barmaid the money for her drink while introducing himself; his name was Mick. They talked for a while, until they were interrupted by an attractive girl with long dark hair.
"This is Mallie, my girlfriend."

Bren's heart took a dive to the pit of her stomach, she hadn't even considered that he might have a girlfriend. He told Bren they had to go and mumbled something about taking in a film; she didn't really hear what he said, she was devastated. As he and Mallie walked towards the exit, he hesitated and glanced back at Bren. Shrugging his shoulders, he turned away and disappeared up the cellar steps.

Staying to finish her drink, she took it to a corner table; feeling very sad and sorry for herself. She was staring into the bottom of her glass, when something made her look up. A good-looking lad with dark chestnut hair, was walking towards her.

He smiled; he really was a stunner.

"Hi. I thought you were with the bloke at the bar, until I saw his girlfriend come in, I was wondering if you fancy going out for a meal with me sometime. My names Mick by the way."

She smiled, more amused than impressed. Then she remembered the last Michael who had asked her to go for a meal, and erred on the side of caution.

"Maybe." she answered. "Anyway, I'm Brenda."

She and chestnut-haired Mick had been going out together for three weeks, when they ventured into the Cellar Bar again. They sat at a table at the far end of the room and were soon joined by his mate's sister. A while later, some other people arrived and sat with them, chatting and drinking.

Bren was on her way back from the bar, carrying a tray of drinks, when Manchester Alan walked in. He was followed, a few seconds later, by gorgeous Mick; who, until now, she had been trying to look upon as a pleasing but fading memory. Her heart was so far up her throat she thought if she spoke, she might spew it out onto the tray. Nodding to them, she carried on back to her table; collapsing into her seat with a sigh. Relieved that she had made it without her legs folding under her. Luckily, someone struck up a conversation, and they all joined in. The conversation ended suddenly, as a voice said, "Hello Brenda."

She looked up; her knees went to jelly. It was her gorgeous Mick, standing there looking down at her. He was with a shorter lad with a shock of curly ginger hair.

"This is Mick."

It was obvious that he had been drinking; quite a lot it appeared, as he slurred his words.

"We've got this hotel room; do you want to come back with us?"

Not the sort of invitation she had hoped for; she stared at him. What the hell did he think she was, a cheap tart or something?

"Can I bring my friends?"

Obviously, not the answer he was hoping for.

"Didn't realise you were with anyone; I'll see you later."

He was gone as quickly as he appeared.

Hands shaking, she raised her glass to take a drink, but her mouth had relocated. Beer spilt down her chin, like ribbons of drool on a dog's jowls. In an attempt to wipe it away before anyone noticed, she slammed the glass back on the table; which, to her horror, caused a mini tidal wave of golden liquid to cascade over the edge of the glass and into her lap. She was glad when the evening came to an end.

That night, she broke up with chestnut-haired Mick. He looked a little upset, but said that he had guessed she might. He was nice, but he wasn't what she wanted. Then she thought about what he said. Was her attraction to her gorgeous Mick so obvious?

With the intention of going clubbing, Bren was wearing a brand-new pair of over the knee boots, with red hot pants, a red stretch lace shirt and a black tank top; first she was going to have a quiet drink.

In the Comedy, a crowd of lads playing some kind of drinking game, broke the silence of an abnormally quiet Monday evening. The juke box battled to be heard above the noise of glasses rapping on the table, and the shouts of drunken encouragement. Ironically, the song playing was Dawn's, 'Knock Three Times'.

She didn't expect anyone she knew to be in the pub, so she was surprised to see gorgeous Mick standing at the bar talking to the barmaid. Making an excuse to talk to him, she asked.

"Can I borrow one and thruppence, to buy a light ale?"

He carried their drinks to a table, while taking in her whole body, in one appreciative glance. His voice soft.

"Sexy boots."

They sat opposite each other.

"Sorry about the other night, I was a bit drunk. So, are you a working girl then?"

"Yes, I work for a crystal company, Swarovski, as an accountant."

He looked amused.

Then, she realised what he meant. Her shoulder length hair hid her embarrassment, as she lowered her head. His hand, exceptionally gentle for its size, reached across the table, tilting her chin upwards.

"Sorry."

Almost whispering, as though he was about to share some dark secret, he told her he worked as assistant manager, for the London Pride pub.

"I'm from Yorkshire originally."

He was speaking so quietly, she moved closer to listen.

What followed, she didn't expect from someone who was almost a stranger.

"When my mother was happy, she would hold me on her lap and sing to me, I was her favourite. She was Scottish, but very softly spoken. Later, she became a nervous, pill popping wreck."

He told her how he would cover his ears to shut out his mother's screams, as his father punched her repeatedly; holding her by her throat, across the kitchen table. All because she hadn't ironed the *shirt he wanted to wear; to go out with his mistress. Her heart felt for him and his mother, as she knew too well what his mother had gone through. Mick continued.*

"Of course, I was too young to know what was going on, too little to help her. But not too young to remember."

A sullen expression crept across his face.

"I found her with her head in the fireplace. I thought she was asleep. They told me she was dead."

Mick went on to tell Bren how his step mother, Annie, hated him, because he caught her with his father's cousin. How she would lie, to get him into trouble.

"I left home at fifteen, because I couldn't take any more beatings, and went to work with my friend on the trawlers in Grimsby."

He studied Bren's face for a reaction, and appeared reassured when he saw her teary eyes. They sat in silence for a while.

"I've got to go; my girlfriend finishes work in a bit. Mallie, you've met her, haven't you? That's her sister behind the bar."

Bren's heart sank into her 'sexy boots'. So, he hadn't come here hoping to see her. Not only did he think she was a prostitute, he still had a girlfriend. He stood, and paused as though he didn't want to leave.

"See you." He muttered, as he walked off.

His girlfriend appeared through the door, they kissed. He glanced back at Bren, before they moved towards the bar. Pride forced her to finish her drink before she left. As she walked through the tube station, she wondered why he had told her so much about himself. Not feeling like clubbing anymore, she went home.

Over the coming weeks, Bren saw her gorgeous Mick quite a lot, always with some girl in tow, he was quite a flirt. Very often, she would look up and catch him looking at her and sometimes he would ask her to join him and whoever he was with. She usually declined, because she was with friends. Although she really wanted to be close to him, she forced herself to play it cool; she didn't want to be one of his conquests.

After having had a meal with a friend, in the Cockney Pride pub, Bren was finishing her drink when her Mick came over. As he was working, they stood at the bar talking. A mutual friend walked in and came over to say 'hello'.

"You two look really good together."

As Bren looked at Mick, his cheeks reddened, and she could feel hers doing the same.

It appears that Mick wasn't the only one who thought I was a prostitute. Alex and I had met in Playland, around August the previous year. I often went there to play the 'Oxo' machines, as I called them. Being as I spent so much time playing these machines, I got to know the sequences on several of them; I was always very good with numbers, and have a bit of a photographic memory. Watching while other people played, I knew when a jackpot was due. By this time, most people thought they had fed the machines enough money. My predictions were accurate, about ninety-eight percent of the time. Alex would watch me.

We got talking, and became quite friendly, meeting up most days for a chat. Alex had left his home in Lancashire at fifteen and had been living in London for over two years, running errands for some of the West End 'businessmen'.

Often quite a crowd gathered, when I was winning on the 'Oxo's. Sometimes I played four or five machines at a time. As it happened, Alex was not the only person watching me. The manager of Playland looked more like an all-in wrestler. The day he approached me, his face was sombre, and his gait menacing. He grabbed me by the shoulder, and told me I was barred for life.

A month or so later, when I heard they had changed managers, I went back to Playland, to discover that they had changed all the sequences on the machines and that security staff were doing regular patrols. So ended my one-armed bandit gambling career.

It was probably late February when Alex asked me to go and visit a friend with him. Once again, I let the trusting me overrule the loud voice in my head.

The building that Alex took her to had an outside metal staircase, and his friend's flat was on the second floor. When Alex knocked on the door, it was answered by a youngish olive-skinned man, who stood back to allow them to enter. Once inside the room, the man handed something to Alex. At the same time one of the inner doors opened, and seven or eight men spilled out into the room. The first man spoke to Alex in broken English.

"For all." He said, waving his hand to indicate all the others and himself. Realisation hit Bren full in the face. She snarled at Alex.

"You bastard."

Her breath caught in her throat as she felt the sweat beads forming under her eyes.

Noticeably shaking, she backed towards the door, the men were babbling away in their own language. Although she had no idea what they were saying, it sounded angry, menacing. Bracing her body, she expected to be grabbed and dragged off into the other room.

She looked at the boy who had brought her here; that's all he was, a boy. What good would he be against all these men. Glancing at her, Alex gestured for her to open the door; he was now between her and the men. For a moment, she admired his bravery. Throwing the money onto the floor in front of him, Alex shouted.

"That was never the deal. I told you one only."

Edging backwards through the door to the stairs, they turned and ran as fast as they could down to the street. Irritated voices rang in their ears. They kept running, until they were a safe distance away. The threat now behind them, she stared Alex straight in the eyes, and yelled.

"Don't you ever come near me again."

She headed for the nearest pub, needing something to settle her; it was a good half an hour before she stopped shaking.

My problem is that I don't follow my own incertitude. Instinct tells me not to trust, but logic tells me I am being paranoid due to past happenings. Once again, I'd let my guard down and it nearly led me into trouble; as it has done so many times in my life.

Clubs, Pubs and Unrequited Love

I had deliberately avoided Piccadilly and the Comedy bar for weeks, so as not to bump into my Mick, as every time I saw him it hurt; it's hard to want something you can't have. But there were plenty of other places to go. The West End offered many good clubs and coffee bars, there were also some that weren't so good but which opened after the others closed; offering a safe haven until the buses and tubes started running.

The Apple Club was one such safe haven. It was a dive, at the top end of Wardour Mews. The ground floor was a games room with a football table, one armed bandit and a dirty glass cabinet containing a huge slab of corned beef. Mould crept across the surface of the meat, forming a woolly khaki and white floral display, that would look at home on a Women's Institute craft stall.

A coffee bar occupied the middle floor. Selling greasy bacon sandwiches, on stale bread and coffee in unwashed mugs. Grime and black gunk clung to the wall above the cooker, sliding downwards with each input of heat and coming to rest in staggered mounds, along the top of the wall tiles. Your hands stuck to the table tops, glued firmly in place by years of wet sugar and cold fat; forcing you to buy something, in the hope that the owner would free you if you did.

The top floor was the nightclub, if you can call it that. A twenty-foot square room, with a drink-less bar and a juke box. Bench seats ran around the walls, as far as the communal toilet. Communal, because it had most of the wall missing. It was pointless closing the door, because everyone using the club, could see you on the throne. On a plus side, the music was good and you could dance until seven in the morning.

It was in the Apple that I met a Scots lad, who asked me out on a date. Andy was lovely; his only fault, was being head over heels in love with a Scots girl named Brenda. He was so hung up on her, the only thing I had in my favour was having the same name. Even so, we had a few dates and we seemed to get on quite well. Until the night we went to the cinema.

Bren was on her way home to NW London, and she and Andy were stood at the bus stop at the top of Regent Street; waiting for her bus to arrive. Bren heard voices behind them, and turned to see Manchester Alan and her Mick and they were pretty drunk as usual. Mick had a camera, and was snapping everything in sight. He grinned at her before stepping into the middle of a very busy Regent Street, where he began taking photos of oncoming taxis; dodging out of their way when they got too close. Mick ran up to her.
"Give us a kiss, and tell us you love us."

Bren turned her face away as he tried to brush his lips against hers and moved closer to Andy. Mick didn't appear to be bothered that she was with someone. It didn't matter how gorgeous he was, he was being a plank.

Mick and Alan began showing off, dancing and acting like idiots.

Mick came back again and put his arms around her. Bren pushed him away but he said something that made her laugh. Andy was getting annoyed and she couldn't blame him. Mick was openly flirting with her, desperately trying to get her to respond.

It was then that Andy decided to make a stand. He looked angry.

"I've had enough, perhaps you should be going out with one of them."

Then he walked off down Regent Street and out of her life. Mick and Alan started laughing. Mick turned to Bren.

"Looks like someone spat their dummy out. I've got you all to myself now."

Just then the bus arrived, and she got on it; once again leaving the catalyst of probable heartache behind.

Mick shouted something after her, but she clearly didn't hear right, as it sounded like, "I love you." Come on now, how could you love someone you hardly knew? But she wasn't really the person to answer that.

The bus journey home was full of mixed emotions. Andy was nice, but it was never going anywhere and she had been entranced by her Mick from the first moment she saw him. But he was already with someone and he was too full of himself for her liking.

Bren was very popular with the gay and transvestite community, often helping them with their make-up and sometimes lending them clothes. It was a few days after the bus stop incident and she was sat in the Comedy putting the finishing touches to a young lad's eye make-up, when Mick walked in. He nodded to her and went to the bar. Her gay friends left and she got up to buy another drink.

"Already got you one." Mick said.

They sat at the corner table, Mick took a sip of his drink, and studied her face.

"Last time, we had a drink alone together, I told you about my mum. It was the first time I have ever spoken about it to anyone, except family."

What was he trying to say to her? That he trusted her, or felt comfortable enough with her to tell her something so personal? She smiled.

"The other night at the bus stop, it was my 18th birthday. Mallie had arranged a party for me here, and we had just walked her home. When I saw you again, I decided that it wasn't right with me and Mallie anymore, so I told her yesterday."

Bren was just about to answer, and tell him she wasn't interested, when some of Mick's friends arrived, and put their belongings on the table.

Chapter 9
Spiked Drinks and New Love

It was the tenth of April 1971. I was sitting at a table in the Cellar Bar with our mutual friend Manchester Alan, when my Mick came in and walked to the bar. A few minutes later, he came across to the table and set drinks down in front of us.

It was then that their attention was drawn to an argument between two men at the bar. Bren thought that one of the men looked familiar but she couldn't remember where she had seen him before. A while later, Alan made his excuses and left to go home to his wife and baby.

Now that Mick and Bren were alone, he told her again that he had split with Mallie, and wasn't seeing anyone. He asked if she was still with Andy and she replied that she hadn't seen him since the night at the bus stop. Mick apologised, for causing problems between them.

Mick's friend, Aussie Mick, arrived and went straight to the bar. They got up to join him, leaving their half-finished drinks on the table. Aussie Mick got served first and put his drink with theirs, while he went to the toilet.

They all sat at the table drinking, chatting and laughing at silly jokes. After a while, Mick started to trace his finger over the knots in the wooden trestle table, remarking on how big and bright they were. He said that they were growing bigger. Bren told him he was tripping, but he assured her that he couldn't be because he hadn't taken anything.

When Bren looked up, someone at the bar was picking their nose, as she looked around the pub everyone was picking their noses; then she realised that she was tripping too. Bren remembered where she had seen the guy at the bar twice before, it was on the two occasions that her drinks had been spiked. That was more than a coincidence.

When the pub closed, they were still tripping. Actually, over sixty people had their drinks spiked with LSD that night; a very foolish and dangerous prank, initiated by someone with more money than sense.

They had been walking around the West End for ages, and it was getting cold. Her Mick suggested that they went to a friend's house in Tottenham, but when they got there the house was in darkness. Mick managed to rouse one of the lodgers, who let them in. Looking for somewhere to spend the night, they went into the living room, her Mick put the heater on to keep them all warm. Bren was wearing a full-length leather trench coat. Her Mick told her to take her coat off, but she refused. Once again paranoia had set in, leading her to believe that removing her coat was an invitation for the boys to ask her to remove the rest of her clothes. Determined, she was definitely not going to have sex with anyone; she stayed fully clothed. Too full of LSD to sleep, they talked for hours.

As soon as it got light, they went back to the West End, so that Bren could get a bus home. By this time, she was experiencing a major 'come-down', it felt like her stomach was being ripped out. The boys seemed to be reasonably okay, apart from being quiet. It was decided that they would all go home, to sleep and bathe. Her Mick asked if she would meet him that evening and she said she would. He kissed her gently on the cheek and waited until her bus pulled away, before walking towards the Underground.

Travelling to town on the bus that night, fresh from sleep, bathed and dressed in clean clothes, she felt ready to get her life back together. Since her 'lost Christmas' Bren had eased up on the drinking, and had come to realise that she no longer relied on drink or drugs to get her through, she didn't need either anymore; now she drank from choice and not necessity. For the first time in a long while, she actually thought that she might be able to apply to get her children back.

When she entered the Comedy, her Mick was already there, standing at the bar talking to Mallie's sister, Kathy. He turned and smiled at her, greeting her with a kiss on the lips. His lips were so soft she thought her knees would give way, or even worse, that he would hear her heart pounding. They sat and talked, hardly taking their eyes off each other.

Except for work and sleep, over the next few weeks they were hardly ever apart. They would do crazy things that made them laugh. Sometimes, in the early hours of the morning, they would feed the ducks in St. James' Park.

Some weeks later, Mick and Bren decided they wanted some time alone, so they booked into a bed and breakfast in Kings Cross; that was the first time they made love. The room was clean and tidy, with a door in the corner, which they presumed was some kind of storage cupboard. They had been in bed a few hours and had already got the intimate stuff out of the way, so they turned out the light and lay there cuddling and talking; too hyped up to sleep.

It was about 11.30pm, when the room door opened, and someone put the light on. They both instinctively clutched at the bed clothes, making sure they were covered. A young Chinese man stood in the doorway.

"Excuse me, I'm just going to my room."

He walked across to the door in the corner, unlocked it, and put the light on; then retraced his steps back across their room to turn their light off.

"Goodnight." He said, and disappeared into his room, closing the door behind him. They both burst out laughing, agreeing that it was a good thing he hadn't arrived earlier.

It seemed that they couldn't get enough of each other. Mick was crazy, he made her laugh so much, they were like a couple of school kids. Bren couldn't remember the last time she had felt so happy.

Bren and Mick had been together just over two months. It was about 8pm, and she was walking down Shaftesbury Avenue to meet him, when a man stopped her to ask the time. She glanced at her watch, told him, and carried on walking. Suddenly a police car screeched to a halt, three burly policemen jumped out, grabbed her and bent her arms up her back. They told her she was under arrest. When she asked what the charge was, they told her soliciting for prostitution.

They said that she had stopped a man in the street, to ask if he wanted sex. She explained what had happened, and told them that she was on her way to meet her boyfriend at the pub. The police said they had a witness. Then they bundled her into the back of the car, and took her to Vine Street police station. When they arrived, she was cautioned and read her rights. They took away her belt and cigarette lighter, and locked her in a cell.

I heard later, that someone had told Mick and he came down to the police station, but they wouldn't let him see me as he knew me by my maiden name and I had been charged under my married name.

They kept her there all night, sleeping on a stone bench with no blanket, in a cold cell with a stinking toilet in the corner. At 8am she was taken from the cell, put in a prison van and driven to Bow Street Court. Where she was put in the cells under the court to await sentencing; when the court was in session at around 10am.

Around 11am Bren was taken into court, and placed in the dock. The charges were read out, and they called for the police witness. It came as no surprise that the policeman giving evidence was the same man who had stopped her to ask the time.

The magistrate said, that as it was her first offence she would only

be fined, but the money had to be paid before she was released or she would have to stay in the cells. She knew that she didn't have enough money on her, as she rarely carried much in case she got robbed. She couldn't phone her family, so when the magistrate asked her if she was paying the fine straight away. She replied.
"No."
They took her back down to the cells and locked her up.

About twenty minutes later, a policeman came and opened the cell, told her the fine had been paid, and she was free to go. They gave her back the things they had taken from her and she left the court. While she was walking towards the bus stop, she heard a familiar voice calling her. Mick had been in court and had heard her legal name, so was able to pay her fine. He put his arms around her, and held her.
"In future, I will meet you at the Underground."

Although she wasn't a prostitute and had only ever had intercourse with two men in her life, one of whom she was married to, she now had a conviction for prostitution; which she presumed would probably ruin any chance she had of getting her children back. The only thing she was really guilty of, was being lonely and stupid. She couldn't ward off the intense feeling of sadness and self-hate, so she told Mick she needed to go home for a bath and some sleep. They arranged to meet the following evening, in the underground station.

Here We Go Again

It was the day after the court hearing and Bren was longing to see Mick, as she really needed cheering up. She'd had a crap day; her boss had threatened her with the sack for taking a day off without letting them know and when she got home her parents were arguing.

Instead of taking the bus to Regent Street, she had walked to Queens Park and caught the tube to Piccadilly where she and Mick had arranged to meet.

After waiting in the underground for forty minutes she presumed she had got it wrong and took the exit for the Comedy. Ginger Mick was in the bar, so she asked him if he had seen her Mick.

"He's upstairs, he'll be down soon." He replied.

She bought a drink. East End Alan was stood at the side of the bar with some of his friends, she nodded to him and joined Ginger Mick at his table. After about half an hour, she decided to go and see where Mick had got to.

Bren climbed the stairs, looking forward to surprising him; but she was the one who got the surprise. Mick was at the other end of the bar, full blown snogging with Mallie. He never even noticed she was there, but Mallie did because her eyes held a smirk as she looked at Bren. She wondered, why men felt the need to use her and then throw her away like last night's chip wrapper. Determined they weren't going to see the tears in her eyes, she turned and left. When she got to the bottom of the stairs, she automatically wanted to run for the door, but she didn't want Mick to think she cared as much as she did. Spotting East End Alan, who was still stood at the bar, she went over to him.

Bren knew that he was keen on her, since the night they shared the Marble Arch Mescaline trip. Standing on tiptoe, she cupped his face in her hands and kissed him, slipping her tongue in his mouth. He grabbed her arms and pushed her away.

"What are you doing?"

He looked so upset, she felt terrible.

"I'm so sorry. I shouldn't have done that."

Mick's voice broke the silence of the awkward moment.

"What the fuck?"

157

She turned to him, angry, as much at herself for hurting Alan, as at him.

"You finished snogging Mallie then?"

"What you on about?" Mick protested.

Ginger Mick looked at him and shook his head.

"Don't deny it, I saw you. I've had enough shit in my life, I don't need any more."

By now the tears were rolling down her cheeks, she tried to hold them back, but her heart was being ripped apart. Mick looked at her, there were tears in his eyes too.

"Please listen, I don't want to lose you. I've been drinking most of the day. I went upstairs to help Mallie clear up after a party. I always kiss all the bar girl's goodnight, as you know. So, I gave Mallie a kiss and then she started undoing my trousers, I got a little carried away, that must have been when you came up. When I realised what I was doing I pushed her away. She asked me if I wanted sex with her, but I said I didn't because I was with you now. You can ask her if you like. I promise I won't kiss any of them anymore. Just give me another chance, please."

He looked like he was genuine, but so had Carl, Tex, Edward and all the others who had hurt her; but she had kissed Alan. She looked to Ginger Mick for his input, but he just shrugged.

"Being drunk is no excuse. If you truly want to be with someone, you don't go snogging someone else, no matter how much you've had to drink. But because you stood by me when I got arrested, I will give you another chance. I won't pretend it doesn't hurt, because it does. But if you ever two time me, I will walk. I won't be a doormat again."

Mick looked relieved and he hardly let go of her hand for the rest of the night. She didn't think he even noticed Mallie leaving; although she tried hard to get his attention. When he took Bren to the bus stop, he held her in his arms.

"You know, when I saw you kissing that bloke, I have never felt so hurt in my life. I couldn't bear the thought of losing you."

"Well, you know how I felt then, don't you? I've been shit on too many times before. I won't stand for it again, no matter how much I care about someone."

He held onto her until the bus came and when she moved to board the bus it felt as if he didn't want to let her go, in case she walked out of his life forever. After that things seemed to get better between them. They spent every available moment together.

The Problem Is, You Tried

Late one night, being extremely drunk and having missed our last trains, Mick and I found ourselves in Kensington Gardens. Mick built us a shelter out of deck chairs and lined it with some newspapers that he had found in the bin. We crawled in, to sleep off our drunken stupor.

The following morning, I was awoken by a something wet touching my face. Opening my eyes, I was surprised to see a large German Shepherd dog standing over me; at the other end of the lead was a brawny park keeper. I shook Mick to wake him. The park keeper stated.

"This is the Queen's Park."

To which Mick replied.

"She's not using it, is she?"

Needless to say, we were told to leave immediately.

I can't say that our first few months together were a bed of roses. Mick was definitely a charmer and there were several times, when I doubted that his feelings for me were as deep as mine were for him. One such time, was when we took a friend of mine back to our hotel room, because she had nowhere to stay. The friend, Terri, just happened to be a prostitute whose pimp had beaten her up. Naturally, I felt sorry for her and wanted to help.

There was only one bed in the room, so we all slept in it. Mick suggested I should sleep in the middle and that we should all wear something in bed. Terri took her dress off and slept in her slip with her bra and panties underneath. Mick and I slept in our undies, snuggled up together as we always did.

When I awoke the next morning, both Mick and Terri were asleep. I went to get a cigarette but the packet was empty. Knowing that Mick liked his early morning cigarette, I decided to get washed and dressed and go to fetch some. Mick stirred and asked me where I was going, so I told him.

I got to the corner shop but it was closed, as I had forgotten it was Sunday. Remembering that the kiosk on Marylebone Road was the most likely to be open, I quickened my pace as it was quite a walk; I was gone about 45 minutes.

When Bren got back, Terri was still asleep, and Mick was in the bathroom. Mick came out of the bathroom, just as Terri stirred and moaned. Checking her watch Bren couldn't believe anyone could sleep so long.

"Has she been asleep all this time?"

Mick nodded.

Bren looked over at the bed, Terri had kicked the covers off, but she was still asleep. There was something not right. What was it?

Staring at Terri as she slept, Bren tried to figure out what was different, then it came to her. Terri wasn't wearing her bra. Bren turned to Mick. He looked away, taking a cigarette from the packet that she had tossed on the dressing table when she came in. Grabbing his coat, he stuffed the cigarette packet in one of the pockets.

"Come on, let's go." He said, picking up their bag, grabbing Bren's

arm and leading her to the door.

"What about Terri?"

"Let her sleep a bit longer, she can hand the key in when she goes."

They walked up to Marylebone Road tube, in silence. Mick was the first to speak.

"What's wrong?" He said, pausing and grabbing her arm to stop her walking on. No longer the trusting little fool, she answered.

"Just tell me why Terri had no bra on, when she was supposed to have been asleep all the time I was out."

Mick looked down at the ground. She really didn't want to hear his answer, but she knew she had to. He told her how Terri had woken up, taken off her slip and bra and started kissing him, then she had begun feeling him. She wanted him to stop right there.

"I didn't have sex with her, I tried but I couldn't, because I love you."

She turned to him.

"It's funny how these women throw themselves at you. No; I guess I can understand that because I wanted you from the first moment, I met you. But I can't let you treat me like this, I told you after the Mallie thing that if it happened again, I would walk."

"I didn't have sex with her."

"But you tried, don't you get it? I gave up everything to be with you. I had a good job, I could have made something of my life, but I fell in love with you and I let my heart rule my head."

Turning her back on him, she walked away. He followed.

"Please don't do this. I've made mistakes."

"And you keep making them, I can't keep taking all this pain."

"I promise I won't do it again, I'll be with you all the time, twenty-four hours a day. I'll prove myself to you. Please."

His tears made tracks around his cheek bones, to the side his mouth, where he wiped them away with the back of his hand.

Her head told her to keep walking, but her heart wanted it to work, she would rather die than lose him; but if she stayed, there was a chance that he would break her in to so many pieces that she couldn't be put back together. She should have known better than to take Terri to the hotel, after all Terri was a prostitute; she was the one that had left them in bed together.

"This is against my better judgement, and this is definitely the last chance."

He moved to hug her, but she pushed him away.

"Don't touch me; not today."

They walked on to the station, without another word. Once again, she felt like she had been betrayed. Perhaps she wasn't worthy of being loved.

The Things You Do for Love and Money

Mick was true to his word, he didn't so much as glance at another girl, he seemed to only have eyes for me. Things were really good between us, but being as neither of us had a proper job anymore, we needed to earn some money. Mick was still working part time as a bouncer at London Pride, with German George, but it didn't bring in enough for the type of lifestyle we were leading. Sleeping in B&B's and eating out wasn't exactly cheap.

We had been together around ten months and were managing to scrape a living working in pubs, flat sitting and doing little jobs for some of the local 'businessmen'. One weekday night, we had hardly any money and nowhere to stay. It was February 1972 and still quite cold, so sleeping in St. James' Park without sleeping bags, was definitely a last resort.

That night, Mick was approached by a man who offered us £100 to go for a ride with him in his Bentley saloon; it seemed like a wish come true. I knew there had to be some kind of catch because no one gives you that kind of money for nothing but we are talking about the West End; where people had all sorts of weird fetishes and fantasies. Anyway, we decided that if we didn't like what was on offer, we could always walk away.

They were instructed to sit in the back seat, while the car owner acted like their chauffer. He drove them to a little village in Kent where he parked up in a dark street.

"Can you look after the car, while I go and do some business?"

It was more of an instruction than a question. He asked Mick if he could have a word with him. They both got out of the car, and talked for a few minutes.

Once the guy was gone, Mick got back in the car and started to kiss her. His passion rising, he caressed her breast; grabbing his hand, she told him to stop.

"It's okay, he told me he is going to be gone for about an hour, which is why he didn't want to leave the car unattended."

They carried on kissing, and Mick's hand wandered inside her top. Although she didn't feel comfortable, she wanted him as much as he wanted her. Mick had pushed her skirt up and was trying to slip his hand inside her panties, now she really was feeling uncomfortable. She shifted slightly, sitting up, that was when she saw it. Someone moving along the side of the car, with a small light. Trying to keep her voice low, and under control, she grabbed Mick's hand.

"Stop. Someone's watching us."

"It's okay, just carry on. That's what he's paying us for."

"It's not okay." She almost yelled, trying to push Mick off her.

"Just pretend, please, we need the money."

That was certainly true, they did need the money. So, although it didn't feel right, she played along. Mick told her he couldn't get an erection, knowing they were being watched. So, they fumbled with each other's clothing, moaned and groaned, screamed out words of passion and pretended to have sex; while a head bobbed up and down, outside the misted windows, trying to get a better view. When they thought their act had been convincing enough, they sat up and straightened their clothes.

A few seconds later their chauffeur appeared, and got into the driver's seat.

"I'll drop you off at the station."

"Where's our money?" Mick asked.

"I'll give it to you tomorrow."

Grabbing the man from behind, his left forearm across the man's throat, Mick threatened.

"You'll give it to us now, or you won't be able to use your dick for a long while."

The man tried to protest, but Mick tightened his grip. The man fumbled in his trouser pocket, and pulled out some crumpled-up notes, which he handed to Mick. Mick checked it.

"There's only £80 here."

"That's all I've got."

She could hear the anger in Mick's voice, as he told the man what he thought of him.

"Enough, Mick."

She addressed the man.

"Take us to the station."

As soon as he had dropped them at the station, the man put his foot down and raced away. She faced Mick.

"Don't ever expect me to do anything like that again, contrary to what some people might think, I'm not a prostitute and I don't expect to be treated like one."

"Aww come on, you've got to admit it was funny."

He gave her one of his lopsided grins. Any other time she would have melted, but she was furious with him. Mick looked at his watch, it was just gone 11.30pm as they entered the station.

The ticket office was closed, so we walked through to the platform where a man in railway uniform was standing.

"You've missed the last train to London. Next one is at 7am."

We looked at each other.

"Can we wait on the platform?" I asked, indicating the bench at the far end.

"You can wait in my box, it's a lot warmer."

He pointed to a wooden hut, with a sign saying 'Station Master'. We thanked him, and followed him up the platform.

Station Master Jim made us welcome. He related funny, horrific, and ghostly stories while sharing his coffee and doughnuts with us. Jim showed us the scenes of the ghostly happenings and even took us down the line to his mate's station, to hear more stories and play darts.

When seven o'clock came, we thanked Jim for his hospitality, purchased our tickets and boarded the train back to London.

Roofied

One evening while wandering through Playland, Mick stopped to talk to a man who appeared to be of Arab descent. They obviously knew each other quite well. Mick introduced us, and told the man I was his missus. Rudy, who was pleasant and well educated, invited us to his flat for food.

When we got to the flat, another man was there cooking a meal. He welcomed us, and took out two extra plates. The two men were obviously in a relationship. They dished us up stuffed cabbage, served with naan bread, and water to drink; the food was delicious.

165

We laughed, and exchanged stories about places we had lived and had visited.

Rudy excused himself, and left the room, returning a few minutes later minus his hair, which I hadn't realised was a wig; he looked a lot older than I first thought. Placing a deck of cards on the table, he asked if we liked to play.

"Fun only, no money."

We had been playing cards for a few hours, Rummy I believe, when there was a knock on the flat door. Rudy opened the door and two more Arab looking men walked in.

"To play cards." Rudy told us.

The men appeared to be pleasant enough, and made polite conversation as we played. Rudy got out some bottles of spirits and some glasses, and placed them on the worktop. One of the other men began to pour drinks and handed some to us. A few minutes later the man turned to me.

"You are not drinking."

It was more a request to do so, than an observation. I told him that I didn't drink spirits, but would love a coffee. He asked Mick if he wanted another drink and Mick said he would drink mine but the man poured him one anyway.

The man, who said his name was Ishi, put the coffee in front of me. I took a few sips, it was awful. It was probably Turkish coffee. Not wanting to appear rude, I drank some more. A short while later the two men left and Rudy and his partner stepped outside the door with them. I heard them talking in the hallway and seized the opportunity to pour the rest of the coffee down the sink.

Rudy returned.

"It is late, you must stay, I will make a bed up for you here."

He indicated the large floor space, in front of the settee. Mick was already looking very tired, so we agreed. Rudy made up the bed, then he and his partner wished us goodnight and retired to their bedroom. We undressed to our undies and went to bed. Mick fell asleep almost straight away.

Bren awoke, to Mick having sex with her. Her knickers were gone, and he had put her legs over his shoulders; not their normal way of making love. She put her hand up to stroke his hair but instead of his silky tresses she touched a crop of course curls. Pulling her hand away, her mind tried to process where she was and what was happening.

Wide awake now, her conscious mind screamed at her, 'Fight back'. Surprised at her own strength, she shoved her hands hard against the man's chest. Losing his balance, he fell backwards making hard contact with the floor. She brought her feet down, and groped around for her knickers, then realised they were hanging from her right ankle.

After pulling her knickers back on, she sat up, just as the room flooded with light. The man that had been molesting her sat, dazed, on the floor between her and the table.

Beside her, Mick was still fast asleep facing her. The other side of him, a man was kneeling down, penis erect. He was tugging at Mick's pants, trying to pull them down. Luckily, Mick was over six feet tall and quite broad and the man was probably her build so he was struggling with the task. Bren's fist made contact with the man's face, knocking him off balance. Leaning over Mick, using her body to keep the man away, she dragged Mick's pants back up as best she could; before glancing around the room.

Including the two that were interfering with them, she counted six men; all in various stages of undress. There were at least two other voices, coming from the bedroom. Her whole body trembled, she wanted to vomit. They kept looking at her, laughing and talking in their own language; she thought they were planning something.

Unable to rouse Mick, she was determined, they weren't going to touch either of them again.

Loud enough to wake the whole street, she shrieked at the men to keep away and miraculously they did. Although she wanted to run, she wasn't going to leave Mick. Rudy emerged from the bedroom, yelling something in his language. The other men grabbed their belongings and left. Rudy busied himself with tidying up and getting pans out for breakfast, he said nothing to her. Finally, she felt confident enough to let go of Mick and put her clothes on; then she went back to trying to wake him.

Over an hour later Mick finally came to and was able to get dressed. By this time, Rudy had made a huge plate of scrambled eggs. She didn't say anything to Mick about what had happened as she just wanted to get them both out of there. Afraid, that if they caused a scene, the men would come back with re-enforcements. Rudy invited them to join him and his partner for breakfast. She declined; she wasn't taking any chances but Mick agreed. As soon as he had finished, she told him they had to go.

It was another hour or so, before she was able to speak about what had occurred. They had met Manchester Alan for coffee in the Comedy and he asked her why she was so quiet; that was when she broke down.

Mick was shocked, as he was totally oblivious to what had gone on; as she would have been, if she had drunk all the coffee. Obviously, they were supposed to be 'out cold' throughout the whole act and should have awoken in the morning with no knowledge of anything untoward happening. When she finished relating what had transpired, Alan marched them off to the police station.

After having to go through the whole thing again, they were both taken to the hospital for examination. A nurse told her to use a douche, for two or three days, for all the good that would do, *because it couldn't wash away how tainted she felt inside.*

Whether she was raped several times that night or awoke with the first penetration, saved by her loathing of bad coffee, she would probably never know. She did know that Mick probably got her dose in the Bacardi, as well as his own.

Although they both gave as much evidence as they could, the culprits were never brought to justice. Naturally, Rudy didn't deny that they were there and agreed on the series of events leading up to bedtime; but he did add that they had all consumed a lot of alcohol.

Unfortunately, DNA testing was not available in 1972 and the police couldn't understand Bren's reasons for not leaving straight away. Surely the hospital would have tested their blood and urine samples for alcohol and drug content. All the hospital could say, was that she had indulged in extremely rough sex one or more times recently.

About two weeks later, both she and Mick had to be treated for gonorrhoea as she had contracted it that night and could possibly have passed it to him; neither of them had been warned by the hospital that they should be tested. Luckily her period came as normal as she had been worrying about pregnancy.

Being no stranger to the drug scene, I'd heard about people taking 'Roofies' but date rape drugs were a fairly new thing in this country and were not widely publicised, so I didn't form a connection. I never thought for one minute that it was something I would fall foul to, as I was always very careful with my drinks after having them spiked with LSD.

Working for Gangsters

One of the main businesses in London is tourism and tourists love souvenirs, no matter how tacky. So, street traders and souvenir boards, were a big thing in the 1970s. Most of the boards were owned by a pair of East End businessmen, with some very dodgy connections. Mick and I started working for them sometime around March 1972.

We had heard several tales of board sellers being nailed to the boards, or kneecapped (shot in the knees) for stealing even the smallest amounts of money. Always presuming that it was a rumour spread as a deterrent, we were extremely shocked when we heard it had happened to someone we knew.

We would collect the board and stock from a lock-up on one of the back streets and bring it up to the top of Regent Street, where we would pitch up. Our route took us past the Café Royale, and one morning the Queen Mother was due to visit, so they had rolled out the red carpet for her.

Mick came along with the sack barrow loaded high with boxes and not noticing the carpet wheeled the trolley straight across it, just as the Queen Mother stepped out of her limousine. A security guard moved forward to stop him, but the Queen Mother said,
"We must not hold up the workers."

Running a pitch was not as simple as it sounds because most of them were unlicensed. If we saw a policeman coming, we had to put a cover over the board because we could be charged with obstructing the pavement if people were buying from us. At some time during the course of a normal day, we would get charged with obstruction and would have to appear in court the following morning. Once in court, we would pay a £5 fine and then go and open up the board to begin the whole process again.

Eventually, we were given a permanent licensed pitch on the corner of a very busy street in Central London. This board was a lot busier than the previous one. We sold tinned London fog, guardsmen dolls with busbies, badges, London taxis, phone boxes, and various other cheap and tacky, but overly priced, items. The takings would be paid in every evening on close of business, apart from over the weekend, when the money would be paid in on Monday morning.

One Saturday it was unusually quiet. During the day, Mick had talked a lot about Yorkshire. He told me about his local football team, his dad's full name, the pub his dad drank in and the address of the house where he was born and where his sister still lived. Repeating himself numerous times during the course of the day. I presumed he was feeling a bit homesick and steadfastly listened while he talked. What did make me feel good, was that he kept telling me how much he loved me.

We stayed late that evening, trying to sell some more of the trashy souvenirs. At 9pm we called it a day and locked up the board. Mick gave me the keys and I put them in my pocket, then we headed off to find a B& B for the night.

That night our room was in quite a large B&B, with a big dining room. Our night was spent much the same as normal, making love, talking, laughing and generally enjoying each other's company. The next morning, we washed, dressed and made our way to the dining room for breakfast. Mick said he needed the toilet and told me to go and order our breakfast.

Bren went into the dining room and sat down but she wasn't feeling right; her gut kept churning, a sicky lump lodged in her throat. Deciding to wait for Mick, she didn't order the breakfast; as she knew how long he could spend in the toilet.

Mick was taking his time, she waited for about thirty minutes before she decided to go and see what was keeping him. She visited every toilet in the B&B, before returning to their room, only to find that it was empty and Mick's bag was gone. Fighting against the floodgates, she took a last look in the dining room; it was over an hour now since he told her to order breakfast.

Somehow, she managed to hold back the tears while she handed the keys to the receptionist and thanked her. As soon as she was out on the street she began sobbing. It wasn't until she went to get the tube that she realised the takings were gone and she hadn't got much money; so, she walked to St. James' Park and sat on a bench, trying to sort her head out.

Later in the day, back on Shaftesbury Avenue, she grabbed some food and walked around until the Comedy opened for its evening session; where she hoped she would find Mick. Deep down, she knew he wouldn't be there.

Once inside the Comedy, she bought herself a half pint of light ale which she made last most of the evening. By now, she knew that Mick wasn't in London; so much for him telling her that he loved her more than anything. Luckily, her gay friend Brandy came in and she crashed at his flat.

By the following morning, after crying herself to sleep, she had made up her mind that she probably wasn't going to see Mick ever again; so, practicality stepped in and she started to make plans. Rebuilding her life would be fairly easy; mending her shattered heart, she was not so sure about.

It was Monday and she was back in the West End. Too dazed to think straight, she foolishly went and opened up the board in the hope of earning some money. Not even considering that when they didn't go to pay in the weekend take, the bosses would come looking for them; which of course they did. News travelled fast, and by the time the bosses got to her they already knew that Mick had left London.

She couldn't have been open more than forty minutes, when a car pulled up alongside the board and a big muscle-bound man got out. "Keys." He demanded.

It was pointless to argue, she just gave him the keys.

"Now get in the car."

He stayed with the board.

    Running was not an option. Opening the door, she sat in the back of the car with one of the bosses, the other was in the front with the driver who was a very hard-looking man. They drove her to the lock-up, where the driver opened her door and dragged her out by her left arm; frog marching her inside. Standing cross armed in front of her, they asked how much money she had taken that morning. Untying the market apron, containing the takings of roughly £35, she handed it over. They demanded to know where Mick was; she told them she didn't know.

    The driver, pushed her arm as far up her back as it would go, and then some. Despite her being quite flexible, he pushed it way past the uncomfortable point to a place where she thought it was going to snap. She still said she didn't know. The driver spun her round and punched her in the face, blood dribbled from the split in her lip. She guessed she had a lot to thank Carl for at that moment, because that punch was nothing compared to some of the beatings that she had received in the past. The second punch connected with her cheek bone, and she knew that the swelling on that one was going to take more than a few days to go down. They pushed, shook, slapped, punched, and threatened her, but she couldn't tell them anything; as she really didn't know where Mick was at that stage. Finally, one of the bosses spoke.

"He took our money."

She answered.

"It was only just over £50. If you do a stock check, you will see I'm right, in fact I wrote down what we sold. Give me a few weeks, and I'll pay it back to you."

"Too late. We've already taken a contract out on him and it can't

be revoked. You can tell him that when you see him again."

Bren knew that no matter how bad she was feeling she had to warn Mick; she loved him and she certainly didn't want to see him hurt or worse. While wandering the streets, her mind was doing somersaults trying to think how she could get in touch with him. Then she heard his voice in her head.

"My dad drinks in the P………."

There was just a chance.

Having found a phone box and dialled Directory Enquiries asking to be connected, she put the last of her money in the slot and waited. The number answered and she asked for Mick's dad by name. When he came to the phone, she told him who she was and asked if he had any way of contacting Mick. There was a pause and then she heard Mick's voice. Her heart flipped, sending warm ripples throughout her body, try as she may she had no way of controlling it; at the time, she didn't realise that she was going to experience that same feeling many more times over the years.

She told Mick about the hit man and he said that he already knew, because someone had spoken to his dad on the phone the night before. She swore to him that she hadn't told anyone being as she hadn't seen the bosses until that morning; and had only just remembered about the pub name. It was then he told her he loved her and asked her to go to Yorkshire to be with him. When she said she didn't have any money, he told her to get it, catch the first train to Yorkshire the next day and he would be at the station. How was she going to get the money? Perhaps she wasn't supposed to, maybe something was telling her that Mick wasn't right for her. It was now out of her hands and for the universe to decide.

That night she bumped into a gay friend, another Alex, and told him what had happened. Alex hated the bosses of the souvenir boards because his boyfriend, Jason, was the one who had been *kneecapped. He said she could stay the night with them, that he would give her the money she needed and get her to the station. She found it hard to sleep, wondering if she should be going to Yorkshire. If Mick loved her so much, why did he leave her behind? When sleep finally came, the Hippos were joined by masked bandits.*

It was 9.50am, when the train arrived in Yorkshire. There was no sign of Mick. Alone in a strange city, she pondered her options. She could get something to eat, or spend the last of her money on a taxi going to the street Mick grew up on; looking for a house, the number of which she couldn't remember. Really, they were the only two options open to her as she didn't have enough money for a train home. Taxi it was. Telling the driver her destination, she got in the back and closed the door.

Seconds later, the door opened, and there stood Mick. He apologised to the driver and helped her out of the cab. He looked at her face which, by now, was extremely swollen and bruised.

"I'm sorry, but I had to make sure you weren't followed. Did they do that to you?"

She nodded, and he hugged her tightly.

"Come on, let's go. I'm glad you remembered what I told you."

They caught a bus to his sister's house. She wanted to ask him why he left without her but her face was just too sore to say anything much.

Mick's family seemed to be nice enough. We went to the local pub with his dad and uncle, and visited the working men's clubs where Mick introduced me to some of his school friends and his cousin.

After a week, we travelled to Lincolnshire to stay with Mick's brother, Ronnie and his wife Mary. Mick showed me around the docks and told me stories of when he was on the trawlers. We stayed a week in Lincolnshire. Mick had picked up his bank book from his dad so we had a little bit of money. We left Ronnie's and went to Market Harborough and other Lincolnshire towns, doing little bits of work, here and there. Then we came back down country and stayed at a posh hotel just outside London.

All night she was on edge, because she thought that Mick was going to disappear again. The next morning when he suggested she order breakfast, while he went to the toilet, she refused saying she would wait so that they could go in together. Even so, she still wondered if he might sneak out while she waited in their room. There was a knock on the door and when she opened it, he was there smiling down at her.

The dining room was huge and full of people. The waiter showed them to a vacant table which was covered with a cloth and laid up for eight people, with plates, cereal bowls, and glasses for orange juice. There were large linen napkins, which she noticed that all the other ladies had placed over their laps. She picked hers up and put it on her lap. Then for some reason she tucked it in the waistband of her jeans. The waiter came and took their order and when it arrived, they ate heartedly. While they finished their coffee, the waiter cleared their plates.

When they were ready to leave, she placed her napkin on the table, stood up and started to walk away. What happened next was like a scene out of a slapstick comedy. As she walked, the tablecloth went with her, all the dishes and cutlery flew up in the air and clattered back down onto the bare table. Everyone in the room stopped talking and stared at her. Mick pulled the tablecloth from her trouser waistband and threw it onto a vacant chair. Then he grabbed a large French breadstick from another table and began hitting her on the head with it while chasing her out of the restaurant, leaving a trail of bread crumbs behind them. Everyone watched open mouthed, she was so embarrassed that she wanted to curl up and die. Luckily, they had handed the keys in before they went in for breakfast, and left their rucksacks in the foyer; so, they were able to make a quick getaway.

Once they were outside, Mick burst out laughing. He grabbed her hand and they ran off down the street. At that moment she knew, no matter what he did or whatever happened to them, she would always love him.

Chapter 10
It Appears This Is for Keeps

After spending about three months working around the country, washing in public wash-rooms and rough sleeping with only a small blanket between us, we ended up back in Lincolnshire. From there we went to work in a holiday camp in Bognor Regis, for closing down of the season.

When we left the camp at the end of the first week of October, we already had jobs to go to, working as trainee chef and trainee hospitality manager in a hotel in Surrey. By the time we got there, I was already over two months pregnant. The hotel was a big rambling building on a common at the end of a country lane.

We had been interviewed by telephone and wondered if we had bitten off more than we could chew. Our worries were unfounded as the owner and staff were great. We had our own little cottage, which was like having our first home together.

Mick worked in the kitchen as assistant chef and went to catering college one day per week. My job was to learn all aspects of the hospitality trade including the assistant manager's duties; the days were long but fun.

Outside catering was one of the hotel's specialties, on these occasions Mick would double as a waiter. One such event was a wedding reception with silver service. The food was lovingly prepared by our chefs and stored in big aluminium trays which were stacked on racks in the back of an old blue transit van. Mick sat in front with Paul, the manager, and the rest of the waiting staff piled in the back with the food.

The guests had finished the main course, we had cleared away the plates and had bought in the sweet, which was trifle. We had served all but one of the tables before we discovered that we were a bowl of trifle short. Mick set to work scraping out all the nearly empty trifle bowls into one, and then covering the gruesome mess with lashings of whipped cream. I was given the job of serving it.

Rushing around the table, Bren spooned the make-do trifle into the serving bowls. Luckily, by this time, most of the guests were too drunk to see what they were eating. She got to the last person on the table, but just as she was about to drop a spoonful of trifle into his dish, he moved. His arm caught the spoon, which tipped sideways, depositing a huge dollop of trifle in his lap. Mortified and not knowing what to do, she took an unused soup spoon from the table, scooped the trifle out of his lap and deposited it in a serviette. As she scraped the rest of the trifle from the bowl into his dish, the man said,

"That was nice, you can do that again, any time you want."

Face glowing with embarrassment Bren gathered up the serviette, plonked it in the trifle bowl, and made her exit. By the time she got back to the kitchen she was almost in tears.

When it was time for us to head back to the hotel, we piled all the dirty dishes and left-over food into the van, then climbed into the space that was left. Mick was in the front with Paul, who was driving. Paul was in a rush to get home so he floored it, flying along the twisting country roads. He had just taken a particularly nasty bend when everything in the back started to move. Trays of vegetables and meat in gravy hung precariously above us for a few seconds, before depositing their contents all over us. There was a very long queue for the shower that night.

Eventually my bump began to show and I was confined to the office to do bookwork. I decided if I was going to work with accounts I might as well be paid a decent wage, rather than the £14 per week we got between us. So, we gave our notice and went to live with my Mum and Dad. I knew things would work out for us, Mick and I were a team and together we could do anything.

I Thought Things Were Going Too Well

Living with my parents wasn't an ideal solution, but at least we could earn a proper wage. Mick was working as a milkman for United Dairies; the same yard that Carl had worked for and robbed. As I was nearing the birth of our baby, I had a part-time job in a material shop. Mick had made some friends and everything appeared to be going well.

When I lived with Carl I did very little psychic work, as he didn't like me 'knowing' things; I wonder why? Now, for the first time in my life, I felt really safe and loved and was once again giving readings to supplement our income.

It was May 1973, and I was in hospital having the birth induced. Mick was working when our David was born but he turned up soon after, holding a bunch of bananas which he had bought for me on the way in. He peered at Michael in his cot and when he turned to look at me his eyes were wet. Looking at the smile on his face I could even forgive him for the bananas; which he ate, by the way, as I hate them.

Mick was a natural father, changing nappies, feeding, giving hugs when needed and even when they weren't. At first, because of what had happened with my other two boys, my mother was quite distant towards Michael; but as the weeks went by, she doted on him.

Michael was about four weeks old on the day Mick and I arranged to meet after work, we were going to do some shopping in Harlesden. Just after lunch I put Michael in his pram and took a slow walk to the milk yard. We got there a bit early, so I went into the office to tell Mick I was there. The manager was the only person in.

He told me Mick hadn't been in to work for two days. Totally confused, I was sure he must be wrong, and I said so. The manager replied.

"You certainly know how to pick 'em."

I hung about outside the yard for a while, but Mick didn't appear. So, I went home and waited, but he didn't return that night. For the first time in a few years, I cried myself to sleep in my old bedroom. *The Hippos had been unusually quiet and placid for some time, but that night they wailed in unison with her own anguished cries.*

When Bren awoke the next morning, she knew what she had to do. After dressing Michael, she packed the baby bag with nappies and bottles, put some money in her pocket and walked to Queens Park station; where she bought a ticket to Muswell Hill. By a process of elimination, the only person that Mick was still in touch with in London was his gay friend Ian; who he used to lodge with, before he and Bren became an item. Michael slept for most of the journey, and was still asleep when Bren left Muswell Hill station and began the ten-minute uphill walk to Ian's house. Michael was a dead weight in her arms and the bag was cutting into her shoulder, but she kept going determined to see this through.

Bren got to the house and knocked on the door. One of Ian's lesbian friends, Lou, opened the door and asked what she wanted. Bren told her she was there to see Mick. Lou said he wasn't there. To which Bren replied.

"I know he is, because I can see his jacket hanging on the banister".
Lou then said he had gone out, and she didn't know what time he would be back.

"That's ok, I'll wait." Bren answered. Sitting down on the door step, and laying Michael in her lap. Lou closed the door.

About ten minutes later, Lou opened the door again and told Bren to come inside. Lou showed her into the kitchen, where she sat down at the huge pine table and fed Michael his bottle. While feeding him, she decided what she was going to say to Mick.

Lou sat opposite her, watching her in silence. Bren ignored her; she had been used to such treatment from Carl's mother. After a while Lou began reading a newspaper, at least she wasn't staring at Bren anymore. Bren had to admit that in their early days together, she had wondered if there was more to Mick and Ian's relationship. It's hard enough competing against another woman, let alone a gay man; especially one with a lot of money and an extremely rich sugar daddy. Yet she knew that Mick was very much into women; then again, she knew everything about Mick, including secrets that even his closest family didn't know.

It was about an hour later, when she heard raised voices. One of them was Mick, the other another female who told him that a woman with a baby was waiting in the kitchen. The argument went on for some time but because they had lowered their voices, she couldn't make out what else was being said. It ended with a door slamming, and the sound of footsteps coming down the stairs.

Mick appeared looking as though he had only just got up. He stood in the doorway grinning, not his usual grin, he looked nervous. "I'll leave you to it." Lou said, as she pushed past Mick to get to the hallway. Turning back to him she spoke again, her voice angry. "You'd better get this sorted; we don't want this kind of trouble coming to our door."

Mick sat down opposite Bren, who looked at him blankly. It wasn't that she didn't love him, it was just that she didn't care anymore. You can only take so much hurt before you decide that maybe it's time to give up. He opened his mouth to speak, she interrupted. "Before you say anything. I only came here to ask you a question and if your answer is no, we'll walk out of your life forever. If the answer is yes, then it's for keeps, you can't keep hurting me and expect me to welcome you back with open arms. The question is, do you love us enough to want to be with us?"

Mick sat there in silence.

Bren took that as his answer. Her tears were dripping onto Michael's face, causing him to screw up his eyes. Pushing the bottle into the bag and not bothering to zip it up, she wrapped Michael's shawl around him and stood up to leave. Holding her baby tightly against her, as though she feared he would disappear in a puff of smoke and that all she had left of Mick would be gone forever. She was in the kitchen doorway when Mick spoke.

"Yes, I do want you, both of you. I just got scared, I needed to get my head straight. Let's go."

Ushering her towards the front door, he grabbed his jacket from the banister. Then he fumbled in the pockets for the door key, which he dropped on the bottom of the stairs. She was aware that he had kept Ian's key, so the fact he had left it behind was like he was severing ties.

He never said a word to any of them before we left. Although Bren didn't know what had been said, she guessed they'd also given him some kind of ultimatum. At least she now knew she was not prepared to take any more shit from anyone, no matter how much she loved them.

When they were a little way from the house, he grabbed Bren's arm and brought her round to face him.

"I do love you." He said, and kissed her gently.

Then he took their Michael from her and hugged him tightly.

As far as I know, he was never in contact with any of them, after that day.

Arrest That Baby

A family once again, Mick went to work for Co-Op dairies. The early hours of most mornings were spent pushing Michael's pram through deserted streets, trying to get him to sleep. No matter what hour of the night, Mick would be there with us.

Our Michael was around six weeks old, when the police came to arrest him. Yes, you read that right. The police knocked on the door of my parents flat at around 8am, and asked if Michael Joseph Robert lived there. I confirmed he did, and asked what it was about. One of the officers, a ginger-haired six-footer, told me that they would rather discuss that with Michael, so I took them to the bedroom and pointed to our Michael laying in his cot.
"There he is, now perhaps you can tell me what this is about."

The policeman looked puzzled and started flicking through the pages of the notebook, in his hand. Apologising, he started fumbling with his collar; he must have been hot because his face was redder than his hair. It was then he told me, that it was my Mick he was looking for. By this time, Mick had appeared in the doorway. It was his day off and he had been cooking breakfast.

It turned out that they had a warrant for Mick's arrest, for stealing the board money. Mick had to accompany them to the police station, where they made him swear a statement and then released him on bail under my mother's recognisance. They wouldn't let me post bail because I also had a police record, even though it was fabricated.

You can imagine what it was like, trying to persuade my mum to post bail money that she didn't have, especially when she kept asking why I couldn't do it. It turned out that the board bosses were trying to claim £1000 that Mick was supposed to have stolen. Luckily, I had a habit of keeping account of all money earned and paid out. Even though we had moved around a lot, I still had the records of the money we took on the boards, and what we earned from it; I even had lists of what we had sold each day.

I composed a letter to the magistrate explaining that we had a baby, and that Mick would lose his job if he was convicted of stealing money. Enclosing a copy of my accounts, I mentioned that there was a discrepancy in the amount owed, and that I had offered to repay the amount taken. Going on to describe my brutal treatment and that we had been told that there was a hit man after Mick.

The magistrate looked at all the evidence and took into account that Mick's job was at stake. He accepted, that there appeared to be some controversy over the amount owed, because the board owners had agreed all the other cash amounts. Mick was ordered to pay £50.17 ½ p plus court costs. As we left the court one of the board owners snarled.

"He's still after you."

They Don't Get Colic in Lincolnshire

With the court case out of the way, we decided to disappear to Lincolnshire for a week or two, until things calmed down. We had recently discovered that the reason that Michael was not sleeping, was that he suffered badly from colic[5]. It was only our second night at Ronnie's house, when Michael had a particularly bad attack.

Bren and Mick had gone to bed about midnight, and as was normal they slept in the nude, neither of them possessing any nightwear. They had been asleep a couple of hours, when they were woken up by their Michael screaming in pain. Bren sat on the bed, cuddling him and rubbing his tummy, trying to pacify him. Mick sat next to her, talking to him softly, but the crying increased in volume. Michael had only been crying for about five minutes, when Ronnie burst into the room, demanding to know what they were doing to the baby.

Mick got up and walked around the bed to where Ronnie stood. He explained that they weren't doing anything to Michael, and that he had colic. Ronnie punched Mick, knocking him to the floor. Then he began kicking him, swearing, and telling him he was a waste of space.

Bren screamed for Ronnie to stop, which made Michael cry even more. Clutching Michael, she ran around the bed to where Ronnie had Mick on the floor, still kicking him. Grabbing Ronnie's arm, she tried to pull him away, but he elbowed her off.

"Fight back you coward, or do you have to get your bitch to fight for you?"

"I don't want to fight you, Ronnie." Mick replied, flinching from a kick to the stomach.

Now Bren was sobbing, because her baby was in pain, Mick was getting hurt, and she was embarrassed at being naked in front of Ronnie. She knew Mick was no coward, as she had seen him stand up for himself. He just didn't want to hit his brother. Mary finally made an appearance. She managed to calm Ronnie down and get him to leave the room with her. Dressing Michael and themselves, they gathered their things together ready to leave.

When they walked out of the bedroom with their bags Ronnie told them to stay until morning, but Mick was adamant that they were leaving there and then; and Bren was inclined to agree with him. Putting Michael in his push chair, and wrapping him up warmly, they moved towards the street door. Ronnie tried to give them money, but they refused as they had enough of their own. After what he had done, they didn't want his money anyway, they would have preferred an apology.

They left the house and spent the night walking around the town before catching the first train in the morning. It was a long while before they saw Ronnie again.

Once again at home with my parents, we settled back into our lives. Mick gave his notice to the milk yard and we took on a temporary job managing the fish and chip shop in NW London; while the owners were selling it. We took our Michael to work with us during the day and Mum looked after him in the evenings. It took the owners about six weeks to sell the shop, after which Mick got a job in a local builder's yard.

Mum's brother Harry, my favourite uncle, was suffering from early onset dementia, so we all rallied together to help him. This went on for about three years until Uncle Harry's daughter had him committed to Shenley Mental Hospital where he died from bowel cancer a few months later.

Spooky Goings On

After I left the coven at the age of 16 years, I had become involved with several psychic phenomena societies through which I became involved in paranormal investigations. The involvement with these investigations, further advanced my mediumship capabilities.

It was on the first day in our new job managing a fish and chip shop that the first strange thing happened. Mick had lit the range, which is the big deep fat fryer unit for cooking and storing fish and chips. He put a block of vegetable fat in each pan, and set the temperature to low. We were both in the preparation room getting ready for opening. After a while, there was a smell of smoke. Panicking, we rushed to the front of the shop to find the pan smoking and the temperature set to maximum; the door was locked from the inside, so no one could have got in. Mick set the dial to standby and we went back to getting things ready; each thinking that the other must have turned it up.

The evening sessions turned out to be very busy. So, we advertised for staff. Rita started work the following evening. She went into the prep room to fetch a basket of chips and returned looking quite pale.

"It felt like someone pinched my bottom." she said.

Mick joked, saying that he was innocent as he had been stood in the shop all the time. I said nothing because I had experienced the same thing that morning, and put it down to imagination. Over the weeks, we got used to our bottom pinching ghost. It seemed that as soon as we voiced the fact that there were no other problems, things started to happen.

Part of the shop equipment was a fat extractor which we used for getting the oil out of the batter scraps. It looked a bit like an old-style spin dryer and was situated in the prep room on top of a large chest freezer. To operate it, you had to turn it on at the plug which was high up on the wall and then turn a dial on the front of the machine. One morning we were working in the front of the shop when the fat extractor started up by itself. There was no one else with us at the time. A few days later our television caught fire. Being as we had no money to buy a new one, we decided to rent one from Telebank.

It was a quiet Tuesday evening and Mick had brought the TV down to the shop for the first time; he put it on top of the big chest freezer and pushed it well back against the wall. Between serving customers and frying fish and chips, we stood in the doorway and watched whatever was on. Around 9pm, we were working in the front of the shop when there was a loud bang. Dashing to the prep room we found the television in the middle of the floor, a good two feet from the front of the freezer. We tried to convince ourselves that it was a freak accident and that somehow it had slipped, but we both knew that was impossible. Telebank exchanged the television for a new one, but the same thing happened on the third evening that we had it downstairs. Once again, we got it exchanged and this time we decided to play it safe and have it in the front of the shop.

We had both popped into the prep room for supplies, when we heard an almighty crash from the shop. On investigation we found the shop empty, door still closed and the television in several pieces on the floor. It was as though someone had picked it up and thrown it down with brute force. We would have heard if anyone had come into the shop because the bell above the door would have rung. Telebank refused to give us another television because 'damage by ghost' was not covered by their insurance.

A few weeks after we started there, we decided to get married. Just before we left for the registry office our boss, George, came by and gave us a bottle of Champagne; he couldn't have known we were getting married and he gave no reason for the gift. Our stay in Kenton was plagued with weird happenings and strange coincidences and both Mick and I started seeing and feeling strange things. This went on until our boss sold the shop.

Mum and Dad were invited to spend Christmas with us at Mick's dad's flat in Yorkshire. When we arrived, his wife Annie had gone to stay with Ronnie. So, Mum and I cooked the Christmas dinner for us, Mick's Dad and Mick's younger sister Beth. Mick had just gone to the toilet when Beth, who was a spoilt little brat that always liked to upset people, turned to me and said,

"Mick's never going to marry you, you know."

My mother replied for me, "Too late, he already has."

Beth's eyes showed her discontent. Mum smiled.

Chapter 11
Watch Out! Man-Hunter on the Prowl

When you are dealing with staff you need to be prepared for anything, but I didn't expect brainless brazenness from one of my co-workers.

Moving to Twickenham was like a dream come true; I loved it. Every day before work, I would walk down to the river and feed the ducks. Being as the shop was very busy, we had staff who we had inherited from the previous manager. Within the first few weeks we suspected that someone was fiddling the till and after that same member of staff disappeared with the float money, our suspicions were confirmed. Needing a replacement, we employed a woman called Kate. She was plump, around fifty and a very hard worker.

We saw it all in Twickenham, one of our customers was extremely eccentric, she sometimes walked about with no clothes on her upper body, just a nurse's cape with cross over straps around her shoulders. Kate had only been with us a few days when the woman came in to buy a piece of cod roe and she wanted it cooked fresh. Kate explained that we had just cooked some, but the woman became quite aggressive and demanded that she got what she wanted, following up with.

"I have judges in my family."

Kate, who was a little deaf, heard her wrongly and replied.

"Grudges, I don't bear grudges."

Mick was putting the cod roe in the pan, and couldn't keep a straight face. Hearing the commotion, I got to the front of the shop just as an argument ensued, about judges and grudges. I tried to butt in but I took one look at Mick, who was doubled up with laughter and had to walk away.

Kate was not just a good worker; she was very reliable and

extremely loyal. So, when another member of staff left to have a baby and I took on a young woman named Chantelle, she didn't hesitate in giving her opinion. Chantelle was married with a young child and could only work weekday lunchtimes, which meant I could spend my daytimes with Michael.

As I said my Mick was a charmer and most of our female staff flirted with him. One evening, Kate told me that I should watch Chantelle as she was 'after Mick'. Laughing it off, I said that it was okay. Besides I trusted Mick completely as we were nearly always together and he was forever telling me how much he loved me.

It was about a month later, Mum and Dad had come to spend the day with us. Mick told me that being as Kate and the Saturday girl were there, I might as well have the day off. Mum and I were getting food ready and found that we needed a few things. So, we decided to go to the shop, then call in for some potatoes on the way back. When Mum and I walked into our shop, Chantelle was stood by the counter. I asked her if Mick knew she was there, as it was gone closing time and the staff had gone home. She said that she was passing and Mick had called her in. When I went to get the potatoes, I asked Mick what he wanted Chantelle for. He looked puzzled, and when I told him what she had said, he denied it. Saying that he had only waved to her and gone straight out the back to cut the chips. On my way out of the shop, I told Chantelle that Mick hadn't called her and she left. Mum looked at me sternly, and said,
"You want to watch that one."

The following Friday, I got a complaint from the other girls saying although they worked as hard as Chantelle, she was getting all the tips. After the shift I called them all together and suggested we started pooling the tips and splitting them equally at the end of the week. A few days later one of the staff had a dental appointment, so I covered for her. That was when I discovered why Chantelle was getting so many tips. I was in the cloakroom getting myself an overall, when Chantelle came in. She took her top off, put her overall on and left the zip undone down to her bra.

One afternoon, after spending an hour down by the river, I popped into the bank for some change. Knowing Mick would be peeling spuds for the evening, I decided to drop the change in the shop before going to make dinner. As was normal the shop door was unlocked.

"Only me." I called out as I walked in. Tossing the coin bag under the counter I headed to the prep room.

The last thing I expected to see was Chantelle standing in the doorway in her bra and knickers with her overall by her feet. Mick had his back to her, busy tipping potatoes into the peeler.

"What the fuck, are you doing?"

Chantelle visibly shook at the sound of my voice, she turned to look at me. I felt like decking her.

"I was just asking Mick, to see if my earring was trapped in my bra, as I lost it when I took my dress off."

'Was she crazy saying this to Mick's wife'. I could feel the anger making its way through my body. Now I really did want to deck her.

"Well, I suggest you put your dress back on and go home."

Mick heard my raised voice, and turned to me shaking his head.

"I didn't know you were there, Chantelle, I thought you'd gone."

This was feasible because the peeler was very loud, and I had often made him jump by walking into the prep room while he was using it. In fact, Chantelle didn't hear me come in because of the noise.

She was still standing there. I glared at her. Through gritted teeth, I said,

"Get dressed".

Still, she stood there. I put my face up close to hers.

"Are you fucking deaf, or just mental, get your stuff and go."

Shoving her towards the cloakroom as I spoke.

After she left, I told Mick she had to go as she was trouble. He protested saying that she was a good worker and that he wasn't interested in her. Maybe he wasn't but he was a normal healthy man, and she was a pretty girl offering him sex on a plate. How long would it be before she upped the game and perhaps made it impossible to resist? Hand on heart, I can honestly say that I am not really a jealous person but this was pushing the boundaries too far. I looked Mick straight in the eyes.

"I told you years ago, I wasn't going to take any more crap so either you tell her to go, or I will go."

The next day Mick told Chantelle to leave, maybe he blamed it on his jealous wife. But I challenge any woman, finding themselves in that position, to say they wouldn't have done the same.

Things went back to normal after that. The other girls started getting tips again, based on their good service and not their cleavage. Chantelle came in the shop a couple of times and asked to see Mick, but he had told the staff to tell her he wasn't available; and soon she didn't come around anymore.

Over the following few months our boss seemed to be saying some strange things, and I began to think that he was considering selling all his businesses and moving back to Scotland. Then out of the blue our old boss phoned us offering us a position running a fish shop in a busy area of London. The wage was way too good to refuse.

When we handed in our notice, our boss told us the business was sold and we could leave straight away.

Mr B

George's business partner, Mr B, dressed like a Mafioso, but the man behind that formidable exterior was soft spoken and polite.

Our new flat was in serious need of decorating. Mr B told us to do what we liked, and he would pay. As was usual in that area, the property had mice, but we weren't worried because we had our new kitten and she would chase them when she got bigger. Unfortunately, that didn't go according to plan as the cat ran away from the mice.

The flat soon started to look more like home. Our bedroom was quite large, but it backed onto other buildings so I put up some heavy curtains for privacy, as we still slept in the nude.

Early one morning, when our kitten was still very young, I got up to prepare breakfast, and left Mick asleep in bed. I heard Mick's voice and went to see if he was awake. He was still asleep but murmuring.

"Oh, Bren that's nice."

I asked him what was, and he woke with a start looking completely bewildered. He plunged his hand down the bed and when he brought it out again, he had hold of the kitten who had obviously been sucking where she shouldn't have. All he could say was.

"I thought your teeth were a bit sharp."

Mr B was a thoughtful boss; who would call out of the blue, to take us for breakfast or lunch. One morning, during breakfast in the London Hilton, the conversation got around to the souvenir boards, and it turned out that Mr B knew the owners. We thought it best to tell him the whole story, as we didn't want him to hear it from someone else. He nodded but made no comment, and went on to tell us about his time in the Dutch S.A.S.

A couple of evenings later, Mr B came into the shop accompanied by two older gentlemen; all dressed in black trench coats and wearing black Fedora hats. They definitely looked like Mafia and had an air of 'you don't want to mess with us'. I looked at Mick and grimaced, he gave me one of his crooked smiles, but his eyes weren't smiling. Mr B spoke.

"No need to worry about your hit-man he is off the case, permanently".

All three of them turned to leave.

As he reached the door, Mr B asked if we had tried the food at the kebab shop yet. We both shook our heads.

"Tell them B said to give you some sandwiches, no charge as I own it. Make sure you go tonight for your supper."

After what B had told us about the hit-man, and the way they all looked, we weren't about to refuse. We mumbled a thank you and they left. We were later to find out the sandwiches were Doner kebabs and the best I have ever tasted.

That night, we talked about what B may have meant about the hit-man being off the case permanently. Our conclusion led us to think that we may have become involved with people who didn't suffer fools gladly. At least we wouldn't have to keep looking over our shoulders anymore.

George had already told us that B had a finger in several pies, but we didn't realise just how many. A week or so later, B arrived just as we were preparing to open. He bent down, held our Michael's hand and asked him if he liked ice cream as he was going to take us to get some. We got in his car and he drove us to a popular ice cream parlour, in South London. The door was closed, so B knocked.

The manager came to the door and said he wasn't open yet. B pointed out that it was opening time, said that he wanted to buy ice cream for his friends and held out the money; he was being very polite. The manager replied that it was his shop and he would do as he liked and told B to piss off and come back later.

I saw B's face, and he was angry. He grabbed the manager by his collar and said,

"It's not your shop, it is mine, and you don't speak to customers like that. I need to make a phone call."

B disappeared inside the shop. Leaving the manager outside the door. A few minutes later he reappeared.

"You no longer work for me, pack your things. My friend will be here in five minutes for the keys."

Then he whispered something in the now ex-manager's ear.

B walked back over to the car, apologised to us and told Michael.

"We will have to get ice cream another day. Let's go get breakfast instead."

As he went to drive away, another car pulled up and a man got out, he was built like a brick shithouse. He nodded to B and walked towards the ice cream parlour.

As it turned out, Mr B owned most of the buildings on the road that our shop was on, and many more besides. He also owned strip clubs, restaurants and casinos.

Our Michael's third birthday was coming up and Mick and I were discussing what to buy him, and whether he was old enough to wear jeans. When we turned around, B was stood behind us. On Michael's birthday, he arrived with a pair of Levi's for each of us and a tricycle for Michael; he had obviously heard more of our conversation than we realised.

After we had been working in the shop for about nine months, George decided that he wanted to emigrate with his family, so he and B agreed to part company. B didn't like the man who wanted to take over from George and definitely didn't want him as a business partner. We didn't like the new owner either, so when B asked us if we wanted to work for him, we declined and decided to move on instead. B very generously gave us two months money as compensation and said he would be in touch if he decided to take on another fish and chip shop.

Our next job was in Basingstoke and was probably one of the best places we had worked. Tom and Brian were good bosses, but towards the end of our second year I got bad vibes about the future of their partnership. While having our morning coffee, I told Mick that the partnership was coming to an end, and that Tom would sell the business because of it.

Whenever I said something outright like that, without thinking, it always happened. This has continued to happen throughout the years and, over time, I have learnt to trust it. Often it is in the form of a statement which just spills out of my mouth for no apparent reason and usually in the middle of a totally different conversation; sometimes, I am not aware of having said it. Other times, it is a thought that pops into my head and refuses to leave until I acknowledge it, or act upon it.

About two weeks later, Tom announced that the partnership was being dissolved, and that he could not afford to run the shop on his own.

Chapter 12
Homeless

While Mum and Dad lived in North-West London, they had a capped rent of £7 per week. The landlords wanted to triple the rent, but they couldn't do it while Mum and Dad were sitting tenants. So, they offered them £1000, and a new build rental in Neath Hill, Milton Keynes; which my dad eagerly agreed to even though it was in the middle of nowhere, and they had no form of transport.

They had been living in Neath Hill for about four years when we secured a managerial position in a fish and chip shop in Lincolnshire. The shop was split in two; half was a bakers come coffee shop and the other half was the chip shop. The flat wasn't ideal, as it was very small and had poor ventilation which caused mould in the bathroom and kitchen.

It was around this time that my mum became ill. Dad phoned to say that Mum was passing blood, so I told him to ring for an ambulance straight away, and we would be there as soon as we could. We didn't have a car at this time and the bus service was terrible, taking us halfway around the country to get to Milton Keynes. It was evening when we arrived and Mum had already been taken to Stoke Mandeville hospital. Off we went by bus.

When we got there, the hospital was doing tests and there was nothing we could do but go back to our flat, ready for work the next day. They kept Mum in for a few days, stemmed the blood flow and sent her home, with a referral to Bletchley. After spending almost an entire day trying to get to Milton Keynes we decided, as it was likely to be a regular trip, we needed a car. The following day we bought a second-hand car on Hire Purchase.

Michael had been at his school for about four months and had just got settled in, when the owner decided that instead of employing us, he wanted to rent us the shop; we agreed to talk about it. A few days later, while Mick was cleaning the shop, the owner came by with a contract; which he tried to get Mick to sign. Mick told him that he wanted me to see it first. I glanced through the contract and didn't like what I was reading. The owner kept looking at his watch and saying all was fine, and we should just sign. He seemed too eager to get a signature, so I told him I wanted a solicitor to take a look at the document. He wasn't happy, but said that he would be back the next evening.

We managed to speak with a solicitor the following afternoon, and my fears were confirmed. The owner wanted money for a 10-year lease, payable monthly, plus £500 per week rent; the shop was barely scraping £250 per week. There was no chance of expanding into a restaurant because the owner still wanted to run the bakers and coffee shop; so, it was a definite 'no'.

When the owner arrived that evening and we told him we didn't want to rent the shop, he gave us our notice; effective immediately, including vacating the flat. We put our furniture in storage the following day. Packed our personal belongings into our newly acquired car, put Michael and our dog in the back, then drove to Boston to look for work.

Now officially homeless, we were unable to sign on for full benefits as we had no address; so, we had to sign on at the job centre daily. This meant that we had to stay in the Boston area; the benefits were under £5 a day for a family of three. We had a little bit of money left from our wages, but knew that we needed to economise, as we were unsure as to when we would get another job

There they were redundant, without any severance pay and homeless. The severity of the situation slapped Bren in the face that first night, as she huddled up with Mick, Michael and the dog in their car. Shivering and unable to sleep, she tucked the covers tightly

199

around her loved ones, feeling to make sure their bodies were warm. Staring into the darkness beyond the windscreen, she checked the doors were locked; aware that they would need to rise early, before the workers invaded the industrial estate they were parked on.

There was no work in Milton Keynes as businesses were still being built; so, they slept wherever they could find a place they could park, without being disturbed. They couldn't move far from Boston and could only afford a limited amount of fuel. They survived on the minimum amount of food, usually chips and bread, which they shared with their dog.

Bren felt dirty and scruffy because they couldn't change their outer garments daily, as they had nowhere to wash their clothes; or themselves. Because her child didn't have a proper place to sleep and proper food in his belly, she thought she was being a terrible mother. Most of all, she was terrified that someone was going to take their boy away from them. She slept very little, always vigilant, watching for any sign of police or nosey passers-by; heart in mouth whenever she heard voices.

It had been fifteen days, and the weather was getting colder. While Michael slept on, she and Mick talked about their situation. Mick wrapped his arms around her, stroked her hair and brushed away her tears. He looked so sad.

"I'm sorry."

"It's not your fault, it was that money grabbing arsehole that caused this, not you."

By the time Michael woke, they had decided they needed to move nearer to London; if they were to stand a chance of getting a job fairly quickly.

It was the middle of winter and snowing, and they were camped out in the car at Heston services. Using the heater and the engine in bursts, they tried to keep warm without running out of fuel. They all *bunched together, covered with two quilts. Being as it was so damn cold, her teeth chattered. As they lay there, she considered that they might not make it through the night, she supposed that Mick was probably thinking the same.*

The following day, surprised that any of them had woken up, they drove to Hounslow station and bought a newspaper; to search the job section. Lady Luck must have been on their side, as they spotted an advert and managed to find a phone box. They were overjoyed when they were asked to go for an interview that afternoon. They went in search of public toilets with washrooms, where they all had a strip wash and changed their clothes. Clean, and with a bit of make-up on her eyes, she felt the best she had in weeks.

That afternoon they made their way to Basingstoke. The shop was on a very rough council estate, it was horrendous. But, as Mick said, if they could get the job then they would be able to start looking for something better straight away. They were over the moon when they were asked to start the following day; and accommodation would be available.

Being as they were not far away, they decided to pay their friends Sharon and Gavin a visit, maybe they could even stay overnight. They were so lucky that they had a car, as they definitely wouldn't have survived without it; she knew that she never wanted to be in that situation again.

When they turned up to start work the following day, their new boss Danco, was waiting to show them around and give them the keys; it was then he dropped the bombshell. The promised flat wouldn't be available for a week, as the last manager had not yet moved out. Knowing they couldn't sleep in the car any more, they were at a loss. They had no money for fuel to go anywhere, so Mick decided they would take a chance and sleep in the shop. If they got up early, they could have a wash in the prep area, so if Danco came around at opening time it wouldn't be a problem.

They cleared a space under the counter and made Michael a bed underneath. They could have the dog in the shop in the evening and he could stay in the car during the day. Danco left them alone all week. On the Saturday he came to give them the keys to their flat, which was not particularly nice, but it was furnished and a roof over their heads. They slept well that night.

Looking for a Permanent Home

Although the Basingstoke job got us out of a sticky spot, the flat was never going to be home; what we wanted more than anything was somewhere we could call our own. Around five months after we started in the shop the owner decided to sell. He gave us a month rent free, to find another flat.

We used that month to go to Yorkshire, with a view to perhaps getting a council house and jobs. We had tried several times to get a council place in London, but to no avail. Over the years we were given a range of excuses, one bright spark suggested that my mum evict us from her flat; but if she did, they would take her to court for wrongful eviction.

We arrived in Yorkshire on Saturday evening and went to Mick's dad's flat. Mick's step-mum, Annie, said we could stay for a week. Annie had hated Mick since he was a child.

On Monday we visited the council offices. We told the clerk that we had been in Yorkshire for some time and were now without a permanent place to live. They offered us a house straight away and we were due to view it on Wednesday. But for some reason, Annie decided to tell the council that we had only just arrived in Yorkshire; and the offer was withdrawn. Then she told us we couldn't stay anymore, even though we were paying our way.

From there, we went to Beth's house. There was only her and her infant son living there, as she had separated from her husband. We only intended to stay for three weeks, until we had to move our belongings from the Basingstoke flat; meanwhile, Mick looked for work and a place to live. Never having sponged off anyone, we were paying for almost everything, even though Beth was claiming benefits. She just kept telling us she needed more money, and because we had nowhere else to go, we kept giving it. I even sold my beautiful Victorian ring, to give her more cash.

Then at the end of the second week, it all came to a head. Beth, who was a very big woman, had taken a liking to the leather jacket that I had bought Mick for his birthday; and she asked Mick if she could have it. When Mick refused, she told us we owed her more money. Over the two weeks we had been there we had given her more than an average man earned in three weeks. We had practically nothing left, so we decided to leave.

Michael was hungry and Beth had refused to let us eat breakfast at her house, so we had little choice but to spend money we couldn't afford, eating in a café in the Market. After breakfast we popped into the local pub to see Mick's dad, and tell him that we were going back to London, but Beth had already beaten us to it.

Mick's dad came at us guns blazing, he told us we had been sponging off Beth for weeks and she was in tears because she couldn't afford it. Beth had told their dad that we had stolen her key, when we walked out that morning. She had actually given us the key; in case she wasn't there when we needed to get in to collect our belongings. Even though Mick tried to explain, Mick's dad threatened to kick shit out of him and told him he was disgusted with him.

Mick was upset because his dad had never taken his side since he was a child; preferring to believe Annie's lies. Because of that, Mick had taken many beatings he didn't deserve. Now his dad was taking Beth's side, without listening to the full story. Ronnie was there for the weekend and decided to stick his nose in; but we already knew where that would lead, so we left the pub.

Beth's house was empty when we got back, so we let ourselves in and packed up our stuff. Although we searched everywhere, we couldn't find Mick's leather jacket, so we had to leave without it. We later found out, that Beth had worn it when she went out that day and Mick's dad said she should keep it in lieu of the money we were supposed to owe her; Mick never got his jacket back.

Back in the town centre, Mick sold his wedding ring so that we could get fuel for the car; we didn't have any other choice. For twelve years after that day, we had no communication with Mick's family, whatsoever.

Mick drove us to Milton Keynes. Where Michael and I stayed with Mum and Dad for a few days, while Mick went to sign on in Southall and look for work. I was devastated at our family being apart. After a week or so, we were offered a job in a fish and chip shop in Southall. The accommodation was horrendous. It was one scruffy room, in a flat that was used for storage. Although we were the only people staying in the flat, the bathroom and toilet were shared with the rest of Choudhry's staff and often there would be a thick black grease mark around the bath when we went to use it. We hated it, but it was money and a roof over our heads.

Our boss Choudhry looked down on women. If he phoned the shop for anything and I answered he would hang up. Southall was not a safe place for women, and some men, at night. There were rapes, shootings and stabbings, none of which got into the newspapers. Often there was trouble between rival gangs of different races and castes. One Monday, Patrick and Stanley, two young Jamaican lads that we were friendly with, told us not to come into Southall on the following Friday evening. That was all they would tell us.

We were working in the shop on Friday 3rd July 1981, and there was a very strange feeling in the air. Nothing was said, but our usually friendly Asian customers appeared distant and restrained. It was like everyone but us, knew what was brewing.

That evening coach loads of skinheads arrived at the Hambrough Tavern for a concert. Apparently, around tea time, certain skinheads had daubed National Front slogans on shop windows and verbally abused and threatened Asian female shop keepers. Later that evening, groups of Asians had retaliated, by blocking the fire exits of the pub and pushing a blazing coach through the front doors; putting 110 people in hospital, and injuring 61 policemen. This resulted in a huge riot. After the riots, our boss was no longer willing to employ white people; we just wanted to get away from Southall.

One of the Asian lads who was still friendly with us, told us about a little ploy that they used to get homed. He told us to find somewhere for our Michael to stay while Mick and I got a live-in job in a pub. The idea being, that after a few weeks of working in the bar we would get ourselves sacked and go to the council as a homeless family.

Finding a live-in bar job was a lot easier than we could have imagined. Within days, we had lodged our Michael safely with my parents and landed jobs in a night club come bar. We moved in on the Friday and started work Saturday evening. Although we hadn't worked in a bar for years, it soon came back to us. Mick was a big man as when I got pregnant, he had piled on the pounds. So, by this time, he was around eighteen stone but still good looking. The manager was pleased that we both 'turned a few heads', as it encouraged the punters to come to the bar to buy drinks.

If I thought that finding the job was easy, then getting the sack was a doddle. Like I said Mick was a big man and the bar was very busy, so after a couple of hours Mick was drenched in sweat; not smelly, just soaking wet. The manager didn't like that at all and told Mick to stop sweating which, considering that the club was hotter than a tropical jungle in the height of summer, was an impossibility. Perhaps he thought we could just turn off a tap and Mick would be dry again. Mick pointed out that sweating was a natural reaction to working in this type of environment, so he was asked to leave. I was told I could finish the evening, but being as Mick was not being paid for the work he had done, I said I would leave straight away. We gathered up our things, and finding ourselves out on the street at 3am, we spent the night in the car.

As soon as the weekend was over our Asian friend, Binji, accompanied us and our Michael to the council office and told us what to say. From there, we were sent to a bed and breakfast at Ealing Common.

The Grange Hotel B&B, was nowhere near as grand as it looked from outside. The rooms were dirty with no facilities and the hotel was full of druggies and alcoholics. There were fights, overdoses, and definitely no breakfast. People would bang on our room door in the early hours of the morning, asking for food or money.

You didn't venture to the toilet during the night, no matter how desperate you were, in case you got mugged for your bedroom slippers; you might think I'm joking, but it really was as bad as that. Mick got a temporary job as we had to pay £18 per week towards the rent and were not entitled to draw benefits to cover it. Michael was not in a school as we had moved areas, so we stayed in the room most of the day. You didn't leave the room empty in case you got robbed, they would take anything, including your clothes.

Most of the people we got to know moved out in the first month. We were there eight weeks before we were offered a place. A second floor, two storey maisonette in Ealing; we moved in straight away with nothing, in case they changed their minds. The council gave us a blanket and a two-ring hob, to help us out until we raised enough money to pay for a van to fetch our furniture from Mum and Dad's garage in Milton Keynes; where we had moved it when we could no longer afford the storage in Lincolnshire.

Work and Untrustworthy Friends

Finally in April 1981 we had somewhere to call home, even though we had to sleep on the floor for a few weeks. We were ecstatic, no more having to keep bosses happy, just to keep a roof over our heads. We got our Michael a place in the local school and worked at whatever was going; until we could find proper jobs.

We started up a window cleaning round, which gradually earned us enough to live on. While cleaning the windows on an old lady's house, she happened to mention how badly her bathroom and toilet windows needed painting. Mick, forever the knight in shining armour ready to aid the damsel in distress, volunteered to do it for her free and gratis. I dutifully held the ladder while Mick painted; which took about an hour tops. When I stood back to survey his handywork I was quite taken aback.

"You did realise she only wanted the frames painted, didn't you?"
He just flashed me one of his lopsided grins. We spent the rest of the day scraping the excess paint out of the bubble glass (the forerunner to frosted glass); I never let Mick and his paintbrush near another window frame after that.

Besides having our own window cleaning round, Mick worked for a window cleaner in Ealing. All was going well, until one day I got a phone call from a very distressed housewife to say that Mick had fallen off his ladder onto a stone patio, while cleaning a window above her French doors. Worried that he may be seriously hurt, I rushed to his aid. Luckily, it was not far from where we lived, so it took me less than ten minutes to run there. Apparently, the ladder had slid backwards on the stone surface and Mick had landed heavily on both ankles. I loaded the ladders and helped Mick to get to the car. He managed to drive home, although he was in a lot of pain; after which he couldn't walk for about five or six weeks and was going up and down the stairs on his backside.

Mick's window cleaner boss wasn't happy, as he needed someone to do the round. Off Bren went, carrying a long aluminium ladder over her shoulder, through all the back gardens and down alleyways. It turned out that the man was a complete arsehole. He had taken on a row of three-storey town houses, but he didn't like doing them, so Bren was told they were hers. They needed the money, so she didn't have a lot of choice.

The main problem with three tier ladders and high buildings is that you have to climb almost to the top of the first part of the ladder and edge the extension up, then repeat for the next tier. At some stage, throughout this process, the ladder is not leaning against anything. Each time the ladder tilted away from the wall Bren held her breath and hung on tightly to the ladder; for all the good that would do. Bren really didn't like doing it. She felt so sick, it was a miracle that she managed to finish the round. When she went home and told Mick, he said that she was to tell the bloke to shove it and they would manage somehow.

We did manage, homework putting inserts in magazines, giving readings and demonstrating cast iron saucepans and Tri-Chem fabric paints.

When it came to wheeling and dealing; Trotter was my middle

name. For a while, we worked on local car boot fairs; and that is where we met Troy. He was an ex-policeman, who lodged with a policeman and his wife. We became quite friendly and would go to auctions together. Troy was always pleasant, and as a scout leader he got on really well with kids.

One day, when Michael was just turned eight, we were working at a collector's fair in Slough. Troy arrived, and said there was another fair in Maidenhead and asked if he could take Michael. We told him it was fine, but we would need him back before we were ready to pack up.

After a while I began to feel uneasy. I told Mick that I wished Michael would hurry up and come back, I think he was feeling uneasy too. About an hour later, Troy and Michael appeared. When I asked Michael if everything was alright, he just gave me a wooden Ladybird that he had bought for me. Troy left and we packed the car to go home.

While travelling home, Michael told me that Troy had showed him some photographs. It was a wonder Mick didn't crash the car. My heart was in my mouth when I asked him what sort of photographs. Michael told me, they were of naked men and women - I presume porn. Fighting to keep calm, so as not to scare him, I asked him what happened next. Michael said that he told Troy he didn't like them and didn't want to look at them.

From as soon as Michael could understand, I had always been very open with him. We had a lovely gay man living on our block who I trusted completely, but it led me to raise the subject of perverts with Michael. I told him that there were people out there who were not nice and who might make inappropriate suggestions to little boys, and that he was to tell me if anyone ever did this.

The day after the collector's fair, I visited the couple who Troy lived with and asked them if there was anything that I should know about him. They told me that he had been in prison for molesting a little boy. I was livid and asked why they hadn't warned me, as I would never have allowed Michael to be alone with him; they said they thought I knew. But, being as the couple had two children, the thought never crossed my mind. It turned out that Troy was having an affair with the wife, behind the policeman's back.

Later I discovered that Troy's modus operandi was to target a single mother under the pretence of wanting a relationship, just so he could get near to the children. The next time we saw Troy, Mick told him if he ever tried to do anything to our Michael, he would kill him; I honestly believe he would have done, unless I beat him to it. We kept Troy at a distance after that.

Several years later, Troy's picture was on the front of the local newspaper; after being arrested for molesting two boys from his old scout group. I left the paper on the coffee table. Michael came home from school and went into the living room. A few minutes later he came into the kitchen.

"I see Troy's been done for molesting children. He never did anything to me, apart from show me photos."

Breathing a sigh of relief, I thought, 'you were one of the lucky ones'. I believe the photos were meant to groom Michael for other things but, luckily, he had remembered what I had told him.

A Double Death

My mother had become quite ill, so Anna arranged to bring her and Dad back from Milton Keynes to a flat in Harrow. Although Anna took charge of the move, and Mum's bank book, Mick and I were left to do the chores and take Mum and Dad to St Bartholomew's hospital in the city.

So that we could still work while caring for my parents, we started running market stalls selling babies and children's clothes. Mick bought a van so that we could transport our market stalls and stock. One day while travelling back from a Sunday market, alerted by a loud roar, we found that we had lost the centre pipe on the exhaust. So, Mick, definitely no mechanic, found a length of rubber pipe by the roadside and decided to use that. I told him that the pipe smelt of petrol and that I didn't think it was a good idea, but Mick said it would be alright. He crawled under the van and secured the pipe with jubilee clips.

We started back on our journey and all appeared to be fine. I was just beginning to think I had made a fuss about nothing, when there was a loud bang and the rubber pipe shot across the road at about ninety miles an hour. It was a good thing there was nothing or nobody in the way.

Mum was gradually getting worse. She had been diagnosed with thyroid problems, lack of calcium, crumbling bones and stomach cancer. Being as Anna worked all week, we agreed that we would look after Mum and Dad during the week, and Anna would do the weekends while we were working. To help boost our income, weekday evenings I worked in a fish and chip shop from five until midnight, and was also giving tarot readings as and when I could.

Mum was taken into Park Royal Hospital and while in there, it was discovered that the cancer had spread to her liver. After three weeks Mum was discharged from hospital, and went back to her own home. We continued to look after her during the week and work at weekends. Sadly, the weekend arrangements failed miserably; often my parents didn't get any food and we would have to take them something after we finished work.

We were travelling to Mum's every day. I was caring for Mum and keeping two homes going; as well as working and looking after

Michael. Mick and I decided, that being as we were now looking after my parents seven days a week, it would be a good idea if they moved in with us; then I could just check on their flat every other day, which made a lot more sense.

So, Mum and Dad moved in. Mum had Michael's room and Michael and Dad slept in our bed. Mick and I slept downstairs on the living room floor, with a baby alarm connecting us to Mum; in case she needed us in the night. During the day I would tend to Mum's needs. In the evening while I was working in the chippy, my Mick would sit in the bedroom and talk to Mum. When Mick and I were first together he and mum didn't get on very well but, after they actually sat down and talked, they realised they had a lot in common and actually enjoyed spending time together. Anna didn't like Mum living with us, as she said she wouldn't be able to see her. I gave Anna a door key, so that she could come and go as she pleased.

About a week later, on January 21st 1983, after tea, Dad got out the Yellow Pages and marked off the insurance companies they were with; he told me I was going to have a lot of 'running around'. At bedtime Dad said,
"Thank you for the lovely food, and the lovely warm. Goodnight, God bless." Then he went upstairs to bed. The next morning, I found him dead on our toilet.

Then came the funeral arrangements. The undertakers wanted to know whether Mum and Dad were going to be buried in the same plot, as they had to inform the cemetery how deep the grave had to be. Being as mum always said that she didn't want to be buried with Dad because he had made her life a misery, I had to pose the question.

Firstly, I asked her whether she wanted to be buried or cremated, to which she answered.
"Is it possible that I might get buried alive?"

I relayed what the undertaker told me.

"If by chance, you were still alive when we put you on the slab, you certainly wouldn't be after we had finished embalming you."

"In that case I will be buried, as I don't fancy being burnt alive."

Next, I needed to know if she wanted to be buried in the same grave as Dad and explained why I had to ask.

"Will I be on top?"

"Yes." I replied.

"Good, because I want to be able to get out if he starts with his old nonsense."

By this time Mum was little more than a skeleton covered with flesh. The Macmillan nurse arranged for her to go into Michael Sobell Hospice while we buried Dad, as she was too weak to attend the funeral. We had taken her to see Dad in the chapel of rest the day before. Surprisingly, she had kissed him goodbye. We arranged for Mum to come home on New Year, but she passed away on the morning of 31st January, nine days after Dad's passing.

Now, the only contact I have from Anna is a very cold and formal Christmas card every year.

Mad Axe Woman

Just after Mum and Dad died, a new neighbour moved onto our block. She was a young Asian girl called Anika, who had a little girl about eighteen months old. I gave her curtains and furniture and sometimes babysat her little girl. Anika seemed fine for the first few months or so, but then she became very strange. The whole block was constantly being disturbed by very loud music and men callers, all hours of the day and night. I think Anika was also using drugs because she became quite aggressive.

A while later, Anika started throwing dirty nappies out of her window, into the clothes drying area. Our Michael, who was just eleven at the time, was walking home from school when Anika slapped his face; because he was supposed to have looked at her. While we were at work, she attacked our elderly neighbour, hit her in the face, stamped on her spectacles, and threw her potted plants over the balcony.

Anika's living room window opened level with the communal balcony and she gave us all a tirade of abuse every time we came to, and went from, our properties. While she was throwing one of her tantrums, she ripped my washing from the line in the communal drying area and dragged it up the street; then reported us all to the council for being racist. We took months of abuse from her. She was even physically abusive to her own child.

My parents had been gone about four or five months and I had never really mourned properly, as I had been too busy arranging two funerals and sorting out everything else. I think it had finally hit me, as I had been feeling raw for a few days.

On the day the incident occurred, Anika had been taunting us all from her window, as we went about our business. Mick was using an axe to chop firewood in our porch, while I was peeling potatoes in the kitchen. I took the rubbish to the communal chute and as I walked back along the balcony, Anika put her head out of the window and screamed that my husband fancied her. Even though it angered me, I ignored it, as Mick had never shown the slightest interest in her. Our next-door neighbour George came out to see what all the noise was about. So, I stopped to talk to him and Mick. Anika came out of her flat and started to walk towards us. Looking at Mick, she shouted.

"You want to fuck me, don't you?"

Before anyone could stop her, Bren grabbed the axe, and sprinted along the balcony. Anika saw her coming and ran. She managed to get in and close the door, just as Bren brought the axe down. It smashed into Anika's door, and stuck firmly in the wood. Mick grabbed Bren from behind, spun her round and held her tightly, as she sobbed uncontrollably. Anika called the police.

The policeman asked Bren why she put the axe through Anika's door, and she answered.

"Because I couldn't get to her fucking head."

The policeman told her Anika wasn't going to press charges, even though he had advised her to do so. He said that he would be taking the axe away, and if Bren wanted it back, she would have to get it from the police station.

Anika went surprisingly quiet after that, and moved out not long afterwards. As for me, I had to pull myself together and get on with life.

Getting Our Lives Back on Track

After my parents died, I suddenly found myself with a lot of time on my hands, so I applied to work for the RSPCA, in the cattery. The first week I was there we had an outbreak of ringworm and had to burn all the old cages. It was all hands-on-deck, building a new cattery, shampooing all the cats and treating them for the skin disease. I did most of the shampooing and was the only member of staff who didn't catch the disease. Apart from working in the shelter and fostering motherless kittens, I also ran one of their shops for a while.

I saw some terrible sights while working at the home and found myself constantly crying over one animal or another. It really got to me and even though I was torn by the need to help, my mental health was suffering, so I decided to help with fundraising instead; via Tarot readings.

It is very rare that I predict money or wins, but if I do, it is because I am absolutely certain that I am right. One such incident springs to mind. It was a Saturday and I was giving charity readings on an RSPCA gala in Uxbridge, when a woman sat down at my table. Her body language told me that she was not going to be very responsive. There she sat, poker faced, arms folded across her chest, grunting in reply to my comments. Just before I concluded her reading, I said to her.

"You're going to win some money."

"I'd better make sure I do the football pools this week, then."

"It's not the pools, it's premium bonds, £100." I responded.

She threw her head back, raising her eyebrows in disgust.

"I only wanted a reading to see if you were a Gypsy Rose Lee."

She said, handing me £5 and then tutting as she walked away. I breathed a sigh of relief, and carried on with reading the next person in the queue.

The following Saturday, I was giving charity readings for the RSPCA again, this time in Slough. I looked up to see the same arrogant woman walking towards me. 'What now?' I thought.

She marched up to me and leant over my table, her face close to mine.

"I had to come and see you, just to let you know that on Monday I won £100 on the premium bonds."

She didn't wait for a reply, but instead, just turned and walked away.

Things appeared to be going well for us, we had just acquired a mortgage on our property. Mick had a job with a plant hire company, and I now ran a café on a building site, from 6am until early afternoon.

Three evenings a week, I worked at a chippy in West Ruislip; it was called Cockney's. We had our regular customers and one was a rather tasty biker, who always came in for rock salmon and chips. One evening, we'd had a rush on rock salmon and only had cod left. The biker came in, and I greeted him in my usual friendly way. Then I said.

"I'm really sorry, we haven't got any rod, but I've got a nice bit of cock."

I realised what I had said, and tried to correct it.

"I mean I've only got cock."

Barry, the bloke I worked for, was doubled up with laughter; so much so, he couldn't say anything. By this time, I was in hysterics and apologising like mad. The biker stood there with a completely deadpan expression.

"I know what you mean, just give me the cod."

Obviously, he had no sense of humour.

Chapter 13
The Psychic Stuff and Bi-location

My Mick and I thrived on laughter. He was a terrific husband and father and was spontaneously funny. Yes, he had a temper sometimes, but he was never violent; I was living with someone who made me truly happy.

Many moons ago, a friend of mine and I were asked to do a private reading for an Emir in an extremely plush hotel suite, in a very expensive hotel in Knightsbridge. My friend was an elderly lady from Yorkshire who could be quite outspoken. A limousine picked us up from her home and drove us to the Knightsbridge Hotel where we were escorted up to the suite.

An ornately dressed, turbaned man with a huge sword reclined on the floor across the doorway. On our approach he stood up and placed his hand upon the hilt of his sword, moving to the right-hand-side of the door to allow us access.

Once inside, we were summoned to a table in the centre of the room where two gentlemen sat. One introduced us to the other; the second man turned out to be the Emir. The first man waved his hand in a downward motion, indicating that we should sit on the chairs at our side of the table. He introduced us, explained that he was an interpreter and told us we were to address him and that he would convey what we said to the Emir.

My friend M was asked to begin. After the first few sentences had been passed backwards and forwards, M, in her broadest Yorkshire accent, said.

"Chuff this, I want to speak to the organ grinder, not his bloody monkey."

The interpreter looked absolutely livid and started to rise from his seat; I buried my head in my hands, too embarrassed to look at any of them. Then the Emir spoke in the poshest Oxford Uni accent I had ever heard.

"Adi, that is completely alright, there really is no need for you to act as a go-between. Now order the ladies some refreshments."

I glanced at Adi, who shifted in his seat and forced a smile. Picking up the phone on the small side table, he spoke to reception and then replaced the phone in its cradle. The coffee arrived, and we continued with our readings. When we had finished the Emir thanked us, bid us good-day and left the room.

Once again Adi phoned reception and a few minutes later the concierge arrived with two envelopes on a silver tray. Adi took the envelopes and handed one to each of us.

"You did not state your fees so the Emir hopes that this is agreeable, £400 each?"

We nodded and thanked him as he ushered us to the door.

"Your car is waiting downstairs."

I think it was probably around 1987 when I joined Bob's Psychic Fair circuit; where, over the years, I had the pleasure of being asked to read for many well-known personalities and business entrepreneurs.

Although I had worked as a psychic for many years giving one to one readings and demonstrations, until joining Bob I had never worked on a psychic fair with other readers. At first, I just attended as a seller, as the thought of working with so many professional readers was really quite daunting.

The first reading I gave on a psychic fair, was in a small, town hall in the south of London. A large Jamaican woman, began walking towards my table. Suddenly feeling very nervous, I dived under the table and pretended to be looking for something in my bag;

in the hope that she would give me a wide berth. When I popped up again, to my dismay, she was sat at my table. Not knowing what else to do, I started to give her a reading, but she answered 'no' to the first three things I said. Smiling, I apologised and said I didn't appear to be tuning in to her, so perhaps she would like to go to someone else. To my horror she said.

"No."

Wishing the ground would swallow me. I started again; she grunted. Unsure as to whether this was a yes or no, I carried on. By this time, I had decided that the worse that could happen, was that she would say I was rubbish and not pay me; in which case I would never read on the fairs again.

I muddled through the thirty-minute session, after which I asked her if she was happy with her reading. There was a pause and I waited for the 'no'.

"That is the best reading I have ever had; you were spot on with everything."

I stared, aghast; then asked her why she said 'no' at the beginning.

"I just wanted to see what you would do." She replied, handing me my fee and an extra £5. She took some business cards and said that she would recommend me. Believe me, after that, every other reading was a doddle.

Around this time, a member of my development circle was having some problems with a 'psychic', who was trying to extort huge amounts of money from her. I promised that I would talk to the 'psychic' a few days later. That evening during our group meditation, I suggested that we all focus on the unscrupulous woman, to see if we could glean any knowledge of her intentions.

To my amazement, my circle member phoned me the next day to say that the 'psychic' had contacted her asking how I had got into her house. Apparently, during my unannounced visit, I had told her to give my friend her photographs and money back and then left before she had a chance to answer. A few days later, my friend received a registered letter containing everything she had given the 'psychic' and a request never to contact her again.

I don't know who was more shocked, me or the 'psychic', as I hadn't even set foot outside my front door; let alone travelled to Bayswater. Yet she described me exactly, even down to what I was wearing the day before. Was she a better psychic than we thought? Or did I somehow, bi-locate to her house during the meditation?

I was always very busy with private readings and to make sure I got the right person from 'spirit', I would ask for something of theirs as a link. Over the years, I have had some really weird items given to me. But, by far the most bizarre and unpleasant was presented to me on a visit to a lady's house.

When I walked in, I was a little surprised by the décor, as there were pieces of motorcycle mounted on the wall above the fireplace. Settling down to do the reading, I asked for the object.

The woman left the room and returned holding a crash helmet, which she handed to me and I closed my eyes. After giving the information she was looking for from her son, I opened my eyes again. That is when I noticed the blood and other matter inside the helmet. The woman explained that the helmet was returned to her in that condition after the fatal accident. I don't know whether I was more repulsed at being given such an object, or at the condition in which it was returned to the poor mother. The bike pieces on the wall were actually from the fatal crash.

Over the years, I have been privileged to visit several interesting places and meet numerous fascinating people. I have also had some very unusual requests through my psychic and spiritual work. By far, one of the strangest was being asked to do was an exorcism by post; needless to say, I didn't do it.

During my years working spiritually, I have done some quite unusual things, including: Readings in the Dean's house at Westminster Abbey for a huge star-studded charity event, giving readings at Olympia and having a story published in the Brixton prison magazine; I wasn't an inmate, by the way.

One evening when giving a service in Hayes church, someone in the audience asked where my power came from. I don't look on what I have as being 'a power', I believe it to be a natural gift. So, I replied, tongue in cheek, that for all I knew it could be aliens beaming messages through the fillings in my teeth. Needless to say, it went down like a lead balloon. The whole church stared at me in silence. Trying to mask my embarrassment, I said.
"Joke, you know, ha, ha, funny, funny."
They still stared at me, expressionless; so, I made my escape while I still had a miniscule amount of dignity left.

A Huge Error of Judgement

The letter from the Salvation Army arrived one Tuesday morning. Although, we hadn't communicated with Mick's family, for over twelve years the Sally Army had somehow managed to trace us, using Mick's National Insurance number. Mick's sister Beth wanted to inform us that Ronnie had cancer and that their dad was in hospital after suffering a heart attack.
"I don't give a fuck."
Mick threw the letter onto the kitchen worktop.
"It'll be the same as it always was, me getting the blame for everything."

"You should go, you'll never be able to forgive yourself if anything happens." I reasoned.

Mick was adamant, but I persuaded him that it was the right thing to do. Later events, proved that to be the worst decision that I have ever made.

When we arrived in Yorkshire, Beth greeted us like we had returned from the dead. Ronnie had been operated on for prostate cancer and was now back at work.

Mick's Dad, Jack, was propped up in his hospital bed, when we visited

"What do you want?"

He asked, adopting the normal aggressive tone that he reserved for Mick. Grabbing Mick's arm as he turned to leave, I addressed Jack. "We didn't have to travel nearly two hundred miles to see you. Just because you don't get on with someone, doesn't mean you stop caring about them."

Jack took a deep breath, before asking.

"What have you been up to?"

Mick gave him a brief summary of our lives since our last visit to Yorkshire

For years, all Mick, Michael and I had, was each other, so we became very close as a family. While in a WMC that night we were stood together laughing and joking, when Beth said.

"It's not right for a family to be so close and so happy."

After spending a few days in Yorkshire, we left for home.

Not long after our family reunion, Mick started wrapping himself in a sheet and pushing a pillow between us. Our very active sex life dwindled to a light kiss on the lips. Remembering that the same thing had happened with Carl, so many things went through my head, from Mick not loving me anymore, to him being gay, or having an affair. When he was finally diagnosed with diabetes and I was told that it sometimes affects sex drive, I was so relieved. It didn't make any difference to our sex life, but at least we started cuddling and kissing again.

A while later, a thought drifted into my head that Mick was going to die and leave me. Although I tried to shake these thoughts off, every now and then they would haunt my dreams. I was so in love with my husband that it actually hurt.

Weird Happenings and the Funny Stuff

One of the girls who worked Bob's fairs was called Amelia, she was into the healing arts and practiced Reiki. For Christmas that year, one of her friends had bought her a 'Grow Your Own Willy'. It was a kind of foam penis, about one-and-three quarter inches in length and when you put it in water it grew. Amelia decided to put it in a large, clear glass jug on her bedside table; to see just how big it would grow.

One weekend, we were having a healing session in her flat. It was sometime in January and very cold. By this time the 'willy' was around nine inches and still growing. The girl upstairs had gone away for the holidays, so there was no heat in her flat.

We were in the middle of healing, when water started dripping from the ceiling; a little at first and then faster. We tried to get a response from the flat above, but obviously she was still away, so we called the fire brigade.

About half an hour later, three burly young firemen arrived to break into the flat, and turn the water off. When they had stopped the leak, the firemen came into Amelia's flat, to assess the damage. One of the firemen, who was drop dead gorgeous, asked if he could use the phone to submit his report to the station. Amelia brought him through to the bedroom to use the phone which was, as you probably guessed, on the bedside table. The fireman reached out to grab the phone and caught sight of the huge willy in the jug. He stared at it for a few seconds, then said.

"I hope that's not all that remains of the last fireman who came in here to use the phone."

My Mick and I worked well as a team we were always thinking up new ways to make money. We came up with a good idea for a TV programme and sent it to quite a few TV companies; only to receive refusals. A few months later, I was cooking dinner when Mick called me in to the living room.

"Your programme is on the TV."

So it was, with exactly the same name I had given it, being aired by one of the big TV companies; and to add salt to the wounds, a friend of mine was appearing on it. Obviously, I couldn't do anything about it, but I learnt a valuable lesson that day - to always send myself a sealed, time and date stamped copy of everything that I wrote.

In April 1991, I began working full time at a company on Western International Market, as credit controller/litigator. I loved my job. My working hours were from 4 or 5am until lunch time; and I still worked the psychic fairs most evenings and weekends. With the job responsibility and working the fairs, came a new found confidence and independence.

When I was younger, I always tried to keep myself as fit and active as possible. Most of my exercise, was walking, which although good for the legs, doesn't really tone the stomach. So, I invested in one of those muscle toning machines. I stuck all the electrodes in place and tried it out on the low to medium settings. It seemed to work, although it was a somewhat slow process.

One day, everyone was out, so I decided to have some 'me time'. I went into the bedroom, stripped to my undies and attached the electrodes. Laying back on the bed, I turned the dial to medium. After a while, I thought I would try it on a higher setting, so I turned it up full.

My arms and legs shot out at 45°angles from my body. No sooner had they relaxed slightly, then they shot out stiffly again. It was a horrible sensation. I tried to grab at the control knob, but the process was so rapid that it was impossible to get a grip on the control. It was quite scary, as I had no way of stopping it. I couldn't even detach the electrodes because they were strapped in place. All I could do was lay there, enduring constant muscle spasms until someone came home.

As soon as I heard Mick's key in the lock, I screamed for help. Mick came rushing to my aid, but when he saw me, he collapsed in fits of laughter, while I continued with my self-inflicted torture. What sweet relief when he finally released me.

In the spiritual and complementary therapy business, correct wording is very important. My friend Iris was the first person to acquaint me with Reiki, back in the 1980s. She also taught me Indian Head massage. Iris was German and despite knowing her for over ten years, her understanding of the English language had never really improved. I had introduced her to Bob's psychic fairs because in those days, Reiki and Indian Head Massage were still fairly new to most people. She had a good little setup, with professional posters, and a sign written van, stating
'Indian Head Massage'.

After meeting for lunch, Iris was taking me home and we were driving through London. As we pulled up to a set of traffic lights, a car full of young blokes pulled up next to us. They pointed to the writing on the van and one shouted.

"Do you give head?"

Iris replied that she did and asked them if they wanted a business card. It took me quite a while to explain to her, that what they wanted was not an Indian Head Massage but something quite a bit lower in the body.

My friend Peter Richards, who was a brilliant medium, would often accompany me to events. We catered for student balls, birthday and hen parties and what Peter lovingly called 'Grab a Granny' nights. These were usually disco buffets for aging singles. We loved doing them, as we had great fun. Peter and I worked in similar ways and we had the same warped sense of humour. Sometimes we would go straight from an evening Psychic Fair to a function and give readings until three in the morning. The highest number of readings that I have given in one session is fifty-seven, at a charity function for Du Cane Road Hospital.

One of my spiritual gifts is my ability to work in trance. This is when a spirit speaks through me, using my voice box. My trance sessions are always carried out in a very controlled manner, and I would never consciously use trance with children present. Slipping into trance accidentally, has only happened to me four times since I first realised that I had trance ability, at the age of sixteen. Three of these times, were when the people I was working with desperately needed it.

Once on a psychic fair, I was giving a reading to a lady when I started to feel myself going in to trance. Overcome with a desperate need to urinate, I excused myself and dashed to the toilet. Upon my return the lady told me that I had channelled her daughter who was incontinent.

Another time I was working at a fair in Grays, Essex. The usual 'star' readers were absent from the fair so when we opened, I got the first reading of the day. The woman wanted to contact someone who had passed, so I asked her if she had an object for me to hold. She handed me a lock of hair. The next thing I remember, was that a crowd had gathered around my table. According to several people, I had taken on the appearance and voice of the woman's dead child. The woman was overwhelmed, so I didn't charge her; but I was busy for the rest of the day.

While visiting my friend Trish and her two young boys, one Saturday evening, the conversation became focused on her family; and those that had passed. I drifted into a trance and someone came through for Trish. The 'spirit' told her things she particularly needed to hear, some of which actually involved the children. Luckily the boys were none the worse for wear and after an explanation they quite happily settled down to a good night's sleep.

When Trish's eight-year-old, Jonathan, went to school the following Monday, his teacher asked if he had a good weekend. He said he did and then excitedly added.
"My Auntie got possessed."
I have no idea what his teacher thought had happened.

It was around 2am on an autumn night in 1992, and I was walking our German Shepherd dog. Just as I drew level with the door to our block of maisonettes, my dog started to growl. Glancing around, I couldn't see anything, so I gave the lead a tug and led the dog into the block. As I reached the centre landing, I glanced out of the window and caught sight of a strange looking figure, which seemed to tower above the garage rooves. The figure was looking straight at me and holding something up to show me; it looked like a baby. After a while, the figure disappeared. My dog's hackles were up, so

I took her indoors.

It was then that a thought struck me, why was I the only person to have seen this? Surely there must have been other people about, even at two in the morning. For days, I kept asking people if anything strange had been reported in the news; but nothing.

Occasionally, I would sit in my friend Christine's circle, which I called, 'me time'. On the evening of 29th March 1993, I was meditating, when Bruce Lee came through to me as clear as anything. He said he was concerned about his son, Brandon, as he was in danger. I told the others in the circle, but none of us were sure what to do with the information. There was no real social media, at the time, so making contact with someone in America was still quite difficult. Anyway, what exactly would you say? That your dead father's spirit came through to a complete stranger, because he was worried about you?

Two days later, Brandon Lee was shot dead, on the set of his film The Crow. Throughout the following day, Christine and several members of her circle phoned me; all as astounded by the news as I was.

Obsession

I first met Al on a fair at Hendon Halls Hotel, in either 1991 or 1992, when he came for a reading, he was a member of a very popular group. A while later I gave his aunt a reading, but after that I heard nothing from him for a few years.

The call took me by surprise, Al asked if I would do a reading from a photo for him. I explained that if he didn't know anything about the person in the photograph, I couldn't guarantee that the information would be accurate.

When he arrived at my house the following day, he produced a photographic print in a frame that he had bought from a junk shop. He placed the photo face up on the table, and I proceeded to tell him that the girl pictured was a photographic model. I gave him some very detailed information, and described a seaside town in Yorkshire, including a lighthouse inland. Being a Londoner, I had never been to Yorkshire, and wasn't even sure if this seaside town existed. Al went off to investigate and found everything, just as I said and confirmed that the information I had given about the girl and her mother was correct. The only thing he couldn't find was the lighthouse, but while driving home, he stopped to ask someone about it and was told that it was on the girl's family's land.

Al was so impressed that he asked if he could come and see me on one of the psychic fairs. He turned up a couple of weeks later and said that he had written me a song. To me it sounded like a love song so, feeling a bit creeped out, I played it for my son Michael and he joked about it being a bit romantic. I didn't tell Mick as I thought it was just me being paranoid, being as Al seemed to be obsessed with the girl in the picture; even though she had been dead for decades.

A little while after this, things started getting a bit weird, as Al kept turning up at the fairs that I was running. One evening he told me that he wanted a selling stall at my events and asked if he could buy my stock. I wasn't using it, so I sold it to him at a reduced price. After that, he still turned up at the fairs but never hired a stall. Al was always hovering around me and over the weeks he told me some quite personal things about his life. Just to be safe, I made it very clear that I was devoted to my husband.

One afternoon, Al showed up at Bren's workplace, even though she didn't remember telling him where she worked. She couldn't have made her disinterest any plainer but after a psychic fayre one night Al appeared just as she was about to get in her car. Grabbing hold of her, he tried to kiss her. She pushed him away, telling him that he was out of order.

It was around summertime 1993, Bren was asleep in bed next to her husband, who was snoring away merrily. She was awoken by the feeling of someone on top of her. As she was aware that Mick was next to her, she wasn't sure what was going on. Startled she reached for the bedside lamp. As the light flooded her side of the bed, she was surprised to see that nobody was there. But whatever it was had changed position to kneel over her. Unseen hands ran up and down her naked body. But what was more disturbing was, that in the light from the lamp, she could see indentations in her skin as though invisible fingers were applying moderate pressure. Not only unnerved by what she was experiencing, she felt violated. Fear turned to anger, when a sense of who it might be flashed through her mind; as soon as she quietly said Al's name and told him to go, it all stopped.

When Al phoned her a few days later, professing his love for her, she told him she wasn't interested and that he had to stop harassing her; it wasn't even flattering, in fact it was downright freaky. All went quiet for a few weeks and she began to think that she had seen the last of him.

Bren was organising a psychic fair for the church and was expecting some cheques through the post. Never having had anything to hide from Mick, she asked him to open all the mail and bring any payments with him when he came to pick her up from work.

When Mick came to meet her that afternoon, he was very angry. Al had sent her a letter, saying how much he loved her and that he couldn't live without her; so, she had to explain everything to Mick. Luckily, she had told Michael what was going on. Mick wasn't happy, but he accepted her explanation.

It was then that the phone messages started. Al would leave loving messages on the answerphone, but because she didn't respond, the messages started to become abusive and threatening. Extremely unnerved by it all, she broke down. Mick told her he was going to pay Al a visit, but she asked him not to; as she was worried what the consequences might be. Instead, she phoned the police.

Once the police were involved, all contact stopped, she never heard from him again. Until one morning in 1997, when she received a package, postmarked from somewhere in Scotland. There was no letter included, but it was obviously from Al as it was a CD of songs; including the song he wrote for her.

I had been working at Western International for almost five years and was very happy there, until the company was sold and a partnership took over. The junior partner took a dislike to me; let's just say it was because I did my job too well. He tried everything to get me to leave, but in the end, exactly five years to the day that I started there, they made me and some others redundant.

Starting a Business and the Mystic Maze

The job market had changed considerably during the five years that I worked at Western International. There were plenty of junior positions, but being as I had been working in management and on my own initiative for so many years, the thought of working under someone for a quarter of the salary really didn't appeal to me.

While looking through the 'sales and wants' in the local paper, I came across an ad for units to let in Crowther's Market, Fulham. As the market was situated in an old manor house on North End Road, I didn't need persuading, so I used some of my redundancy money to rent a unit on the 'long gallery'. It was perfect for a small shop;

with a space for a table and two chairs to do my readings. For six months it was fantastic, the whole place was a hive of activity, but come October, the wind screeched through the building. It wasn't just cold; it was brass monkey freezing. You couldn't use electric heaters because the wiring was old and couldn't take several appliances working at once, without blowing the main fuse.

I had recently seen adverts for units to rent in the Mystic Maze in Drummond Street. The next day, I took myself out for a coffee. As I entered 'The Maze' through the main door there it was, the perfect unit for me, separated from the hallway by a floor to ceiling trellis.

The café was at the other end of the building, so I ordered a coffee and told the woman behind the counter.

"I would like to rent that empty unit." Then my bubble got well and truly burst.

"It's already let." She told me.

"Are there any more units to let? I was desperate to become part of this set-up.

"You will have to speak to Kim, in Laurence Corner, she owns the Mystic Maze."

Laurence Corner was an army surplus and fancy-dress shop on the corner of Drummond Street. I went straight there and asked for Kim. She interviewed me, tested my psychic reading ability and told me she would keep my name in case a unit became available. I could actually see myself working in that unit, with my sign above the door so I took the plunge and asked her about it.

"They are coming in, to settle the deposit in a couple of days." Kim said.

My mind completely set on it, I asked her to let me know, if and when it became available again. When I left, I felt quite despondent.

Kim phoned me three days later, to say the person hadn't turned up and the unit was mine if I wanted it. On a sunny day in late

October 1996, I moved into the Mystic Maze.

The Maze was busy from the word go and I found myself giving readings and advice to a lot of big business people, which meant that I had to carry a very hefty insurance in case anything went wrong; but I was loving it.

Most of my work was carried out during the day and a lot of my clients visited on a regular basis; some had even become my friends. One of my regular clients offered to set me up in a psychic reading practice in London's Harley Street. Forever being suspicious of people's intentions, due to past experiences, I refused; a stupid decision on my part.

The Mystic Maze was situated in the Warren Street area of London close to the Capital Radio building and Euston station. The centre consisted of two large buildings, almost opposite each other, plus another four shops. The building opposite us was once a Victorian boys' school and in which people would often hear ghostly voices.

Our building was another that was built in Victorian times or earlier. We had a lot of problems with lights flashing on and off and bulbs blowing. I wish I could say this was due to paranormal activity but it was actually because water was getting into the wiring.

Traders would come and go on a regular basis. People were really nice when they took a unit, but after a few weeks it was as if their entire personality had changed. They would become extremely paranoid, accusing other traders of taking things, psychically attacking them, and generally plotting against them.

Even weirder was that each of those traders packed up and disappeared overnight. We would come in the next morning, to find an empty space. This behaviour wasn't restricted to our building. After a while, the same sort of thing began to happen in the buildings on the other side of the road.

After I had been in the Maze about two months, Elizabeth showed up. Next to my unit was what I called the shoe box, a kind of shed-like building with ranch doors. Being as it had a side door that opened into my unit, it became my reading room. Beyond the shoe box, there was an alcove with a heavy oak table, two chairs, and a curtain that could be pulled across for privacy; this was the space that Elizabeth was renting. Elizabeth would say and do weird things. She never got any readings and blamed it on the other readers.

One Saturday morning Elizabeth arrived shortly after me. I'd had a particularly busy morning, and then four clients booked in on the trot in the afternoon. As I went to greet my third client, I saw Elizabeth directing a West Indian lady to her table.

"At last." I thought.

I'd not long returned to my unit after seeing my last client out and was enjoying a cup of coffee with my nose buried in a particularly good book, when I heard the commotion. My friend Jessica, the transgender who gave readings in the building across the road, was bawling at Elizabeth.

"Don't you ever try to steal my clients."

Her voice was almost a shriek as she brought her fist down heavily on the oak table. The impact was so hard that the legs splayed out in all directions. Elizabeth's Tarot cards flew through the air.

"Next time, it will be your face."

Jessica stormed out.

Elizabeth looked terrified and I don't blame her; it frightened the life out of me too. Apparently, the woman Elizabeth read for had come in to ask where Jessica's unit was and Elizabeth, desperate for a reading, had told her Jessica was on holiday and she was working in her place. When the woman left, she bumped into Jessica's boyfriend Tommy; and the rest you already know.

The following morning, I had someone booked in for a past life regression, so I arrived at around 9.30am. As I turned the corner onto Drummond Street, I could hear the alarm. Leaving the door open I walked in, turned off the alarm, and checked my unit; it was all locked up. Next, I checked Ann's Native American shop; all secure. Then I noticed Elizabeth's alcove was stripped bare, the only thing remaining was the table with its splayed legs and the two chairs, one of which was on its side, where it had fallen when Elizabeth leapt out of the way of Jessica's fist.

Can It Get Any Weirder?

Even after Elizabeth's departure, people in the Maze were still acting strangely, so I mentioned this to my American friend Maureen. That afternoon she arrived fully prepared to carry out some Feng Shui, to try to lighten the atmosphere. Just before she left, she put a load of foil angels in a glass of water on one of my shelves.

When I arrived at the shop the next morning, there were angels scattered all over the floor. The glass of water was still intact, with just two angels in the bottom. No one else had access to my unit as I had the only keys and there was no room to climb over the gates.

Anne and I had always been on friendly terms, in fact I had bought quite a lot of stuff from her. One morning, I came in and found a gemstone animal fetish on the floor of my shop. It wasn't mine and it certainly wasn't there when I checked round the night before; it was virtually impossible to have thrown it into the unit through the two gates. Presuming it must be Anne's, I took it back to her when she arrived that day. She began to cross examine me about how I got it, and then said I must have stolen it from her shop.

Angry at the accusation, I pointed out to her that if I had stolen it, I would hardly have brought it back; besides I had spent hundreds in her shop, so why would I want to pinch something that was only worth a few pounds. We never spoke to each other after that day, and I never set foot in her shop again.

In November we had to say goodbye to our beloved Susie dog, because her back legs had stopped working. Although we had other animals, the house seemed empty without a dog. Christmas came and went and I must admit that my business clients were very generous with presents and gifts of money for me.

Michael had gone on holiday to Spain at the beginning of January 1997 and Mick and I decided we were going to look for another dog. We bought a Jack Russell Terrier, from kennels up near Northampton, and when Michael returned from holiday, he named her Chelsea. At the time, I didn't realise how special that little dog would become.

After she had finished her work each morning, Rose, the Mystic Maze cleaner, would come and sit up by my unit to read her newspaper. I deliberately never read newspapers as I always found them to be full of depressing stuff, but Rose liked to point out the murders to me. She would show me the picture and ask me what I thought had happened. Having a big interest in how the criminal mind works I was happy to play along and would tell her what I felt, based on the newspaper photo. Of the crimes that got solved, I had almost a 100% success rate; the unsolved ones, we may never know.

The man looked nervous when he entered my shop. He wanted to know if he had to be a believer, to contact his wife. After explaining that it did help but wasn't absolutely necessary, he sat down at my table. His wife honoured us with her spiritual presence. After going through the usual things that constitute proof, she told him, that knowing that he had never really believed, she had left him a Victorian feather fan in a particular drawer; to show it was really her. The man became angry, saying that his wife had never had anything like that. He assured me, that there was certainly nothing remotely like it in any of the drawers of the piece of furniture I had mentioned.

A few days later, I had just finished giving a reading, when the same man came storming through the door and into my unit.

"How did you get in my house?" He demanded.

"I'm sorry sir, I don't know what you are on about."

He told me that he had gone home after the reading and was adamant that his wife didn't have anything like I had described. But curiosity got the better of him that morning, and he took a look. To his amazement, there was the fan, exactly as I had said.

"Did you put it there?"

I told him that I had no idea where he lived and if I had a Victorian feather fan, I would be keeping it and not putting it in a complete stranger's drawer. He kept mumbling about how it could have got there.

"Just take it as proof that your wife did contact you." I said.

Still looking shocked, he nodded and left.

The most peculiar things happened in the Mystic Maze basement. Due to the water getting into the wiring the bulbs would continuously blow, so more often than not you would end up walking along a dark corridor to an equally dark toilet. Often, while in the corridor, people reported being shoved in the back. But when things happened in the ladies' toilet, I never thought to ask if anyone else had experienced the same, perhaps I should have.

The first occasion was when I was washing my hands. There was a small dirty window above the sink, which let in the absolute minimum of light. I was at the sink when something started to wind around my legs. At first, I thought a cat had got in. I was wearing trousers, so couldn't feel the cat's fur but then I realised that it was too big and strong to be a cat. Looking down, I saw what appeared to be a very large bodied snake-like creature. Not being overly keen on snakes, I must admit that I was pretty freaked and started to back away towards the door; then, whatever it was, just disappeared. This happened to me several times more, while I was in the toilet at the Maze.

While stocking up my shop one day, I happened to glance out of the window to see the local Sufi dowsing outside the front of the shop. When I asked him what he was doing, he said he was dowsing for the dragon that lived in the river under the Mystic Maze. I know London has underground rivers but, as yet, I am not sure if there was one under the Maze. Even so, it got me wondering about what I had witnessed in the ladies' toilet.

It was a Monday evening at the beginning of September, my friend Simon and I were attending a Positive Living group meeting. During a meditation, I received some information that was to lead to a very unsettling period in my life. It was at the time, when a tragic event was being broadcast on the news. The following day, I spoke openly to friends and work colleagues about what I had been 'given'; asking their opinion. It appears that news travels fast.

On Wednesday afternoon, I had a visit from a gentleman in high authority who said that he wanted a 'reading'. During this reading, I mentioned certain things to him that I shouldn't have known. When I finished, he confirmed who he was and then asked how I travelled home. I told him.

"By tube."

To which he answered.

"Do you know how many people fall under the tube in a year? You have a family. I think families are so important, don't you?"

When I went home and told Mick, he said.

"You had better be kidding, otherwise we are all dead."

For years, Mick thought I was joking, until something appeared in a newspaper that confirmed the information I had given.

When talking to my friend one morning, we heard some strange noises on the phone. This went on for a few months and then stopped. I won't say any more on this topic, only that information I received from the 'spirit', put myself and my family in serious danger. This is why, I am now very careful with whom I discuss sensitive topics.

Trade had begun to drop off quite a lot when Capital Radio moved to Leicester Square. Although I still had my regulars; new and random customers had become almost non-existent. As things, had continued to get weirder, and I was now struggling to make a decent living from the Maze, I eventually decided that it was time to move on. That was when something else happened that was very odd.

The tailor from the unit upstairs asked me why I was leaving. I told him.

"The walls are bowing outwards."

When he looked at me in a strange way, I asked him what I had just said. He repeated my words. I was quite shocked, because that wasn't what I intended to say. Two weeks later, I returned to the Maze to visit a friend only to find that the outer walls of the building had been jacked up.

Chapter 14
It will change your life

It was while I was on a workshop weekend with Leo Rutherford and Howard Channing that I met a school teacher, who was based in Wales. I am going to call her Penny. We appeared to form some kind of connection and I told her that my life seemed to be taking another pathway but I wasn't sure where it was going.

About six months after we met, Penny asked me if I would go on Leo and Howard's New Year retreat with her. The person she was going with had backed out and Penny had already paid for two places.

My family and my animals, were my life and I was rarely away from them so wasn't sure if I really wanted to go. I discussed it with Mick, who told me I deserved a break. Being as I'd wanted to do a Sweat Lodge for some time, I relented. On the morning of 29th December 1997, I set off by train to meet Penny at a station en route. My life has been plagued by my bad decisions, but this one launched a chain of devastating events, that were going to lead me to one of the darkest places I had ever been.

Penny met me from the train and handed me a small pouch. I looked inside and found a tiny green stone.

"Moldavite." She told me. "It will change your life."

We drove from the station to Dartmoor, where we arrived at a beautiful, 'olde worlde' three-storey house, in the middle of nowhere. There was no TV and our mobiles had no reception, the only connection to the outside world was a payphone. Entertainment consisted of a radio tuned to Radio 4 and an upright piano. As soon as my belongings were in my room, I rang Mick to tell him I had arrived safely, giving him the landline number and promising I would ring to say goodnight; I missed him already.

The evening was spent taking part in an introductory workshop. When I went to bed that night, I missed Mick's arms around me. My dreams were filled with him, but although I knew he was there I couldn't find him. I flew down staircases and jumped off high walls and buildings while trying to reach him, but he was always gone when I got there.

Before breakfast I phoned Mick, just to tell him that I loved him. The whole day was taken up with a workshop, where we had to search our souls for all the negative things that had happened in our lives. We were asked to pair up with someone and discuss our 'stories' with each other. I was paired up with a young lad and all the awful things that men had done to me over the years, started to surface.

That night I had a similar dream to the night before, waking with tears streaming down my cheeks. Donning my dressing gown, I dashed to the phone needing to hear Mick's voice to make sure he was still there. Right there and then, I should have asked someone to take me to the station so that I could go home; but I didn't.

The morning workshop was an exercise to engage all the senses; which was held out on the moor. You never really appreciate the true beauty of nature until you see it through 'spiritual eyes'.

That evening around 8.30pm, we were instructed to grab a towel and meet downstairs in the foyer. Following Leo, we all made our way to the far field where the fire was already burning brightly. The ground was fairly dry around the edge of the field, so we undressed and left our clothes there. Wrapping ourselves in our towels, we formed a line to enter the sweat lodge.

The drumming had already begun. The ceremony was in three parts, around forty-five minutes each. There were about thirty of us, all naked, sitting shoulder to shoulder. Between each part the flap to the lodge was opened and water was passed round to drink. More hot rocks were put in and herbs were sprinkled on them. It was an amazing and very spiritual experience.

None of us bothered to dress to go back to the house; we just put our shoes on. It was gone midnight; we had been in the sweat for over three hours. As soon as I got back, I had a bath, dressed in clean clothes and phoned Mick to wish him happy New Year. Then I joined the party that was now in full swing.

New Year's Day was spent sleeping in, chatting in the Jacuzzi and saying our good-byes because most of us left early. On the way back, I realised from some of the things she was saying, that Penny wanted more than just friendship from me. I thanked her and told her I was totally in love with my husband and probably had been since the first time I set eyes on him.

I was glad when I reached home, but even though I was now back with my Mick, I couldn't forget those awful dreams, especially as they still continued to happen.

Penny stopped making contact soon after.

A Very Narrow Escape

Changes had been occurring in the energy levels within, and surrounding, my body since the sweat lodge. After a while I managed to channel the energy for a higher purpose and my already strong sense of intuition became even more fine-tuned.

Now that I had left the Maze and was no longer working the fairs, as both Bob and his successor Adrian had moved on to pastures new, I needed some form of regular income. Once again, I found myself job hunting, without much success. I was getting worried because we had a mortgage to pay.

Needing a stop gap, as reading from home wouldn't generate enough short-term cash, I began scanning the vacancies in the local paper. When I saw the ad for a maid in a brothel, it seemed like a good idea. Three days a week for £150 would go a long way towards the bills. I applied for the job and got it. All that was needed was someone to answer the phone and door, make sure there was always clean linen, and generally look after the girl who was working. When I told Mick, he really wasn't happy about it, his actual words were.

"I didn't think there was anything you could do that would shock me."

Being as he had been made redundant for the second time in four years and our Michael was working abroad. We definitely needed the money so he relented, but insisted on taking me and picking me up.

For about four weeks, everything was fine; although, some of the requests from the punters would make your toes curl. As a safety measure, there was a camera trained on the front door so that we could see the clients before we let them in; but it didn't cover a very wide angle. The girls worked alternate shifts. They were nice enough, although a lot more mature than the 'young buxom blond' advert suggested. We did have one young girl, Lou, and she was working that day.

It was very quiet and we were sat having a coffee when the bell rang. Lou looked at the camera and said,

"There's a guy there, I think he's been before, I'll open the door while you finish your coffee."

Lou started for the door.

"Lou, stop."

Bren didn't know whether she had seen something on the camera, or if it was just a gut instinct, but something wasn't right. Grabbing

*the baseball bat, which was left as a precaution behind the door, she
whispered to Lou.*

"Stay by the phone."

By now Lou was terrified.

"Don't go."

"I'll be right back."

*Bren knew she had to find out what was outside that door. As she
crept down the stairs she clutched the bat tightly, ready to strike
anyone who might already be in the building; aware that her
breathing was heavy. Needing to be as quiet as possible, Bren snuck
along the passageway. Trying not to lean against the door in case it
gave away her presence, she peered through the peephole. Clapping
her hand over her mouth just in time to stifle a loud gasp when she
realised, she had been right. There were at least three men outside,
one of whom appeared to be holding some kind of iron bar. Turning,
she moved noiselessly, back along the hallway.*

*The sound of splintering wood made her aware that they didn't
have much time; it was an old door that could give at any second.
Belting up the stairs two at a time, she wasn't worried about noise
now. Locking the upper door behind her, she handed Lou the keys.*

*"Lou, take your mobile, lock yourself in the bedroom and phone the
police. Tell them there are men trying to break in; tell them
everything."*

*She hoped Lou hadn't heard the fear in her voice because she was
relying on that phone call to save them both.*

*Fighting to control her shaking, she placed herself to the right of
the door, the bat raised ready to strike. She listened for the slightest
indication that they were in the building, but at the same time she
wondered how long it would take the police to get there. She
struggled to make out anything other than the loud thumping in her
chest and the rasp of her own breath.*

The door appeared to be tougher than she thought because now they were making way too much noise; she felt sure one of the nosey neighbours would have noticed something. Bren couldn't do anything but stand there and wait, there was no means of escape. She could hear Lou's loud sobs coming from the bedroom, she really hoped the police were on their way. Needing to listen for sounds of entry, she didn't dare shout to Lou to ask what was happening.

Just as the door gave, banging hard against the wall, she heard the sirens and prayed that the men had heard them too. After what seemed like an eternity, someone hammered on the upstairs door.
"Police, open the door."

Glancing over her shoulder at the camera, she was relieved to see a policeman on the doorstep.
"Come on out Lou, the police are here."
Taking the keys from Lou but still gripping the bat, she unlocked the door to allow the policeman to enter. Lou collapsed into her arms.

The police told us that we'd had a very lucky escape, due to my gut instinct. The day before, some men had been let into a brothel in Harrow where they stabbed the elderly maid, beat the working girl severely and violated her with a broom handle; leaving both of the women in a critical condition.

We gave as much information as we could and were relieved to hear over the police radio that they had arrested one of the men, who had taken off on foot. Bren looked at Lou, the poor girl was in tatters and she wasn't much better herself.

"I'm sorry but this isn't for me and if you've got any sense Lou, you'll be out of here too. They couldn't pay me enough to go through that again, I thought we were both done for."

The police took them both home. She walked in the door and fell sobbing into Mick's arms, while the policeman told him what had happened.

Lou rang Bren the next day to tell her that she had moved back in with her parents and was going to look for a job. Lou kept thanking her, but Bren had only acted on a survival instinct. She was no hero she was as scared as Lou, maybe more so; because she had already seen what they were facing.

It's strange because I had always been more afraid of being old and alone than dying; but that day, I looked at my Mick and realised I had a reason to live.

A few weeks later, I started giving readings in an antique centre in Uxbridge where I met a young lad named Rob, who worked at the centre and was about my Michael's age. We struck up a friendship and would often go for lunch at the local pub. We had similar interests and would have some quite interesting discussions.

Things Get Worse

Mick couldn't claim benefits because he was given around £800 redundancy; which was supposed to pay all our living expenses for four months. The bills were piling up and our mortgage wasn't getting paid; but we had an insurance policy to cover the payments, so we weren't too worried. Mick managed to get another job working for 'A Plant', and we thought everything was going to be fine.

A few days later, we were called to attend an appointment at the building society. We were shocked when they told us that our mortgage hadn't been paid for five months, as the first three months arrears weren't covered by the policy; so, the policy had been rendered invalid. We were never told any of this when we took out the mortgage cover insurance. They said we had to pay all the arrears right away, or they would foreclose on our mortgage and take us to court to claim the property from us.

Although we made them an offer to pay, they wouldn't accept it and after a few weeks we received a court date. It appeared that the only option was to ask the court for time to sell our home; so that we wouldn't end up owing the building society. I expected Mick to come to court with me, but he said he had to work; I really needed his support.

When the day arrived, I had to go to the Law Courts in the Strand and my friend Trish came with me. The court approved my request for time to sell; but they only gave us two months. Mick left me to deal with it all and I put our home on the market. I felt like my whole world was falling apart.

In desperation, I took on a unit in South Harrow market at the weekends. A friend of mine, a disabled guy named Richard, was taking on a shop in West Drayton; which was due to open in a few months. He had asked me if I wanted to share it with him. He took me to the shop and showed me the room; which I decorated and furnished with a table, chairs and the trimmings ready for work.

Meanwhile, I was working in the Uxbridge antiques centre Monday to Thursday. So, rather than leave the market unit shut, I asked a member of my circle, Sherry, if she wanted to use it free of charge for healing; on the days that I wasn't there. The only condition I made was that she displayed my board, saying I was there giving readings on Friday and Saturday each week.

Later than she intended, she rushed to open her unit, although she really didn't see the point. The market wasn't busy for any of the traders and it certainly wasn't any different for a Tarot Reader. Although, she really didn't want to be there, she didn't want to be at home either. They had already started to pack some of their things into boxes and seeing them was a constant reminder that they would soon be without a home.

After a few weeks, she found that no one was coming in for readings on a Friday or Saturday, and she wasn't even taking the stall rent - another expense that she really didn't need. Two weeks went by while she considered what she was going to do. She thought about asking Sherry if she wanted to rent the unit full time. Richard wasn't on his stall, so she rang him to ask when his shop was opening and he told her that there had been some kind of holdup. Not wanting to admit defeat, she regretfully asked Sherry if she wanted to rent the unit, but Sherry refused saying that she was going to work from home. So, Bren decided to give up the stall.

While she was there clearing out her things, one of her clients came along.

"I thought you weren't here anymore, the other girl that was doing readings said you had given it up."

"Readings? She was only supposed to be doing healing."

Then Bren noticed Sherry's poster stuck to the reverse of her acrylic sign. Furious, because she had been paying the rent and Sherry had been reaping the profits, she blamed herself for allowing it to happen.

Being as Bren hadn't seen Richard for about a month, she decided to take a trip to his shop to find out what was going on. She asked Mick to take her as her car had already been repossessed; a crooked move on behalf of the finance company, which she had found out about too late.

When they arrived, the shop was fully stocked, open, and displaying a sign for Sherry giving tarot readings. The fuel had been added to the fire, Bren walked straight through the shop into the reading room, where Sherry was in the middle of a tarot session; Sherry was sat at Bren's table, on Bren's chair, using Bren's cloth, Bren's tarot cards and Bren's tape recorder.

Grabbing the bag, she had left in the corner a few weeks earlier, Bren scooped the cloth, cards, tape recorder and ornaments into it,

ripped down the drapes and stuffed them into the bag. Sherry leapt
from her chair and grabbed at Bren trying to stop her.
"Would you mind standing up please."
Bren asked the lady having the reading. She folded the table and
chairs and called Mick into the room. Sherry protested and her
client looked on opened mouthed. While Mick carried the stuff out
to the car, Bren turned to Sherry.
"I offered you an opportunity and you screwed me over, so you can
get your own bloody equipment because you're not using mine."

It turned out that Sherry had been dating Richard since I
introduced them. She had persuaded him to let her give readings in
his shop, instead of me. As it happens, she took Richard for every
penny he had, and didn't even show up at his funeral when he died
a few months later. For me, it was just another person who had let
me down when I needed friends.

Someone had put an offer in on their home, which made her
realise how final everything was.
And the Hippo dreams were back with a vengeance.

Not the Same Me Anymore

It was dark and she was walking home alone. The shadows were
alive with unseen beings walking alongside her; the type of
creatures that exist in gloomy basements, in strange old houses -
hiding round corners, just out of sight. The monster like beings that
cast strange silhouettes, on cobweb infested walls. She knew these
creatures; they followed her everywhere, lurking in the darkness.

Although, she had walked this route many times before at night, it
had never been this late. The shadows moved menacingly, reaching
out, almost touching her. Pulling her coat tightly around her, she
tried to make herself smaller, less conspicuous. She was afraid that

if she was noticed, unseen hands would grab her and drag her down into some bottomless pit; never to see the light of day again. Something loomed in front of her. She jumped, repeatedly telling herself.

"It's only a shadow."

Since the New Year sweat lodge, she hadn't felt right. Looking back on the past, she searched her memory for a clue, some reminder of what troubled her. Somewhere deep within was the reason she felt so afraid. Perhaps it was the aftermath of the cleansing period that had altered her perspective on life. Everything appeared to be unsynchronised, in the wrong place, the wrong time. Sadness overwhelmed her; she loved her family yet she felt estranged from them. The love she felt for her husband hadn't changed but she was scared to love him. So many times, in her life people and things that she loved had been taken away from her.

The Hippos had warned her that this was only the beginning; she knew that there was more to come.

The Beginning of the End

When she awoke that morning, her whole body felt numb. Her head, normally so full of ideas and challenges, seemed to be empty. She foraged deep within her mind for just a tiny flicker of anything that might resemble the normal her. Nothing was the same. The house looked the same, her family looked the same and yet it was like aliens had landed and exchanged everything she knew and loved for some kind of mechanised substitute. The only thing that still seemed real was her little dog.

She was an outsider looking in; to her, everything appeared to be moving in slow motion. Her husband and son were talking, she could hear them, but their voices seemed to be coming from some far

251

distant place. The formation of their words was sluggish, the pitch wavered unnaturally. It reminded her of a scene from 'Twin Peaks', where the midget speaks backwards. She was glad when they left for work, as she didn't want... no... she wasn't able to make conversation.

Mick kept asking her what was wrong. He kept repeating the question, but she couldn't answer because she didn't know the answer. Then he asked her if she still loved him. She wanted to run into his arms, but she couldn't move, she was cemented to the piece of floor on which she stood. He asked her the same question, again and again, her head felt like it was about to explode; but he kept on asking. Wanting to make him stop, she screamed.
"No."

But she didn't know why she said that - it was a lie, she loved him more than life. She wanted to tell him but the words wouldn't form on her tongue. He looked at her with sheer hatred, and walked away. Her voice screamed after him.
'Don't go, please don't go. I love you'.
But it was only in her thoughts.
He didn't want her near him, so she slept on the settee. No, she didn't sleep, as her mind wouldn't let her do that.

The next six months were a blur of constant nothingness. Now she was the subject of the conversation, instead of a part of it. The loneliness was all encompassing, coursing through her whole being like some huge emotional tidal wave. Her head throbbed with the pressure. Unseen hands squeezed and twisted her brain, until it became little more than pulp; but still the pressure built. Leaden legs carried her, begrudgingly, on long arduous walks.

Needing to relieve the pressure in her head, she punched herself until the bruises were visible, but it didn't help. The kitchen knife in her hand, she rolled up her sleeve and dragged the blade across her bare skin. With the flowing of blood came a kind of release. The inner woman was broken, her heart shattered. The outer shell appeared tough, yet it was all a front to avoid getting close to anyone or anything.

"They all leave her, one way or another and with each parting another little piece of her breaks off."

Trying to Be Normal

Trying to survive she was still working in the shop in Uxbridge, giving readings. Going through the motions, doing the only thing she was able to do. She was still trying to look after her family by seeing this house sale through, even though they didn't talk to her anymore. They just talked about her as though she wasn't there. Never had she felt so alone. She just wanted to go back to the loving family they were. The longing to be able to return to her bed at night, to feel her husband's arms around her, was agonising. Alone on the settee, she cried herself to sleep.

When she rose in the morning, she felt like she was still asleep; observing everything in a dream state. At least she still had her work, she was grateful for that. Listening to other people's problems took her mind off her own. She hardly ate anything as Mick and Michael were only cooking for themselves; they had essentially cut her out of their lives. The evenings were the worst, sitting there listening to them sharing a joke, or commenting on something on the TV. Often, she went out on the pretext that she was going to see a friend; the truth was she walked around the streets for hours, having no money to do anything else. The only plus side was that she was extremely fit.

One day Rob suggested that they took the following day off from work, to go to Portobello Road. She didn't need a lot of persuading, as she had no one booked in and Portobello was one of her favourite places in London. They arranged to meet at Rob's flat.

When she arrived, Rob had not long got up. He made her a coffee and went to take a shower. Glancing through a fitness magazine that Rob had left on the coffee table, she was unaware that he had come out of the shower.

Looking up, she was shocked to see him stood in front of her, completely naked, smiling down at her. She couldn't pretend that she didn't look, because she did. He was slim but full of muscle; in fact, it was the first time she realised that he was actually bloody gorgeous. For a moment, she almost forgot that he was just over half her age. She longed to be a teenager again, in love for the first time.

She decided that what he was doing wasn't fair; she so wanted to be close to someone, anyone. The need to feel wanted was working its way through her body, arousing desires that had lain buried for too long.

"Put your clothes on and let's go."

"But you know how I feel about you."

The thought hadn't once crossed her mind that he wanted to be more than friends. She laughed, trying to make out that she thought he was joking.

"Come on, you daft bugger, Portobello Road awaits. I'll see you outside, it's hot in here."

Deep down, she knew he hadn't been joking. He was the same age as her son, for fuck's sake, and she would only be using him. She loved one man and only one man.

They had a good day out. There was even one crazy moment when she did a gate vault over a barrier in the centre of the road, just to see if she still could. That day, she decided that she and Rob would *never be alone again because she wasn't sure that her will power was that great; especially as she hadn't had sex for about twelve years. Her confusion and fear were getting worse. She was becoming more withdrawn, even though she was still giving readings and going through the motions.*

The completion date for the sale of their house was estimated to be the first week in November. Now she wasn't just confused, she was terrified of facing life without her family. It was around early-October when Mick spoke to her.

"What are you going to do?"

"I don't know. Trish did say I could stay there, but now her mother's moving in so that isn't happening."

Before she knew it, she was in his arms and they were kissing. His hands were all over her body and then they were naked on the living room floor, making love. For those few fleeting moments, she felt happy. They carried on talking over the following weeks about day-to-day things, but they never had sex again.

After four weeks the silent treatment re-commenced, she was stupefied, it had seemed that they were trying to sort things out. All she wanted was for Mick to ask her to stay; but all she got was silence. What Mick didn't tell her was that he had given her a month to pull herself together; but that was something she was incapable of doing.

While packing personal items and special belongings in boxes she experienced a really bad moment of déjà vu, and her mind drifted back to all those years before when they were homeless. She wished that she could have her life back; she didn't want to be doing this, she wanted her home and her family.

Trish gave her Chinchilla's a home but she was determined that wherever she ended up, her precious Jack Russell Terrier, Chelsea, would be with her. As the time started to get nearer, she grew more

255

and more anxious and tried to lose herself in studying and research. It was while she was doing some research that she came across an article about depression and PTSD, and a list of the symptoms. As she read through, she realised that she could have been reading about herself.

Chapter 15
Broken

The house sale went through. Bren sorted out the money, splitting what was left into the appropriate bank accounts. She was still hoping that Mick would ask her to stay, as he and Michael were renting the maisonette two doors away from theirs. Luckily, a friend of a friend said she could rent his council flat, as he was going to move to Manchester.

She packed her boxes into the cab, and with Chelsea held firmly in her arms, she closed the cab door. Glancing, one last time, at the place she had called home for the past eighteen years she began her journey to Rickmansworth and a different life. She longed for the security and love she had felt during her time with Mick. Now she knew that she had never felt so scared in her entire life.

In the twenty-eight years she had been with Mick, she hardly ever dreamt of Hippos but now they were back every night and something had changed. Now they were even more scary, because these Hippos had faces.

The dreams always started with her trying to find her husband. She knew he was there but he always seemed to be a few minutes in front of her and she could never catch up. There were always dangerous hurdles put in her way but that didn't stop her; she would tackle them but still she couldn't catch up to him.

Every morning she awoke, heartbroken. Her brain didn't shut down as she thought it might; instead, it went into overdrive. Once again, she was functioning almost normally, but in a zombie-like state.

Joe, the man who rented the flat that Bren moved into, gave her the bedroom and he slept on the settee as he was moving out the following day. The cooker and washing machine didn't work, the fridge was on the blink and the whole place was filthy and reeked of cigarette smoke. She had embarked on a new course and was expecting to stay there some time, so she wanted the place liveable. The next week, she decorated the flat, and ordered some new kitchen appliances, carpets and furniture. By the time she'd finished, she was exhausted, physically, mentally and financially.

She and Mick had begun talking on the phone, as there were papers that needed signing. He would sometimes meet her from her course and drop her off at her flat. At least they were talking. She thought things were going well, as he was allowing her to use his place to do occasional readings from. She knew there was a long way to go, but she believed their love was strong enough. Studying filled her days, stopping her from thinking too much; helping her to survive the empty hours between the weekly meetings with her husband.

Then, out of the blue, Mick announced that he and Michael were moving to Yorkshire. His sister, Beth, had got them a council house. She was halfway through some courses and couldn't leave London, so when Mick and Michael moved to Yorkshire at the beginning of December, she decided she would follow as soon as she could.

She was crying way too much, so she finally relented and sort help. The doctor prescribed Seroxat and arranged an appointment with a counsellor. It turned out to be a marriage guidance counsellor, which Bren proceeded to tell them was a dead loss being as her husband was living in Yorkshire. Her attitude got her a referral to the mental health unit for January. Being as she had never been good at swallowing pills and she didn't like relying on medication for anything, she didn't take the Seroxat.

A few days before Xmas, she took Chelsea and travelled up to Yorkshire to see Mick's house and spend time with her family. Mick took her places and held her hand but they didn't sleep together, even so she felt like they were getting close again. They had been close, the three of them, when all they had was each other.

A large succulent turkey and all the trimmings adorned the table, untouched. Huddled on the couch with her dog, Chelsea, she stared at the food. What on earth possessed her to cook a dinner that she knew she wasn't going to eat; especially one big enough to feed half the population of Rickmansworth. She didn't know how many tears she shed that night.

A few days after Christmas she drew all but £200 from the bank, with the intentions of buying herself a decent car, so that she could get to Yorkshire easier. Somehow, £6000 had disappeared from the flat. No one had visited her and she had only been out to go to college.

The Millennium approached. Its nearing presence, bringing with it a feeling of impending doom. Many of the people she knew, felt that it was going to be a positive time of change; to her it was just another nail in her marital coffin. If she thought that she was going to make it through the day without being upset, she was seriously mistaken.

The carpet must have been rendered threadbare, with all the pacing backwards and forwards. She stopped every twenty or so steps, to rub her throbbing head. By 7pm she was a nervous wreck, convinced that if she wasn't with her husband and son for the Millennium, then they would never be together, as a family, again.

Heartbroken, she rang Mick who was already out enjoying the festivities. She was hysterical, irrational, obsessed with the idea of getting to Yorkshire by whatever means. He tried to talk her out of it.

"It's New Year's Eve, and there is no way you will be able to get

here. I can't fetch you; I have been drinking."

Out of control, she screamed and begged. The next few hours were horrendous; she alternated between phoning her husband and son, pleading, suggesting stupid ideas, threatening and sobbing.

During her last call to Mick, she heard a female voice telling him to hang up; she knew it was his sister Beth. She phoned again, begging him to let her be with him; she said she would get a cab as she had £200 to get there. Mick told her not to be so stupid. This time she was screaming and tearing at her hair. Mick said she was mad and when she tried to ring again, he had turned his phone off. She rang Michael, who told her to go to bed. Once again, she heard Beth's voice telling him to get rid of her, that she was spoiling their night. When she tried to ring Michael again, his phone was off as well.

Distraught, she screamed until her throat was too hoarse to even whimper. There are no second chances, you have one life and you live it; you cannot go back and start again. Alone now, regretful and guilt ridden, she searched for ways to relieve the torment she was feeling. The cold blade felt comforting against her flesh.

Horrendous screams broke the silence of night, alternating with woeful sobs. It took more than a few moments to realise that they were coming from her. Rising from her bed, she sought out the solace of the kitchen knife its serrated blade tearing jagged ridges in her arms. Still the pressure built, until she felt that her head may burst if she couldn't find the release valve. The knife was still in her hand, it was only when she felt the blood dripping onto her bare legs that the pain in her head started to ease. That night, she took the prescribed anti-depressants; all of them and anything else she could find.

She was travelling along a tunnel. Muffled voices appeared to be arguing, some wanted her to follow, others were telling her to go back. Bren could see someone reaching out for her, a woman with a bright halo surrounding her. Confused, Bren hesitated attracted by the light, then a voice she knew from so long ago, whispered.

"Not yet, gorgeous."

Turning around, she hoped to get a glimpse of him.

Daylight peeped through the curtains, she awoke to Chelsea licking her face which was covered in her own blood and vomit. So, she was still here, she couldn't even do that right. It was three days before she realised her phone was dead. As soon as it was recharged, she had a call from Mick asking if she was alright. She was very far from alright.

Now there were two dogs, she couldn't really remember when the second one had arrived, only that it had. She and her dogs would make occasional trips to Yorkshire by train, which was becoming more and more stressful for her, as she wasn't in a good place, mentally or physically.

One day, when she was struggling to get off the train, Chelsea slipped down the gap between the train and the platform. Terrified, she screamed for someone to help, but although the platform was crowded, no one came to her aid. The taste of vomit filled her mouth. Afraid that she was going to lose her precious little dog, she dropped all her bags on the platform. Still holding Levi's lead tightly, she struggled to haul Chelsea back up through the gap, knowing the train could move at any second and that would be the end. Luckily, Chelsea's harness and lead were strong enough to take the strain. One last tug and Chelsea was in her arms. She collapsed on the platform, hugging both dogs to her; just as the train started to move out of the station.

When she emerged from the station, she was trembling violently. Mick was there to meet her and when he saw her, he looked concerned. Mick said he would look after one of the dogs to make her journey back easier. So, when she left to go back to London, Levi stayed behind.

On the journey back to the flat, she had to change trains at Birmingham. Partly because of nearly losing Chelsea on the journey up and partly because she had bad memories of Birmingham, she became hysterical and had to have a nurse accompany her on the two trains back to Rickmansworth.

When Mick phoned a couple of days later, he asked if she was still moving to Yorkshire. She said she was, and asked if she could move some of her stuff straight away. That day she packed some books and other belongings that she wouldn't be using and Mick hired a van to come and get her.

They arrived at Mick's house and unloaded. When she asked where she should put her things, Mick told her there was nowhere to put them. Because of her state of mind, she immediately thought that he didn't really want her there. So, her days were spent playing solitaire on the computer and her nights sleeping on the couch. She lay awake most of the night, hoping Mick would come and get her and take her up to bed with him; but he didn't. She didn't know what to say to him, so she didn't speak.

After a week, she told him she would move her stuff back to Rickmansworth. She left her books behind, hoping that by seeing them there, Mick would realise how much he missed her and ask her to come back. Her books were never seen again, as Beth laid claim to them.

The day after she got back, she got a message on the landline from Joe, saying he was moving back into the flat; but it was alright, she could stay as he would sleep in the living room. By now she was nearly broke and needed to do something.

Her appointment at the psychiatric unit was due. There were bars *at all the windows and they locked the doors behind her. The doctor was German. She kept asking Bren what the problem was. Bren replied that she was hoping someone could tell her. The doctor kept banging on the table and repeating the question. Finally, Bren told the doctor that it was bodies. The doctor asked her what it was about bodies that she didn't like. Bren stared at her.*

"If you really want me to throw up, keep talking about bodies because the thought of them makes me feel physically sick." The doctor just kept banging on the table. Bren needed it to stop.

"Were you Gestapo in a past life?

The doctor looked shocked at the question.

"I want to leave now and I'm not coming back."

Bren desperately needed some money, so she went to try and sign on for benefits, but Joe was already signing on and the DWP said that being as they lived at the same address they had to claim as a couple. Worried about the implications, Bren told the clerk that they weren't a couple and that she was trying to get back with her husband. Furthermore, if he thought she was living with another man there would be no chance of a reconciliation; but they didn't care. So, Joe had to claim for her; but he didn't give her a penny of it. Can you imagine what it is like having to ask a practical stranger to buy you sanitary products? This went on for several months and eventually she just lost track of time.

In desperation, she requested a social worker and asked him to help her find a property in Yorkshire. She also wrote to Tony Blair to complain about the way she had been treated by the DWP. Meanwhile, she was giving readings and Reiki attunements to try to make some money to keep herself and her dogs. She also needed to save some money for when she got her own place.

Hypnotherapy

Anatomical forms mingled with erratic thought patterns, stumbled over each other, trying to win pride of place in her mind. For three of the longest hours she had ever experienced, low attention span versus gastric flu loomed over her. The thought that she might have to do the embarrassing fifty-yard dash, before the "pens down" request, would be a fate worse than death.

How I passed that exam still amazes me.

Bren had decided to try taking the anti-depressants to see if they would help her. The Seroxat tablets had a strange effect upon her. Rather than becoming 'more normal', she swung between periods of being calm and lucid, and times when she was completely out of control and a gibbering mess. In fact, she nearly got arrested for assault in the benefits office because she threw a Bic pen at someone and it hit them on the back of the head.

During her lucid periods, she would give readings, Reiki sessions, and run development circles. There was no other choice, as it was the only way that she could get any money towards her move. One member of her circle was a man named Ailean, he was Joe's friend. Ailean was a teacher who was very heavily into chaos magick, and was studying to be a hypnotherapist.

Being as she was stressed about an upcoming exam, Ailean offered to give her a hypnotherapy session to help calm her. Finding it hard to concentrate, she agreed to try anything that might help.

They went into Bren's room, where she kept her therapy couch, Chelsea followed her in. That was quite normal as she was a very placid dog who sat in on Reiki sessions and circles, but when Bren laid on the couch Chelsea started growling and showing her teeth. Ailean shouted to Joe to get the dog out.

When she first succumbed to the hypnotic trance, Bren could see herself giving birth to a full-grown man. Then, as she listened to Ailean's voice, there was a series of weird events where she seemed to be battling for her life. After that she didn't remember anything until Ailean was telling her to come back.

It seemed like she had fallen back onto the couch from a great height, landing with her left foot under her right buttock, her toes up near her waist. Although she was quite double jointed when she was younger, there was no way that she could have got into that position. Ailean told her to rest awhile, and left the room.

When she got up a few minutes later, she heard Ailean and Joe whispering to each other; something she had witnessed them doing several times before and that she hadn't really thought about until that moment. On more than one occasion, Ailean had asked her if she would do battle on the astral plains. Although she thought it strange, it had never really bothered her. But after what she had experienced during the hypnotherapy session, she was beginning to question his motives.

The following day when she went out, she only got a few yards before her left knee gave way. From that day her knee grew weaker and she was struggling to walk far. It wasn't until months later that she connected it with the hypnotherapy session.

A Different Side to Joe

When Bren first met Joe, she thought he was quite pleasant but now, after living under the same roof as him for some months, she was beginning to form a different opinion of him.

Although Joe was claiming money for her as a partner and she was paying him rent, she had the bare minimum to eat. By this time, she hardly left the house, partly because her leg was getting progressively worse and partly because of her fears. Confusion and anxiety would leave her unable to focus on her surroundings and even the familiar would appear unrecognisable; often she couldn't even remember how to get back from the local shop. When Joe went shopping, he would buy certain foods just for him. Frequently, he would hide in the kitchen and eat a full packet of chocolate biscuits. Because he couldn't see Bren, he thought she couldn't see him.

Being as Bren was working practically every day, she should have had money in her savings, but she had nothing and couldn't understand why. In her confused state, she relied on Joe to make sure her clients paid. Later, she found out from a friend that Joe was taking the money she earned from the clients and keeping it. When she did have money in her hand, she would give Joe a banknote to buy dog food or other stuff she needed but she never got the change back.

At this point I should probably mention that Joe was quite a well-known medium and was also giving readings himself.

Finally, one morning in February 2001, Bren got a letter from Tony Blair's office telling her to revisit the benefits office as her claim was going to be reassessed independently. A week later, she was offered a house in Yorkshire and she asked her Mick to look at it for her. A couple of days later, the man in the house decided that he didn't want to move after all. Bren's hopes were dashed once again. Around the end of the first week in March, she was offered a two-bedroom modernised house but told she had to take it there and then without viewing. She agreed because she was so desperate.

Being as Bren had disposed of Joe's broken furniture, she knew that she would have to leave what she bought to replace it. While packing, she told Joe she was going to take the Victorian wardrobe and chest of drawers, which were her own personal purchases. He said that she would have to replace them or leave them behind.

Her benefits claim hadn't been processed as she now had to wait until she moved to Yorkshire. So that week, she carried out a Reiki Master's Attunement to buy Joe another wardrobe and chest, and get the money to move with. This time she made sure that she took the payment herself and hid the cash.

During one of my more lucid moments, I informed all my clients and friends of my impending move, refreshing their memories of my mobile number; I knew I would be relying on the readings to keep me going.

It was mid-March when Mick and his cousin Andy, helped me to move into my house. The council very kindly helped out with the necessities from their second-hand furniture stock as I had practically nothing.

In a moment of complete madness, I left the landline for Joe as he couldn't get one connected because of bad debt. Months later, I received a demand for over £1500 from BT that Joe had run up in my name and being as I couldn't afford to pay, I had to go bankrupt.

Yorkshire at Last, Heartbreak and Regrets

When Bren arrived in Yorkshire, her leg was causing her severe problems, she could hardly stand, let alone walk. When she sat down, she would have to hold onto something to stand up again. She had to go up and down stairs on her bottom using her arms for leverage; she feared that she might end up in a wheelchair.

Mick visited her most days and would take her shopping. He was civil towards her and helped where he could, but never showed her the affection that she so desperately wanted. His actions were understandable, being as he thought that she had stopped loving him. Her behaviour was horrendous, but she couldn't stop herself from acting the way she did.

When he visited, she didn't want him to leave her so she would scream hysterically and claw at her face and arms. Neither he, nor Michael, could handle the way she was. She wanted so much to get better, because she still believed she and her Mick had a chance. Hating herself for being such a horrible person, she would turn to the only thing that eased her pain; the knife.

One day while Bren was putting the rubbish out, Chelsea wandered into next door's garden through a hole in their fence. She went round to the front of the house where she was met by a very nasty young woman.

"Get your fucking dog out of my garden, or I will set my Rottweiler on it and he will tear it apart."

Chelsea was all Bren had left; she broke down. Sobbing, begging.

"Please don't kill my dog."

Mick's family treated her like an outcast, she wasn't included in their Christmas and New Year plans. Instead, she was confined to the house with only her dogs for company. Mick and Michael had cut her out of their lives, now she was more of an inconvenience; at a time when she needed them most.

It was 2002 and she had now been in Yorkshire for a year. Mick's forty-ninth birthday was on April 3rd and the whole family went out for a meal; she wasn't invited.

The thing that completely broke her heart and her spirit, was when Beth told her that Mick didn't want to be with her ever again, and was only seeing her out of pity. She didn't want his pity she wanted his love. Foolishly, Bren believed what she was told and never asked Mick whether it was true.

But Beth didn't stop at sticking the knife in, she twisted it until it tore Bren apart.

"I've got this friend who is on the game, she is very pretty and a lot younger than you and I've paid her to spend the night with Mick."

Heart crushed; Bren made up her mind to end it that night. But she looked at her little Chelsea, the only living thing who had stood by her through the outbursts, the tears and the pain and realised that her dogs needed her to give them a better life. So, instead, the knife became Bren's friend again; but something had changed. The cutting had gone from being a form of release, to a punishment for all that went wrong and she blamed herself for every little thing.

No matter how much she loved Mick, he had now had sex with someone else and that was obviously his way of saying it was over between them. All those sexless years, waiting for Mick to want her again; never allowing herself to be a complete woman, even when temptation was put in her way. Now she needed to stop taking the anti-depressants and get her life back together, for the sake of her dogs.

When she woke on the morning of April 6th, she decided that she wasn't going to end up confined to a wheelchair. Over the next few weeks, she shut herself away and refused to see anyone; she thought that no one would be bothered anyway. The only contact she had was with the people she gave readings over the phone. All her shopping and bills were paid for online.

That morning, she had flushed all her medication down the toilet. Determined to make her legs work, she forced herself to exercise. It was sheer willpower that helped her overcome the problems with her legs. By the end of the second week, she was actually able to walk around the house and get up from the chair without struggling. Gradually her legs started to get stronger. During this time, she felt very vulnerable because she was craving love. It wasn't sex she wanted, she just needed someone to hold her in a loving way. While she was feeling like this, she refused to open the door to anyone;

269

especially her Mick, as she couldn't trust the feelings stirring in her body.

She wanted to hurt Mick in the way that he had hurt her, but she was afraid that she would be the one that would end up in pain; that was the last thing she needed when she was trying to mend. By now, she desperately needed male company. Although she had always been a little wild, she was now thinking of doing something that was totally against her moral principles. That Friday night, she made two phone calls.

The following day, she dropped the dogs off at Mick's, promising to pick them up on Sunday afternoon. As she spoke to him, she kept her head bowed not able to look at him, as she knew all those old feelings would bombard her; and she wouldn't be able to hold back the flood.

She boarded the train to London and arrived in Rickmansworth late Saturday afternoon. She knew Joe fancied her when they first met and she thought that because he was such an arsehole, she would be able to detach herself from any romantic feelings. When he opened the door, she greeted him with a kiss. Not a friendly peck on the cheek, but a lingering lover's kiss. He seemed surprised but responded, his tongue finding hers. After some fumbling with each other's clothes, they finally ended up naked in his bed. They had sex several times and he whispered the right words, but what she was looking for wasn't there. Right then she knew it was a mistake; she wanted to vomit, wanted to run to her Mick's arms, beg him to love her again. It was too late to get the train home, so she had no choice but to stay.

The following morning, Joe seemed to be in a rush. She barely had time to bathe before he told her he would walk her to the station, as the first bus wasn't until 10am. As they walked, he kept looking around him, she tried to ignore it but finally she had to ask.

"Are you afraid of being seen with me?"

He looked shocked. Then he told her, he was meeting his girlfriend at 11. He could have told her when she arrived that he had a girlfriend, he could have pushed her away, but instead he had sex with her, not once but several times. No wonder he didn't want to bump into his girlfriend. He was never good at concealing guilt. She couldn't wait to get away from him, she felt used; no, more than used, she felt cheap. But isn't that what she had done, gone there with the intention of using him?

The tube to Kings Cross was crowded, but even her fear of stranger's bodies pressing against her faded in comparison to how dirty she felt. When Mick answered the door to her, three and a half hours later, she still couldn't look him in the face; but for a different reason this time. Afraid that he would see the guilt, she knew she had to get away from him quickly, before she burst into tears. Now she knew she loved and wanted him more than ever. She felt ashamed because she had wanted to pay him back for breaking her heart; but all it had done was make her feel worse about herself. She took the dogs and left, not even stopping for the coffee he offered her, or the lift home.

When she got back to her home, she cried; but she didn't punish herself because she had already done enough of that on the train.

When all the feelings for her Mick were so strong, when the opportunities had presented themselves, why didn't she just grab them? Why didn't she just throw herself into his arms, and tell him how much she loved him? Because her stupid, screwed up, depressive mind wouldn't allow her to do so. It wouldn't allow her to take the chance that she may be rejected, yet again.

Chapter 16
How Do You Stop Loving the Love of Your Life

My benefits never did get sorted because right from the moment that I moved to Yorkshire, my London, International and business clients started phoning for readings.

Depression had helped Bren to start writing again; putting down her darkest thoughts and fears onto paper helped her to gain some kind of perspective on life. Although she occasionally saw her Mick, she wasn't part of his life anymore, Beth saw to that. Beth was the one he took shopping and to the working men's clubs; the one who shared his birthdays. Mick wasn't seeing any other women, maybe that is why Bren still had hope that one day he would come back to her; she missed him so much.

Mick didn't want her anymore, he had told Beth as much, but she was still totally in love with him. So, when she felt herself about to rush round to his house and beg him to love her again, she would throw herself into something that would occupy her mind in a big way. Deep down she knew that she had to try and rebuild her life without him.

Throughout her life, anything that she had ever loved or been close to had been taken from her, as if by some kind of hellish intervention and now Mick was gone too. A memory flooded back to her. It was 1994 or 5 and she was on a psychic fair. Suddenly feeling extremely sad and uneasy, she turned to the reader next to her, and asked if Mick was going to die. The reader told her 'yes'. Although she must have buried this in her subconscious, she believed the awful feeling that Mick was going to die and leave her was still there, gnawing away in some dark crevice within her brain. She loved him so much she couldn't bear the thought of being without him.

Rather than face losing her Mick forever she thought about killing herself but how would Michael cope without both his parents and who would look after her Chelsea. She had tried several times before and failed, maybe the universe wasn't ready to let her go; perhaps it had some mightier plan for her. She hoped it had, otherwise she had wasted all that time being away from the man she loved, still loves.

After the Joe incident, I was quite wary of becoming involved with anyone. I think it had finally dawned on me that words can be very superficial, and can slip easily off the tongue. Many people will tell you what they think you need to hear, just to get what they want. Nevertheless, I was very lonely so I decided to have a go at dating.

Somehow, I started conversing with a guy online. We both had a love of poetry so when he suggested meeting up, I thought that it might be a good idea. He sent me a photo of himself: he was tall, slim and good looking, with longish fair hair. He looked a little younger than me, but I still looked quite young for my age, so I wasn't bothered. Erring on the side of caution, I suggested we go for coffee at the shopping mall and would meet up at the bottom of the waterfall escalator; one of the few places I could find easily since the disorientating effects of the depression.

Bren made her way to the escalator. Nobody of his description was anywhere to be seen. Thinking she had been stood up, she was about to leave when she noticed a man with longish grey hair stood by the shop opposite. He was only slightly taller than her and looked nothing like the six-foot man who she was supposed to meet. When he saw Bren looking at him, he started to walk towards her, and introduced himself as the man she had been waiting for, Paul. They walked to the Costa coffee shop near the exit, where he bought two cappuccinos and they sat down.

Their conversation centred around his job and life in general but she couldn't warm to him. There was something about him that didn't sit well in her mind; apart from him leading her to believe he was about twenty years younger. It was someone else's voice that broke through her pondering. The one that said.

"Of course, I don't like paedophiles."

Looking around her to see who had spoken, she noticed that everyone else was drinking or eating, and holding their own conversations. Paul was staring at her with his mouth open.

'Oh no, don't tell me I just said that'. She thought.

Paul looked at his watch, muttered something about being late for an appointment, and left. She never saw or heard from him again.

So that ended my attempt at internet dating.

Where Have I Gone? I Want Me Back

Often, I would long for the old me but that me was gone; lost somewhere in the annals of time. No matter how much you want to, you can't go back and relive your life. You can only go forward, often with regret but also with increased knowledge.

One night, I went out with our Michael and his then girlfriend, Debbie. Not being a drinker anymore, I had a couple of drinks that went straight to my head. On the way home I fell over and hurt my knees. It was probably a combination of the drink and the depression that made me feel quite sorry for myself and in need of company.

Bren often chatted to people in the Yorkshire chat room and that night was no different. For some reason, she poured her heart out and told everyone she needed a hug. Just then, Mick T came online and told her she should go to bed as she was attracting the wrong sort of people. He said if she went to bed, then he would come and take her out on his bike the following day. They arranged to meet outside the Gala Bingo at the top of her road.

The following day, she remembered that she was supposed to meet Mick T, but wasn't sure if he was actually going to turn up; thinking it might have been a ploy, just to make her go to bed. But, forever the optimist, she put on her old bike leathers; which she hadn't worn for many years and honestly didn't know why she had kept them. Being cautious, she put moccasins on, in case she needed to walk into town.

On her way up the road, she saw a biker riding slowly past the Bingo. A few minutes later he came back and turned down her road. When he saw her, he stopped, lifted his visor and smiled. He had a lovely smile, but he looked so young. Looking down at her moccasins, he grinned, then handed her a helmet. She was anxious, due to not having ridden pillion since she was fifteen.

They arrived in Matlock and parked up. Mick took her to a café, and bought two cups of coffee; she could tell he was nervous because he spilt most of it in the saucers. After, they walked up onto the hill and sat and talked. Mick T, like Bren, was separated from his spouse. Suddenly, she had the feeling that this was the man she was going to spend the rest of her life with which shocked her, as that was the furthest thing from her mind.

That evening they went for a drink. She mentioned to Mick T about her interest in the paranormal and he said he would take her to a haunted place that he knew. The following night, they set off for Stocksbridge. They parked in a lane above the motorway and settled down to see if anything happened. Thinking it wasn't really important at that time, she hadn't told Mick T that she was a medium, so she hadn't even considered talking about trance. According to Mick T, they had only been there a few minutes when she turned to look at him. He said she looked completely different and began speaking in a man's voice. He was so shocked, that he didn't remember what was said. But the good thing was, although it scared him, he didn't run away.

Being with Mick T wasn't easy at first, as he also suffered from depression. I suppose I thought that he would drift off and find someone else and that by some divine intervention my husband and I would get back together, after which we would forget about everything that had gone on and get our life back. But that wasn't to be.

Come the beginning of December 2002, I received divorce papers through the post and a message via our son Michael, saying that my Mick wanted to see me. I reluctantly went around to his house, knowing that it would hurt to see him as it always did.

They sat and talked. He told her the family had all been out for a pre-Christmas meal and how beautiful his sister Beth looked all dressed up. All Bren had wanted for the past three years was for him to tell her how beautiful she was and how much he loved her. Instead, she got an ultimatum.

"Either you move in here with me now and get rid of that bloke of yours, or I finalise this divorce."

After all these years, did he not remember that she didn't respond well to threats; they just made her dig her heels in even further. All it would have taken would have been, 'I love you and I want you back'. But he was a stubborn man and he wouldn't do anything that he thought remotely resembled begging.

"Okay then, so I will get on to the solicitor."

He stood up, and showed her to the door.

Once outside the tears streamed. Not only had she lost her husband, she had also lost her best friend; her only friend for many years. It was like she had lost him for a second time, but this time it was final.

And the Hippos plagued her dreams……….

She could see her husband in the distance, but every time she tried to reach him the ground opened up in front of her. Reaching out, she tried to grab at the thing she loved. Just like that little girl did all those years before, in the Hippo house at London Zoo; but this time, the screams weren't joyful.

Rejected

It was New Year's Eve 2002 and Mick T and I were out celebrating, with Michael and some friends. When midnight struck, I turned to give Mick T a kiss, and he ran away.

There she was, standing alone, in the middle of a crowded pub room. Embarrassed, and once again wondering what she had done wrong. Having been rejected all her life, first by her mother who wanted her to be more like her half-sister, children at school, work colleagues, previous boyfriends, Carl, then Mick, Michael and now Mick T; she wondered what the hell was wrong with her. She felt the need to hide away and punish herself. But she was designated driver, as she was the only one who hadn't been drinking; so, she went looking for Mick T. Bren found him outside the pub, tearful. He told her he wanted to go and see his wife's aunt, as they usually spent New Year together; like a fool, she offered to take him to the aunt's house. When they got there the house was in darkness, as the aunt was in bed. She took Mick T home.

When they got back to Mick T's flat, she tried to put her arms round him and kiss him; but he pushed her away. When she asked what was wrong, he told her he was overwhelmed by memories of his wife. Hurt, she wanted to know why he was rejecting her, after appearing to be so keen for the past six months. He asked her if she would have sex with his dad. Thinking he meant literally, she was angry and repulsed; due to deep rooted problems with old men that she didn't fully understand. But he went on to say that the difference between his dad's age and hers was the same as the difference between her age and his. Wounded by his words, she lashed out. "My age didn't seem to bother you before."

It was then he told her he still loved his wife and probably always would. She knew what it was like to love someone that you can't have, but she thought they had both moved on from that.

She'd had almost six months of feeling nearly normal, now once again her whole world was crashing down around her. She had stuck with Mick T because she couldn't let someone else down; giving up any chance she ever had of getting back with her husband.

Within a few days, she had relapsed into deep depression. Repulsed by herself because of being rejected yet again, she felt angry and bitter, completely alone with no friends; used for what she could give people. It was an extremely bad relapse which left her stuttering and unable to form a sentence without blubbering; but worst of all, she began self-harming once again. She became a virtual recluse, so her doctor referred her to a Psychiatric nurse.

When she was alone in the house, she would tear at her flesh and scream until her throat was raw. There was no one she could turn to, she was unwanted, lost and terrified. Although she had a Psychiatric nurse, she couldn't get any support when she was having a really bad day. She lost all confidence and started to self-deprecate, criticising everything she did or said; even her ability to do her spiritual work.

She had always taken pride in her appearance but unfortunately that also suffered, she piled on the pounds because she hardly ever left the house. When she looked in the mirror, she hated what she saw; what she had become.

Levi was a boisterous dog who needed a lot of walking and she was unable to leave the house, so she had to find a home for him. Another thing that she cared about was gone.

Mick T stayed around, although she knew he was having serious thoughts about moving on. He also relapsed into a deep depressive state, which didn't help her state of mind. Mick T had said some very hurtful and spiteful things to her over the months since New Year; every word tore deep into her soul. She knew that people could say a lot of 'spur of the moment' things when they were hurting. After all, she had said some pretty nasty things herself.

Perhaps he was doing the same as she did, when she was getting too close to people. Lashing out, trying to make them hate her and leave, protecting herself from more heartache; but at the time she blamed herself for everything.

Bren's referral to the Psychiatric nurse was only for eight weeks and because there was no way she was going to be better in that time, the nurse tried to get her to join a special interest group. The options she was given were not too brilliant, so they talked about her going back to something she knew and enjoyed which was paranormal investigations. That was when she and Mick T started up a Paranormal group (SPI).

It wasn't easy, but she started to connect with people again. Although she still couldn't go to places on her own, she was managing to be amongst people without freaking out. Mick T remained caring but distant, and Bren started to believe that they may be destined to part.

Learning that not Everyone Is a Real Friend

It was sometime in August 2003, in the early hours of the morning, that Bren got a phone call from her Mick. He told her their Michael had been involved in a serious car accident and had been taken to Rotherham hospital. Being as her Mick didn't have a car at the time,

Mick T said he would take Bren and they would keep her Mick posted. She was terrified that she was going to lose her remaining son.

When they got to the hospital Michael was sat in a waiting room along with the driver of the car. Michael was in a lot of pain, but the doctors wouldn't see him because he had been drinking. Apparently, the car had hit a kerb, overturned, rolled across the road, hit a lamppost, and then rolled again.

"I thought I was going to die Mum." He told her, tears streaming down his face. Bren put her arms around him. His arm was broken so the hospital gave him painkillers, put his arm in a sling and told him to go to Royal hospital the following day.

When he arrived at Royal hospital, they found that his arm was completely shattered. He had to have reconstructive surgery and wear a cage on his arm for six months. Bren was just glad that he was alive.

In September of the same year, I moved to the other side of Yorkshire to be nearer to Mick T for convenience. When we first started SPI, we had a team of five and we had some great laughs; visiting outdoor locations and abandoned buildings. We were getting a huge response to the group, so Mick T set up a website. It was then that we decided to have monthly meetings with a guest speaker, where attendees would contribute £1 each to pay towards the speaker's expenses. In the early days, we managed to find loads of places that we could visit free of charge; and would try to alternate guests, so that everyone got a chance to go on a free investigation. We never made any money from SPI, in fact quite the opposite.

About six months into her relapse and after she had been called in front of a medical panel, Bren was finally granted benefits and disability living allowance. It was around six weeks after she had started receiving benefits, that she was paid a visit.

One day, when Bren was alone at home with Chelsea, a man knocked on the door. She didn't normally have meetings with strangers without someone being with her, because she was still having communication problems, especially with people in authority. The man said he was from the benefits office and showed her his identity card. Stating that he needed to talk to her, he asked to be let in; so, she let him enter.

He asked how she was getting on and she told him that she was trying her best to get back to normal. While explaining what her psychiatric nurse had recommended, she told him about SPI and how she felt it was helping her to be around people. Then he produced a huge pile of paper and asked her what it was all about. It was a list of all her websites, she tried to explain that they were from when she was self-employed in London, before she became ill.

It was then that he told her that someone had reported her for making money from meetings. She explained, as best she could, what the process was and showed him the paperwork related to SPI. By this time, she was getting very agitated and had started to stutter, something she had rarely done recently. He was getting quite aggressive with her and she just wanted it all to stop.

She got up from her seat and ran into the kitchen. Grabbing a knife from the block on the windowsill, she slashed at her arms until she had cut herself quite badly. Blood was dripping all over Chelsea and the floor. The man panicked and asked her what he should do. She told him to leave her house and stick his benefits up his arse; forcibly pushing him out the door. After he left, he went to the mental health unit, to ask them if there was anything wrong with her.

When he was gone, Bren phoned the mental health unit, and asked for someone to come and be with her, but there was no one available. Once again, she felt alone and unwanted; she lay on the floor and sobbed and that is where she stayed until the following morning.

Two days later, she got a phone call from the DLA, asking why she had told the DWP to stop her benefits; as she had been awarded them because, in their opinion, she was unfit for work for the unforeseeable future. They told her that the benefits couldn't be re-instated, as she had said she didn't want them. So, she had no one to support her and no money. It was then she knew that she had no choice but to get better and quickly; or she and her dog would starve. The only thing she could do now, was to go back to giving readings and demonstrations.

As SPI became more popular, we found that there were a lot of people who thought we were making money from it, and who became very jealous. We would return from an investigation and I would spend the following day removing abuse and swear words from the forum. Not long after, the abuse turned to malicious threats. We would receive phone calls in the early hours of the morning, threatening to burn our house down, physically harm us, and even telling us our car was on fire. In the end we deleted the forum, discontinued the monthly meetings, and just continued with about twenty reliable people.

The Worst News Ever

Bren and her ex, Mick, sometimes bumped into each other in town and had a chat. Seeing him cut through her like a knife, because she was still in love with him. As she had moved to the other side of Yorkshire, she hadn't seen him for a while.

She heard through the grapevine, that he regretted listening to his family and divorcing her. He also said that he wanted to marry her again, but this time he would do it properly. If only he had said that a few years earlier. She and Mick T were getting on quite well, so her life was now with him until he decided otherwise; as she couldn't let someone else down.

Bren and Mick T took on a shop in Walkley and he suggested that being as they would be working together, they might as well live together. It was a lovely shop, which turned out be very 'active', and they had many regular clients. They often held evenings of clairvoyance, which proved to be very popular.

One morning in early June 2006, Michael phoned her to tell her that his dad was having a scan on his head. For some time, he had been having severe dizzy spells. She couldn't cry, or show her true feelings because she didn't want to upset Mick T.

The following morning, she was rushed to hospital with a suspected heart attack. Later that day, Michael phoned her with the news that her Mick had been diagnosed with two tumours on the brain, she was devastated. She wanted to see him, to hold him, but she knew she couldn't because it wouldn't be fair to Mick T. So, all she could do was try to hold herself together, as another breakdown wouldn't help any of them.

She was due to give an evening of clairvoyance that night. Her head was filled with thoughts of her Mick, she couldn't bear thinking about losing him forever. She tried to go ahead with the clairvoyant evening, but she collapsed after the first message. So, Mick T told the audience about her suspected heart attack, explained to them that the evening couldn't go ahead and gave everyone their money back.

Trying To Keep Myself Together

Bren's heart was being torn apart, she needed to spend as much time with her Mick as she could, but she also had Mick T to consider. Although she knew it had to be difficult for Mick T, he agreed to her visiting on a weekly basis.

One day, when they were alone together, her Mick said.

"We really made a mess of things, didn't we?"

She knew that if she looked at him, she would break down, so she just nodded and managed a quiet.

"Yes."

"I never stopped loving you, and I am so sorry I divorced you. I just didn't know how to handle the way you were."

Too choked up to answer him, she wished she could just make the rest of the world go away, and fall into his arms; but things weren't that simple.

Because the tumours couldn't be operated on her Mick was given radiotherapy and as a result, he lost all his lovely hair. His eyesight started to fade, until he was practically blind. The Royal Society for the Blind sent someone to teach him how to live as a blind person, how to find his way around his house, and how to make a cup of coffee. Bren hated seeing her beautiful Mick like this, her heart ached for him. Although he was being very brave, she knew that he was falling apart; she felt more helpless than she had ever done in her life. She wished she could bear his pain for him.

A few weeks later her Mick was taken into Royal hospital for some more tests. Michael told Bren, that the day before, his dad had repeated that he wanted to marry her again. She so wished he had told her; she loved and missed him so much.

When Mick T dropped Bren off at the hospital, her Mick was standing outside. He asked her about Chelsea, and Mick T overheard.

"Keep him down here, for about half an hour." Mick T said.

They sat on the bench outside the doors talking. It was quite difficult, as her Mick's speech was becoming quite slurred, and he was muddling his words. A little while later, Mick T came back with Chelsea. Bren sat her on her Mick's lap and she licked his face. He looked pleased.

"She remembers me."

On Bren's following visit, her Mick was confined to bed. His cousin Andy and their Michael were already there. He had deteriorated quite a lot and couldn't speak. The hospital had banned him from smoking, so he was sat in bed smoking an invisible cigarette.

Bren stood at the side of his bed and when he heard her voice, he grabbed her hand and patted her palm repeatedly. At first, she thought that he was trying to give her the invisible cigarette. Then he grabbed hold of her wedding ring finger and started tugging at her ring and then patted her palm again. When she looked at Andy and Michael, their faces told her that they were thinking the same as she was, so she gave him her answer.

"Yes, I will."

She wasn't lying to him, because if he survived, she would find a way of keeping her promise. When she left that day, she kissed him and whispered in his ear.

"I love you, always have, and always will."

The next day, their Michael told her that the results of the tests had come back. The brain tumours were secondary cancers, the primary was in his dad's lungs and it was inoperable. The hospital sent her Mick home and every time she visited it broke another little piece of her heart. Although she wanted to take care of him, she was in a difficult position, so it was left to their Michael and Andy. Bren wanted to spend every last minute with him, but she had Mick T's feelings to consider. In December, her Mick was taken into Michael Sobell palliative care ward.

On the morning of New Year's Eve 2006, Michael told Bren they had to go to the hospital as his dad had fallen into a coma. Michael said he had to phone Mick's sisters, Beth and Laura and then he would be on his way.

Mick T dropped her off and she was first there; it was around 10am. She sat next to her Mick's bed and said her goodbyes. The other half of her was fading away and she had no control over it. As much as she wanted to, she couldn't turn back the clock seven years, she just had to prepare herself for what was to come. Michael arrived about 11am.

When Beth and Laura arrived, Bren and Michael were pushed out of the way so that the sisters could position themselves at either side of the bed, holding her Mick's hands. Andy arrived a little later and he joined Michael and Bren on the seats at the bottom of the bed. It was around lunchtime when Michael went out and spent the last of his money buying them all something to eat. Beth took her food and announced.

"At last, you've put your hand in your pocket for something. By the way, you look like you got dressed in the dark."

Bren and Michael bit their tongues, because it wasn't the time or place for arguments. Beth picked up Mick's dressing gown and put in on.

"I'm having this, and his blanket."

And so, it began.

A few weeks prior, her Mick had asked Beth and Laura to look after Michael when he died and they said they would. During the course of the day, Beth and Laura became more hostile towards Bren and Michael and there were many nasty comments made. It got *to a stage, that by evening, they were taking it in turns to be in the room.*

Around 12.30am on New Year's morning, it was Bren and Michael's turn to be with Mick. They stood at the end of the bed, and looked at him lying there. The nurse had just been in and adjusted the morphine. Michael told his dad that he could go now if he wanted, as everyone was there.

"Can you hear me dad?"

She and Michael looked at each other in amazement, as they both distinctly heard her Mick say.

"Yes."

They thought they must be imagining it. She wanted so much for him to be at peace, so she said.

"You know we will all be together again one day, don't you?"

He answered her by nodding, and saying.

"Yes."

Then, as they watched, a mist-like shape, floated up from his body towards the ceiling. Although his body was still breathing, they knew that they had just watched him leaving. Beth and Laura came back in, and Michael and Bren left.

Bren and Michael sat in the hallway, discussing what they had witnessed, both unsure if they had been imagining it; but if they had, then they had both seen and heard exactly the same thing.

Around 1.45am Beth came to fetch them, saying that it was time. They entered the room just as Mick's body exhaled its last breath. The man she loved more than life itself, was gone forever; there could be no second chances for them. He was fifty-three years old. When he left, he took half of her heart with him.

That night she dreamt about her Mick, and this time he was even further away.

"Come back." She begged.

And the Hippos pain filled roar bounced off her bedroom walls, and tore deep into her soul.

Chapter 17

I Have Another Life Now

Although they wanted to hog my Mick's last hours on earth, when it came to the funeral arrangements Beth and Laura were nowhere to be seen, although they did insist on a Catholic funeral. We relented to keep the peace, but my Mick would have turned in his grave at the thought of a nun sending him off; as he didn't practise his religion and had hated nuns since attending Catholic school. Michael and I honoured my Mick's choice of music, for playing at his funeral; Slade – Thanks for the Memories, Creedance Clearwater Revival – Bad Moon Rising and Roy Orbison – Blue Bayou.

The funeral was a very awkward occasion with all of my Mick's family on one side of the room; and us, our friends, and Andy on the other. Just before she left, Laura turned to our Michael and said, "That's two people I don't have to pretend to like anymore."
So much for the promise to her dying brother.

My advice to anyone who finds themselves in my position is 'don't listen to others', listen to your heart; get the information straight from the horse's mouth, as people lie for their own means. My Mick and I lost out on precious time that we could have had together and I will regret that for the rest of my life.

Fifteen years on and both Michael and I are still having problems coming to terms with my Mick's death. He will always be my Mick because he was the only man that I loved with every part of me; heart, mind, body and soul. The Mick I came to know better than anyone, was a beautiful, funny, gentle giant. Mick and I shared a bond that few people have and at the end, he shared his transition from this earthly life with the two people he loved the most; me and our Michael.

"Sleep well my love, I will see you again when my physical life ends and when that time comes, I won't be afraid to tell you how much I love you."

My relationship with Mick T hasn't been plain sailing, for a while I didn't think we were going to make it. Over the years we have formed a relationship built on friendship and openness and have learned to love each other for who and what we are. We have a lot of mutual interests and he has made me laugh again.

He is my rock, the one who stuck by me through some of the darkest days of depression. He is the one who makes life worth living again.

Coping with the Past and Making the Future Better

Mick T and I have suffered much loss over the years both human and animal but we have faced that loss together. Those that have left the earthly realm, will remain forever in our hearts. Your loved ones are never gone completely while you have still beautiful memories of them. It is the memories that help you to come to terms with your loss.

Although all my animals have been loved equally, Chelsea was extra special as she had been with me through my marriage break up and the subsequent depression. At one stage she was the only living thing that gave me reason to stay on this earth.

One morning in April 2013, Bren was sat on the settee with Chelsea next to her. She had been reflecting on the past, and feeling a little sad. She stroked Chelsea and told her.

"Oh, Chelse, I don't want to lose you."

Chelsea looked at her and it was as if she was saying.

"Let me go Mum, it's time."

A few months later, three months before Chelsea's sixteenth birthday, she began haemorrhaging and Bren and Mick T had to say goodbye to her. Bren was heartbroken, it seemed like she had lost another part of her Mick, but not only that, she had lost her best fur friend and companion. Chelsea left behind a big gap in her life; but she also left so many beautiful memories.

It is just when you think that your life is settled that something you least expect comes back to kick you where it hurts.

While on Facebook, Bren was talking to a woman who created family trees for a living. As a result of the conversation, Bren decided to try and finish the family tree that she had started. For years, she had been trying to find information about her estranged sons but to no avail. The woman she was in touch with, contacted her to say that she had come across some information that Bren might be interested in; namely, a death certificate, which bore the same name as one of the people she was looking for.

Bren applied for a copy of the death certificate. It was then that she discovered that her eldest boy had died in 1998, from Cocaine and Carbon Monoxide poisoning. It took her weeks to get over the initial shock as she had always believed that one day, she would see her boys again.

She had never stopped loving them, or thinking about them. At least she had been a good mother to her boys during the short time that they were with her.

"Farewell my loved ones until we meet again."

Over the years, she had lost so many people and animals who she loved. Yet, although she was able to connect to other people's lost loved ones, she had never received contact from hers. The one person she really expected to contact her was her Mick, because of what they had shared during their time together; but it never happened.

Then on 26th May 2020, in the early hours of the morning, she had a dream.

The dream was clear as crystal, and the colours and detail were vivid. Bren was camping with Mick T in a beautiful field. There was nothing for miles. Near the tent there was a bramble bush with huge blackberries, some of which she gathered and took back to Mick T. The blackberries were so nice that she went back for more but, although there was no one around, the bush had been picked clean; so, she had to venture deeper into the brambles to find them. She became trapped and it took her ages to get out. When she finally emerged Mick T was gone. Her case and bags were under part of an old ripped tent, so, it looked as though he had been gone for some time.

She looked around her, there was nothing, nowhere to go. Suddenly her Mick appeared, he looked fit and had all his beautiful hair; he was solid, because she went to him and put her arms around him. He told her he could get her somewhere to stay while she was there. His arms were around her too.

"Let me be with you." She whispered.

"I can't, but I can find you a hotel room while you are here." He sounded a little sad.

"Please let me be with you, just once, like we used to be. I love you."

There was something unworldly about him. Still holding her in his arms, he spoke softly.

"I love you too." Looking her in the eyes, his voice became firmer. "But I can't."

She felt his tears mingling with her own and then he was gone; as mysteriously as he had appeared.

Maybe he was trying to tell me, it was not my time to be there.

No matter how much I long for what was, my life is now centred in Yorkshire. London is no longer my home but just a place for fleeting visits. My immediate family is now me, Mick T, our beloved animals and my son Michael. I have enjoyed my time working in the spiritual field. Whether the Universe has something else planned for me, I don't know. I am sure if it has, I will be led in the right direction.

Our elders, parents, teachers, and such like, no matter how amazing they are, cannot truly prepare us for life's lessons. For years, I lived in constant fear of my own and other people's demons, always striving to please others, at my own expense. I loved too deeply and I trusted too much. Because of my own insecurities, I allowed myself to be a victim for several years and as a result I succumbed to mental illness.

Depression is merciless, it takes everything from the sufferer, pride, dignity, work, love, life. Family and friends don't know what to do, so they avoid the sufferer; when all that is needed is for them to be there. Caring for a depressive is damn hard work but love and understanding can help to bring them back to you.

When my depression was at its worst, I would exhibit exaggerated behaviour patterns. When I was up, I could cook a six-course meal, dance all night and still have the energy to run a marathon. When I was down, I was afraid of everything. Wanting people to hate me as much as I hated myself, I tried to destroy anything that anyone may have liked about me. You never get over depression, you just learn to live with it and deal with it.

If you find yourself suffering the way I did, don't do as I did and push away the people you love. I learnt by my mistakes, too late to save my relationship with my husband; but not too late to save me from ruining my relationship with Mick T. You may not be able to tell the ones you love what is wrong, because you may not know yourself, but I'm asking you to try and communicate. Not through long drawn-out conversations, because that is impossible when you are depressed. Just try to force yourself to say three words that just might make the difference between losing everything you have and keeping it.

"I need help."

It is somewhere to start. I really wish that I had been able to say those words back in 1999.

Mental illness' legacy to me is overeating, OCD, swearing like a trooper and anger issues. Most days I can control it, but some days it is a lost cause. I still have a lot of bad days and occasionally suffer from panic attacks. On good days I can manage to get on public transport as long as it is not too crowded. It is still scary but I cope. I take each day as it comes. If I have to go somewhere or see anyone, I need plenty of notice so that I can get myself 'psyched up'. I know I will never be fully back to 'normal', but partly is acceptable.

Yes, I miss the life I had but the me that was part of that life is gone. I have changed and I will never get that me back; all I can do is try to accept the me that is left. I miss the warmth of being close to the man I loved for so many years, I miss my special dog. Most of the time I am fine, sometimes things overwhelm me; but I don't allow them to drag me down. Now there are new struggles to face, but I know I will take them in my stride. I can't afford to go under, and I won't allow myself to. There are people and animals that depend on me, so I no longer self-abuse. Occasionally I drink alcohol, but I no longer need to drink. I am a functioning depressive and I am in control.

These days the Hippo's are quiet, and although my dreams are still bizarre, I can normally pinpoint what has caused them. Any bad memories associated with my childhood, other than those I have related, have either been wiped from my memory completely; or perhaps they just didn't happen. Maybe I will never know and perhaps I don't want to.

Now, in my 73rd year, I am about to embark on a new chapter of my life. Whichever way this goes for me, I have a good man by my side who supports me through all my crazy schemes, without judgement. Over the years, I have developed a positive outlook on life and take each new challenge in my stride. I am a great believer that things will turn out the way they are supposed to and that most things will come right in the end; if you just trust. I am determined that I will never go to that 'Dark Place' again, as it cost me so much.

Nowadays, if I feel a grey shadow looming, I either do something that makes me happy or lose myself in my latest project. If you keep doing things to make you happy, sooner or later you start to feel happy. The bad stuff doesn't ever disappear completely, you just learn to live with it and put it in the past, where it should be.

My advice to you all is dwell on the good memories, no matter how small. Try to forgive those who have wronged you; but mostly forgive yourself, for all those things that you have blamed yourself for that were not your fault. I don't hate those who have caused me harm - I pity them; that they are so sick, or so full of self-loathing, that they have to inflict pain and misery on others.

I have been to hell and back and I have survived, and in the process, I have managed to find love and happiness again. Today my thoughts are not about trying to self-destruct, they are about how much life I can cram into the years before I go to meet my maker. If there is something beyond this life, I would really like to be with the people and animals I have loved and lost; to meet them all again in happier circumstances. Unfortunately, we will never know for sure until that day comes. But until then, there is a lot of living to do.

To anyone out there who can relate to any part of my story, my message to you is: Don't give up on yourself. There is hope, it's not easy, but life can be worth living again – one day at a time. I have survived, and rebuilt my life, and so can you.

NOTES

Preface:

Endnote 1:

PTSD or Post Traumatic Stress Disorder is a psychological illness that can occur after witnessing or experiencing traumatic or life-threatening events such as military combat, terrorist incidents, serious accidents, disasters; or violent personal assaults, like domestic abuse or rape. People who suffer from PTSD often relive the experience through nightmares or flashbacks, and frequently have difficulty sleeping. These symptoms can be long-lasting and are often severe enough to significantly impair the person's daily life.

PTSD impacts brain function biologically as well as psychologically. Which results in an overly sensitive and easily triggered survival instinct, often making it difficult to separate non-threatening actions from dangerous events that happened in the past; resulting in an overinflated response. The illness is complicated by the fact that it frequently occurs in conjunction with related disorders such as depression, other problems of physical and mental health, and alcohol or substance abuse. The person may feel detached or estranged. Their ability to function in social or family life may be impaired. They may experience occupational instability, marital problems, divorces, family disharmony, and difficulties with parenting.

Chapter 5:

Endnote 2:

IKE – I know everything.

Chapter 6:

Endnote 3:

Cold Turkey: Complete withdrawal from drugs (or sometimes other substances) without weaning off, or medical help. So called because of the goosebumps people sometimes get in the days after they quit, which look like the skin of a plucked turkey.

Chapter 8:

Endnote 4:

Scratchwood Motorway Services – now renamed London Gateway.

Chapter 10:

Endnote 5:

What is Colic? Inconsolable crying. Things that usually soothe your baby like a feed, cuddle or change of nappy don't seem to work. Baby stiffens or tenses their body, an arched back or clenched fists could all be tell-tale signs of colicky pain. Baby may pull his or her legs up towards the tummy several times in quick succession. Your baby's tummy is swollen or tender and is possibly sensitive to the touch.

Printed in Great Britain
by Amazon

26834395R00175